JOSEF
HOFFMANN
DESIGNS

JOSEF HOFFMANN DESIGNS

Edited by
Peter Noever

With contributions by
Hanna Egger, Rainald Franz, Brigitte Huck,
Ernst Ploil, Elisabeth Schmuttermeier, Jan Tabor,
Angela Völker, and Christian Witt-Dörring

MAK – Austrian Museum of Applied Arts, Vienna

PRESTEL

© 1992 MAK-Austrian Museum of Applied Arts, Vienna,
and Prestel-Verlag, Munich
© of illustrated works: MAK-Austrian Museum of Applied Arts,
Vienna

Illustrations photographed by Elisabeth Kohlweiß, Georg
Mayer, Thomas Römer, Ludwig Schöpp, Marcelo Slama,
and Gerald Zugmann

Front cover: Josef Hoffmann, Chair, 1904 (see cat. no. 26)
Cover design by Anne Marie Friedl
Frontispiece: Josef Hoffmann, photo by Yoichi R. Okamoto, 1951.
From the archives of the Hochschule für angewandte Kunst,
Vienna (Inv. no. 3449/0)

Copyedited by Barbara Einzig
Translated by Eileen Martin and Aleksandra Wagner (Introduction)

Prestel-Verlag, Mandlstrasse 26, D-8000 Munich 4, Germany
Tel. (89) 3817090; Fax (89) 38170935

Distributed in continental Europe by Prestel-Verlag
Verlegerdienst München GmbH & Co Kg
Gutenbergstrasse 1, D-8031 Gilching, Germany
Tel. (8105) 2110; Fax (8105) 5520

Distributed in the USA and Canada on behalf of Prestel
by te Neues Publishing Company, 15 East 76th Street, New York,
NY 10021, USA
Tel. (212) 2880265; Fax (212) 5702373

Distributed in Japan on behalf of Prestel by YOHAN-Western
Publications Distribution Agency, 14-9 Okubo 3-chome,
Shinjuku-ku, J-Tokyo 169
Tel. (3) 2080181; Fax (3) 2090288

Distributed in the United Kingdom, Ireland and all remaining
countries on behalf of Prestel by Thames & Hudson Limited,
30-34 Bloomsbury Street, London WC1B 3 QP, England
Tel. (71) 6365488; Fax (71) 6361659

Designed by Heinz Ross, Munich

Typeset, printed and bound by Passavia Druckerei GmbH Passau

Offset lithography by Gisteldruck, Vienna,
and Karl Dörfel GmbH, Munich

Printed in Germany

ISBN 3-7913-1229-4

This book is a revised and expanded edition of the original
German publication *Josef Hoffmann – Ornament zwischen Hoffnung und Verbrechen*, published in conjunction with the
Hochschule für angewandte Kunst, Vienna, for the exhibition held
at the MAK-Austrian Museum of Applied Arts, Vienna, April 2,
1987 – July 27, 1992. Further venues include:

Hermitage, St. Petersburg (October 29, 1991 – January 7, 1992)

Hoffmann's Birth House, Brtnice, Moravia (August 16, 1992 –
October 18, 1992)

IBM-Gallery, New York (November 24, 1992 – January 23, 1993)

We wish to thank the following institutions for their support of
the exhibition at the IBM Gallery, New York:
Austrian Airlines;
Austrian Cultural Institute, New York;
Federal Ministry for Foreign Affairs of the Republic of Austria,
Vienna;
Federal Ministry for Science and Research, Vienna

Exhibitions and catalogue: Peter Noever
Organization: Christian Witt-Dörring, Daniela Zyman
Contributions: Hanna Egger, Rainald Franz, Brigitte Huck,
Ernst Ploil, Jan Tabor, Elisabeth Schmuttermeier, Angela Völker,
and Christian Witt-Dörring

The editor and the publisher are grateful to the Hochschule
für angewandte Kunst, Vienna, especially to the president,
Oswald Oberhuber, for their cooperation.

Architecture models: Hochschule für angewandte Kunst, Vienna

Contents

Mythos Hoffmann

Introduction

The immediate impression is one of quality, effusive creativity, obsession with form, an uninhibited language of shapes, pathos, monumentality, and many-sidedness, but also of the inconceivable abundance of designs and sketches (the MAK alone has over 5,000 of Hoffmann's drawings in its collection).

In addition to his buildings, including a series of villas, and his ambition to fulfill his mandate for a *Gesamtkunstwerk*, realized with the completion of the Palais Stoclet in Brussels, Josef Hoffmann's renown is fruit of, above all, his string of turn-of-the-century exhibitions in the Vienna Secession, exhibitions at the Austrian Museum of Applied Arts (MAK), held at the beginning of this century, and at the Austrian Biennale Pavilion in Venice (1934). The Purkersdorf Sanatorium near Vienna (1904), his most revolutionary building, is also one of the most significant architectural achievements of the twentieth century. It is striking in its Cubist form, its clearly defined spatial concept, and conclusive in its uncompromising posture.

Hoffmann's incessant stylistic transformations, his "unsinglemindedness," enabled him to adapt his creations to his clients' requirements. This is best evidenced by the Primavesi country house (built ten years after the completion of the Purkersdorf Sanatorium), a compelling, richly decorated building, replete with folkloric motifs, producing an overriding air of artifice.

It is perhaps the very ambivalence of Hoffmann's work – most distinctly apparent in the antithetical examples of the Purkersdorf Sanatorium and the Primavesi country house – which is the basis of his almost timeless presence, his importance, and his "mythos" in Vienna, a city with a special and seemingly ongoing attraction to decoration.

Josef Hoffmann, one of the few Austrian architects who had influenced the international architectural scene during the first half of this century, belongs to the generation of Gustav Klimt, Egon Schiele, and Koloman Moser, which formed the image and appearance of Vienna. It was this generation that was exploited in the worldwide commercial promulgation of "decadent aestheticism" and the "Viennese turn-of-the-century ornamental art."

Hoffmann had never actually intended to endorse fundamental change, but rather to further enhance his l'art pour l'art ideology and to promote the classic Platonic analogy of the "aesthetically beautiful" as the "morally good."

Hoffmann saw himself primarily as an architect, although his most conspicuous, perhaps even dominant, role was that of an object maker. All of Hoffmann's creations – crafts, furniture, monuments, sometimes even buildings – appear to be "objects with individuality" and were designed as in an endless, non-stop, automatic process. This diversity and extravagance, coupled with his extraordinary drive for perfection, all became hallmarks of Hoffmannesque fantasy creations. Most of these arts and crafts objects were produced, over a period of more than thirty years, at the Wiener Werkstätte, of which Hoffmann was co-founder.

This book is a result of the 1992/93 exhibition "Josef Hoffmann Designs" at the IBM Gallery in New York. The exhibition, like the series of MAK Hoffmann exhibitions held in Vienna, at the Hermitage in St. Petersburg and at the house in Brtnice/Moravia where Hoffmann was born, came into being under the premise that the familiar, the old, the widely accepted, and often glorified, are not always worth retaining. Rather, the decisive factor should be to distinguish that which is still valid, vital, and worthy of preservation today.

Only as we begin to address the memorials of the past by shedding a critical light on them, by infusing doubt, by expressing our resistance and refusing to submit, can an opportunity be created for the works of the past to once again acquire meaning, preventing their demise and fall to oblivion. This multifaceted monograph on Josef Hoffmann conveys this proposition, and its contributions reflect the cultural and historical context and reception of his achievements.

Peter Noever

Vienna 1900

Hanna Egger

Europeans have always experienced a strong feeling of fear and discomfort as the turn of a century approaches, a feeling that can rise to feverish intensity.

After the 1848 revolution the Austrian Empire became the Austro-Hungarian, or Danube, Empire, a collection of many different ethnic groups with its capital in Vienna. From 1848 to 1916 this empire of many different peoples, stretching from Venice to Russia, was ruled by a conservative monarch who was bound by tradition and distinguished by an extreme degree of self-discipline: Kaiser Franz Josef I.

Perhaps it was fear of the problems created by neoabsolutism and the multiethnic state, coupled with the industrial revolution, that led people to search for new political agendas, for radically new solutions in intellectual and cultural life during the second half of the nineteenth century, and particularly as the turn of the century approached.

This was the era referred to as the "Gründerzeit," when new industrial enterprises began to thrive in Vienna. The liberal bourgeoisie, particularly the bankers, merchants, and industrialists who were the leading players, opposed the political power of the aristocracy, as did those who supported the growing awareness of an independent national spirit. Franz Josef had to share his power with this ambitious new middle class, which was no longer prepared to submit unquestioningly to the authority of the throne and the church, and he was repeatedly forced to show his willingness to compromise.

The rapid technical changes and the resultant enormous growth in population in the capital brought other problems as well. In 1850 Vienna had fewer than half-a-million inhabitants, but by 1910 it had more than two million. Construction could not keep pace with this explosion, and the consequence was an acute shortage of housing, although the official redevelopment of Vienna was making rapid progress. The Ringstrasse with its monumental buildings was laid out as a triumphal imperial avenue. In 1893 the installation of electric streetlights began in Vienna; in 1894 the electric tram was introduced; and from 1898 river flooding was con-

trolled, the Danube canal regulated, and the city rail network built. In 1899 the first international automobile exhibition was held in Vienna, and it aroused great enthusiasm among the wealthier classes for the new mode of transportation. No middle-class family wanted to be without a telephone and a typewriter. Belief in progress and innovation, designed to guarantee comfort in every respect, became almost a new religion.

The young artists were also filled with the desire to fight for the new. Like the *secessio plebis* used in the Roman

Gustav Klimt, poster for the first exhibition of the
Vienna Secession, 1898

Empire as a combative means of exerting pressure, they left the more traditional institutions, the Academy and the Vereinigung bildender Künstler Österreichs (Association of Austrian Artists) with its Künstlerhaus. New organizations were established: the Vienna Secession in 1897, the Hagenbund in 1900, and the Wiener Werkstätte (Vienna Workshop) in 1903. All had a clearly defined ideology.

A "Sacred Spring" had dawned, and "Freedom for Art and Art for All" was the new cry. In keeping with their programmatic intentions, the Secessionists built their own exhibition hall, designed by Joseph Olbrich, and they also founded their own periodical, *Ver Sacrum*.

The statutes of the new association required an exhibition program that would be "free of Makart characteristics." The Secessionists were referring to the monumental paintings of the flamboyant Hans Makart, who clearly saw himself as successor to Rubens. His name was synonymus with historicism in Vienna, and this was vehemently rejected by the young artists.

Contacts with other countries, until then neglected, were to be greatly intensified "to stimulate creativity at home and to inform the Austrian public of general developments in art." Finally, the barriers were to be torn down between the fine arts and the applied arts.

At the eighth exhibition in 1900 the Secessionists presented the work of Charles Rennie Mackintosh and his group, introducing them to the Viennese public and so providing an intensive encounter with the progressive modern movement abroad. The exhibition consisted primarily of work in the applied arts.

Cafés played an extremely important part in literary life in Vienna around 1900, indeed for intellectual and social life altogether. In 1923 the writer Hermann Bahr compared the café with a "Platonic academy." He and his friends, including Arthur Schnitzler, Richard Beer-Hofmann, and Hugo von Hofmannsthal, met regularly at the Café Griensteidl, where the Socialists also came together under the leadership of Viktor Adler. The more radical representatives of the literary and artistic avant-garde gathered around Karl Kraus in the Café Central. Their group included Peter Altenberg, Egon Friedell, Alfred Polgar, and the architect Adolf Loos. The Café Museum, designed in 1899 by Adolf Loos and nicknamed the "Café Nihilismus," was also a favorite meeting place for artists.

The eighth Secessionist exhibition and the impact of the English and Scottish works shown there undoubtedly provided the major stimulus for the founding of the Wiener Werkstätte, with Josef Hoffmann being particularly affected. When he and Koloman Moser established the Wiener Werkstätte in 1903, with financial support from Fritz Waerndorfer, they gave expression to a growing desire for the "*Gesamtkunstwerk*," the "total work of art."

Josef Hoffmann and Adolf Loos:
The Ornament Controversy in Vienna

Rainald Franz

Josef Hoffmann was born in Pirnitz, Moravia in 1870, and he came to Vienna at the age of twenty-two to study architecture under Karl von Hasenauer, "architect of the Ringstrasse," at the Akademie der bildenden Künste (Academy of Fine Arts). By 1894 the class was being taught by the great innovator Otto Wagner, and after only three years Josef Hoffmann was working in Wagner's office.

With his work as designer of the second exhibition of the Secession in 1898 and with his appointment to the rank of Professor at the Vienna Kunstgewerbeschule (School of Applied Arts) the following year, Josef Hoffmann began to attract the attention of the general public in Vienna, as well as that of the press at home and abroad. Among the domestic commentators was Ludwig Hevesi, a prominent critic writing for the Secessionist magazine *Ver Sacrum* and for *Fremdenblatt*. One of the most ardent supporters of the modern movement in Vienna, he expressed the high expectations held of the young architect:

Hoffmann is one of the founding members of the Vereinigung bildender Künstler Österreichs (Association of Austrian Artists). He is – as one might expect – a student of Wagner....The things he has been doing for the Secession in the past two years have been highly praised and are now attracting a wider public. In him the Kunstgewerbeschule has acquired a real force, someone with something to show for himself who can give students a new direction.[1]

Initially critics favorable to the Secession seemed to find Hoffmann's work most notable for its "simplicity and functional beauty" (Hevesi). His furniture designs were regarded as "novel and yet entirely logical, graceful and yet soundly constructed."[2] During these years Josef Hofmann was recognized primarily as a designer of interior spaces and exhibitions. Hans Folnesics declared in *Deutsche Kunst und Dekoration*: "An interior by Hoffmann is an essential for any art exhibition in Vienna today."[3] Hoffmann's installations were right for the Secessionist exhibitions, "for Hoffmann always derived his design principles from the works of art that were to be shown."[4]

The young Hoffmann soon enjoyed his first success abroad as a designer of furniture and interiors. His rooms for the Vienna Kunstgewerbeschule and the Secession, exhibited at the 1900 Paris Exposition Universelle, met with international acclaim.

Chief honor in this respect belongs to Josef Hoffmann, the architect, who is a professor at the Decorative Art School [School of Applied Arts] in Vienna. He is the very soul of the new movement. Moreover, it may be said without hesitation that no section of the Beaux Arts display is arranged with more taste, or with a keener sense of the merit of the works displayed, than that of Austria.[5]

In the same year Hoffmann traveled to England and met Charles Rennie Mackintosh, and the Scottish architect's furniture was made the centerpiece of the eighth Secessionist exhibition. The fourteenth Secessionist exhibition in 1902 was a particular success. Hoffmann, who had succeeded Josef Olbrich as artistic director, created a "pure geometric" environment for Max Klinger's Beethoven statue. Thus he began to move away from his previous style of "arching curvilinearity."[6]

Up until this time Hoffmann's work as an architect was overshadowed by his furniture and interior designs, by his ephemeral installations. Art critics recognized that such a view of Hoffmann had been limited. As Hevesi declared:

I would like to see a house by Josef Hoffmann. How is it possible that he has never been asked to design one? He is right for Vienna today, one of the architects who can put Vienna at the forefront of our age, and he should be receiving commissions now.[7]

In 1900 Hoffmann designed a series of villas for the Hohe Warte on the outskirts of Vienna, giving him the breakthrough he needed. These villas were built for artists who were Hoffmann's friends, such as the painters Karl Moll and Koloman Moser. As the critic Berta Zuckerkandl described the project:

The architecture has been handled completely in the severe constructivist manner. On the outside each building rises solidly out of the ground. In profile and silhouette these residences radiate harmony.[8]

When Hoffmann, along with Koloman Moser and financier Fritz Waerndorfer, founded the Wiener Werkstätte (Vienna Workshop) in 1903, this collaborative association of architects, designers, and artists represented the next logical step in the path toward the "universality of artistic creation."[9] In 1905 Zuckerkandl's brother awarded Hoffmann the commission for the Purkersdorf Sanatorium near Vienna, a fashionable retreat for the well-to-do; the architect's design was composed entirely of cubic and rectangular elements. Now critics, when attending to Hoffmann's furniture and objects, praised not only their simplicity and clarity of proportion, but also the quality and richness of the materials employed.

Josef Hoffmann's dual gifts as architect and designer for the Wiener Werkstätte are fully realized in the Palais Stoclet, built in Brussels between 1905 and 1910. As the architect Peter Behrens noted, "All [Josef Hoffmann's] conceptions are based on architectural proportions. His designs, even those for the most simple objects of everyday life, have been conceived as part of an architectural whole."[10] The building was compared with Belgian residences in which "the castlelike character of the architecture has been developing as a local tradition from Norman times. … One must admire how the architect has built upon the domestic traditions of his Brussels client…. Every form is conceived on as large a scale as possible, with the intention

Facade of the Purkersdorf sanatorium before completion, 1905

of creating a monumentality equal in weight to the character of the landscape.) Only the best authentic materials are to be used, and the decoration will consist of sublime works of art."[11]

However, right from the start, Josef Hoffmann had opponents within the modern movement in Vienna. One of his fiercest critics was to be Adolf Loos, the other great figure in Viennese contemporary architecture. Originally Loos and Hoffmann had started from very similar premises in their endeavor to give architecture in Vienna a new direction. They were united in their support of the new architecture of Otto Wagner and in their rejection of the Ringstrasse style. Adolf Loos had been a classmate of Hoffmann in Iglau, Moravia, and in 1898 had commissioned drawings from Hoffmann for two articles that he wrote for *Ver Sacrum* – "Die Potemkin'sche Stadt" (The Unreal City) and "Unsere Jungen Architekten" (Our Young Architects). Unlike Hoffmann, Loos was not a member of the Secession. In this early period his attitude toward Hoffmann's work was still friendly, if critical. Also in 1898, Loos wrote an article for the periodical *Dekorative Kunst* that commented on Hoffmann's competitive design for a rental-housing project in the inner-city area of Donnergasse in Vienna:

I find it difficult to write about Josef Hoffmann, for I am utterly opposed to the direction being taken today by young artists, and

Inside the Wiener Werkstätte, 1903

not only in Vienna. For me tradition is everything – the free reign of the imagination takes second place. Here we have an artist with an exuberant imagination who can successfully attack the old traditions, and even I have to admit that it works.[12]

The dispute between the two men was sparked by the controversy over the interior of the new Secession building that arose prior to its opening in 1898. Adolf Loos described the course of events in retrospect in 1913: "Fifteen years ago, I approached Josef Hoffmann to ask that I be allowed to design the conference room of the Secession building, a room which the public would never see and on which only a few hundred Kronen were to be spent. I was turned down flat."[13] Hoffmann's rejection was probably due to his recognition that Loos's position was diametrically opposed to that of the Secessionists. "Were we going to have the old craft tradition? God forbid," he wrote in 1901 in his pamphlet *Einfache Möbel* (Simple Furniture).[14] It was precisely the craft tradition that Loos wanted to continue. "The true path is: God creates the artist, the artist creates his age, the age creates the craftsman, the craftsman creates the button."[15] Adolf Loos came to feel that his rejection of the new movement had led to his being "branded a non-artist"[16] by the Secessionists. In fact, he was still invited to their openings and even invited to exhibit with them. He responded by declaring that "I shall do so when the dealers have been driven from the temple. The dealers? No, those who prostitute art."[17]

Josef Hoffmann became the main target of Loos's campaign against ornamentation, particularly after the Wiener Werkstätte was founded. Nevertheless, for a long time contemporary critics emphasized that which linked the two architects, rather than what divided them.

This furniture [Josef Hoffmann's] takes up the "Old Viennese" tradition and yet is utterly modern; in this it can be compared to the furniture for a large café in the city Café Museum, which another young Viennese architect, Adolf Loos, has recently designed.[18]

Another critic's account of Loos's position at the time makes his attacks more understandable:

He pleased the public – but only the public. Not the artists. He was too modern for the Künstlerhaus and too English for the Secession. He has even more enemies in the latter than in the former. But his attitude is … typically Viennese. He is expressing the saturation with every kind of plush, precious, academic ornamentation.…This attitude is diametrically opposed to that of artists like Olbrich or Hoffmann, with their delight in color and form.[19]

Garden facade of the Palais Stoclet in Brussels, 1903/5

Josef Hoffmann and Adolf Loos   13

In the period before the first public lecture on "Ornament and Crime" (1908), Loos intensified his polemic against Hoffmann's designs, such as his jardinières made of metal grids. "Previously at least a trace of what might be called applied art was evident, but now the grid of our manhole covers are being used for the decor of flower pots and fruit bowls."[20] Schooled in the rhetoric of the magazine *Die Fackel* (edited by his friend Karl Kraus, the satirist, critic, and poet), Loos ultimately claimed that he had actually drawn Hoffmann away from the Secessionist style and manner:

When I showed Hoffmann my first apartment [Stössl interior] thirty years ago he made his first move into the European mode. From then on all his work was influenced by me. And how! A deep armchair is a cushioned crate, a teapot a silver cube. It's painful.[21]

Josef Hoffmann's move away from ornamentation in the fourteenth Secessionist exhibition did not escape Loos's attack: the work was "only ornament" by the "smooth propagator of the new style," Josef Hoffmann.[22]

Josef Hoffmann only once publicly commented on Adolf Loos's attacks, and that was when he responded to Loos's criticism of his work as chief architect for the Austrian section of the 1925 Paris Exposition des Arts Décoratifs.

When, despite my very poor state of health, I had to take over the artistic direction of the Paris exhibition due to my present position in the applied arts in Austria, my first move was to go to Adolf

Facade of the Austrian pavilion at the Werkbund exhibition, 1914

Loos. I asked him very warmly to participate in some way or another.... Loos told me that he wanted nothing to do with Vienna, that he was a Czech citizen and would only consider exhibiting in Prague.... Loos, whose quality I of course have great regard for, did participate in the design of the low-income housing ... despite the differences in our views he fitted beautifully into our group [Josef Frank and Peter Behrens] as a whole.[23]

It was primarily differences in their ways of thinking that split Josef Hoffmann and Adolf Loos; looking back on the major issues in architectural discussions between 1910 and 1930, one can actually find points of agreement in their positions. In 1913 Adolf Loos advanced his pedagogical viewpoint:

Since mankind has been aware of the greatness of classical antiquity, the great architects have been bound by one idea. They have thought: The ancient Romans would have solved this task in the same way as I do today, if they had been in my position. This is the idea I wish to instill in my students.[24]

These same classical principles may be seen in the pavilion built by Josef Hoffmann in 1911 for the International Art Exhibition in Rome, as well as in his pavilion for the Deutsche Werkbund Exhibition in Cologne in 1914. Walter Curt Behrendt, in a contemporary article, remarked that the latter pavilion "borrows ... from the plan of the Roman house."[25]

A preliminary assessment of the work of Josef Hoffmann was undertaken by a number of writers on the occasion of his fiftieth birthday in 1920. The art historian Dagobert Frey wrote:

Hoffmann has only created works in two categories of architecture: exhibition buildings and villas ... and [this] seems not coincidental but rather characteristic of the essence of his art. Exhibition buildings are festive structures for a unique and exhilarating purpose. ... If his exhibition pavilions can be thought of as private interiors of a sort, many of his villas are almost like pavilions. Representative in this sense are his villas for Stoclet, Ast (Eduard Ast, Hohe Warte, 1909/11), and Skywa (Josefine Skywa and Robert Primavesi, Vienna 1913/14). Their monumentality allows them to transcend the character of the domestic dwelling.[26]

Josef Hoffmann's work toward the development of low-income housing in the twenties in his capacity as a city government official is scarcely reflected in the contemporary literature. The "recreator of the elegant villa for the Austrian bourgeoisie, who now also gives his talents to the cause of today's most pressing social challenges – most importantly, low-income housing"[27] remained for most people the designer of expensive villas and luxury goods.

That is still the case with Hoffmann today. No matter what he does, his reputation stays the same. To the vast majority of people, and not only abroad, he is still the man who built the Palais Stoclet. His name evokes ideas of splendor. What he has planned in the way of pure and simple buildings, and has built, does little to counteract that image.[28]

The persistence of that image is all the more surprising when one takes into account the fact that leading architects of quite a different sort, such as Le Corbusier, declared their debt to Hoffmann's buildings and designs for the Wiener Werkstätte:

And among the ordinary productions, often devoted to narrowly circumscribed utilitarian tasks, the works of Hoffmann left a deep impression because he, like myself, starts from the conviction that architectural work must possess a spiritual content, provided of course that it completely fulfills the demands of appropriateness.[29]

In closing we quote from the article that was written by the journalist Karl Marilaun to mark Josef Hoffmann's fiftieth birthday. His assessment is today as relevant as ever:

Josef Hoffmann and his group did away with the Makart sideboard[30] and the dreadful wallpapers of the eighties. They saw quite rightly that the new generation needed a new style….The creators of the modern artifact set up a number of moral guidelines: away with the garbage, use genuine materials, refined craftmanship; but for the most part they created only luxury goods. Here one may recall that Loos, the "grim Antichrist" of the Wiener Werkstätte, was fond of talking not only of a misconception in the applied "arts" but a character fault as well….Of course Hoffmann cannot be held to blame for the fact that the Austrian personality takes the ornament for the essential, that ornament is not a crime but the breath of life for the Austrians, that Vienna is the city of "luxury wares," and this probably for deeper reasons. If this city can be said to have accepted the new spirit, acknowledged that things must be reduced to their essentials, then Adolf Loos would be the leader of the new movement. And Josef Hoffmann, the architect, interior designer, art teacher, and idealist – the last Austrian.[31]

Notes

1 Ludwig Hevesi, "Josef Hoffmann" [1899], *Acht Jahre Secession* (Vienna, 1906): 137ff.

2 Ludwig Hevesi, "Josef Hoffmann" [1899], *Kunst und Kunsthandwerk* 2 (Munich, 1902): 403.

3 Hans Folnesics, "Das moderne Wiener Kunstgewerbe," *Deutsche Kunst und Dekoration* 5 (Darmstadt, 1899/1900): 260.

4 Ibid.

5 Gabriel Mourey, "Round the Exhibition – 4: Austrian Decorative Art," *The Studio* 21 (London, 1901): 114.

6 Berta Zuckerkandl, "Josef Hoffmann," *Dekorative Kunst* 12/1 (Munich, 1903): 4.

7 Ludwig Hevesi, "Die Sezession im Künstlerhause," January 12, 1900, *Acht Jahre Secession* (Vienna, 1906): 214.

8 Zuckerkandl, op. cit, note 6, p. 9.

9 Peter Behrens, "Josef Hoffmann," in Mathilde Flögl, *Die Wiener Werkstätte, 1903-1929:* (Vienna, 1929): unpaginated. Translation of quotation by Eileen Martin.

10 Behrens, op. cit., note 9: unpaginated.

11 Joseph August Lux, "Moderne Kunst," *Hohe Warte* 2 (Vienna and Leipzig, 1905/6): 5-7.

12 Adolf Loos, "Ein Wiener Architekt," *Dekorative Kunst* (Munich, 1898): 227.

13 Adolf Loos, "Meine Bauschule," *Der Architekt* 19 (Vienna, 1913).

14 Josef Hoffmann, "Einfache Möbel: Entwürfe und begleitende Worte von Professor Josef Hoffmann," *Das Interieur* 2 (Vienna, 1901): 37.

15 As quoted by Paul Engelmann, "Ludwig Wittgenstein. Briefe und Begegnungen," in *Alle Architekten sind Verbrecher: Adolf Loos und die Folgen: Eine Spurensicherung*, ed. Adolf Opel and Marino Valdez (Vienna, 1990): 37-42.

16 Undated draft of a letter (1930?), quoted in Burkhard Rukschio and Roland Schachel, *Adolf Loos* (Salzburg, 1987): 53.

17 Adolf Loos, "Keramika," *Die Zukunft* 12 (Berlin, March 5, 1904): 369.

18 Folnesics, op. cit., note 3, p. 260.

19 Unidentified critic ("SS"), "Adolf Loos," *Dekorative Kunst* 4 (Munich, 1899): 173.

20 Adolf Loos, "Wohnungsmoden," *Frankfurter Zeitung* 340 (Dec. 8, 1907): 1.

21 Adolf Loos, undated manuscript fragment, published in Rukschio and Schachel, op. cit.: 63.

22 Adolf Loos, undated fragment from his papers, end of the twenties, ibid: 63.

23 Josef Hoffmann, "Meine Gegner und ich," *Die Stunde* (Vienna, Jan. 10, 1926).

24 Joseph August Lux, "Moderne Kunst," *Hohe Warte* 2 (Vienna and Leipzig, 1905/6): 5-7.

25 Walter Curt Behrendt, "Die Deutsche Werkbundausstellung in Köln," *Kunst und Künstler* 12 (1913/14): 615-26.

26 Dagobert Frey, "Josef Hoffmann zu seinem 50.Geburtstag," *Der Architekt* 20 (Vienna 1920): 65-73.

27 Hans Ankwicz-Kleehoven, "Neuere Bauten Prof. Josef Hoffmanns," *Österreichs Bau- und Werkkunst* 2 (Vienna 1925/26): 45-46.

28 Max Eisler, "Josef Hoffmann und seine Schule," *Moderne Bauformen* 26, no. 10 (Stuttgart, October 1927): 373/74.

29 Le Corbusier, "Die Wiener Werkstätte," in Flögl, op. cit., note 9: unpaginated. Quoted in Eduard F. Sekler, *Josef Hoffmann: The Architectural Work*, translated by the author; catalogue translated by John Maas (Princeton, N.J., 1985) [Salzburg, 1982]: 495.

30 The reference here is to Hans Makart (1840-1884), whose name was associated with a neo-Baroque style of interior decoration. – Ed.

31 Karl Marilaun, "Josef Hoffmann, die Wiener Werkstätte und Adolf Loos," *Alte und moderne Kunst* 113 (Vienna, 1970): 44.

Josef Hoffmann and the MAK – Austrian Museum of Applied Arts

Christian Witt-Dörring

The collections in the MAK – Austrian Museum of Applied Arts include a wide variety of material and afford a detailed and excellent overview of the work of Josef Hoffmann. The collection has been built up over the last eighty years with varying degrees of intensity, and on first examination it appears to be the result of random acquisitions rather than a precisely defined policy. However, examined in the context of the history of the museum, what initially appear to be chance factors prove instead to be reflective of cultural, economic, and political history. As such, the collection is not only the exciting product of subjective feelings but provides information on the history of the institution's priorities as set by individual decisions.

Josef Hoffmann discusses this problem in one of his rare articles, addressing the question of how the museum, in its traditional role as a place where objects are stored and exhibited, confronts the changing priorities of its time through the objects it collects and displays:

Where in this most impoverished of all times are we to find, if not something to emulate, then at least a tradition to follow? We can only take up where the creative impetus stopped for us. Have we perhaps missed that moment? Did we not have the same precursors as in England? Thank the museums for showing you anything, but not for that. Indeed, how much they have not shown us! With the exception of the ethnographic departments, which strangely, despite their highly artistic holdings, are included in the natural history collections, they seem to have entirely forgotten their obligations. Or have you ever seen a fine machine in a museum of applied arts? Has such a museum ever tried to trace the steps of the modern movement in this and other infallible things and sincerely tried to help you in doing so?[1]

Hoffmann was criticizing not only the role of what was then the k.k. Österreichisches Museum für Kunst und Industrie (Imperial and Royal Austrian Museum of Art and Industry), which had hardly changed since it was founded in 1864; he was also raising one of the basic issues for museums: how to set priorities in purchase and acquisition policies. The inventories of the collections are interesting to examine in this regard. Hoffmann's criticism concerning the search for

"tradition" in museum displays is borne out by the fact that it was only in the twenties that the museum began to build up a larger collection of Viennese Empire and Biedermeier furniture. The art of this period was regarded as the expression of the decline of craft and form right up to the turn of the century; it was only re-evaluated by Hoffmann's generation of artists and historians, and it only regained model character nearly seventy years after it was established. The art produced around the turn of the century was to fare similarly, for it was only in the sixties that the first important items of furniture from designs by Josef Hoffmann, Koloman Moser, and Otto Wagner were included in the museum's collection. Again in search of "tradition" – this time, the modern movement of the twentieth century – the young avant-garde of the sixties discovered the products of their grandparents' generation. This cycle of creation, rejection, and rediscovery seems to be repeating itself at regular intervals, through the generations, since the end of the nineteenth century.

May 1, 1898 appears in the files of the Österreichisches Museum as the day Josef Hoffmann was appointed professor at the Vienna Kunstgewerbeschule (School of Applied Arts). The appointment was made two years before the museum and school administrations were separated, and it is our first point of reference in a long and mutual relation that was to prove particularly fruitful for the development of the applied arts in Vienna. The first sign of Hoffmann's presence came with the *Winterausstellung* (winter exhibition) of 1899/1900 in the museum, where Hoffmann exhibited the dining room he had designed for the Paris Exposition Universelle and a number of individual items of furniture. The exhibition catalogue, still in the traditional layout and printed in a Gothic face, hardly suggests the exhibition's inclusion of one of the first examples of modern Viennese furniture. In the winter exhibition of 1901/2 the firm of Jacob & Josef Kohn presented its latest bent-wood furniture in three "modern" interiors, and the role of Josef Hoffmann as designer, which is repeatedly stressed in the contemporary literature on the exhibition, has never been fully clarified. Although Hoffmann regularly exhibited his designs in the museum's exhibitions, it was only in 1908 that the museum bought any of his work, at the Vienna *Kunstschau*: silver artifacts for the Wiener Werkstätte and a wooden jewelry box that had been displayed once before, in Berlin in 1904.

In 1909 Eduard Leisching, an enthusiastic promoter of new art in Vienna, became director of the museum, and through his leadership and the collaboration of the Kunstgewerbeschule, progressive ideas in art finally came into their own. Beginning with the winter exhibition of 1909/10 the museum regularly sponsored a survey of the products of the Wiener Werkstätte. Jacob & Josef Kohn also showed Hoffmann's latest furniture in bent wood. The Kunstgewerbeschule featured its first comprehensive survey of the work of teachers and students in the applied arts exhibition of 1911/12, and the Wiener Werkstätte was first able to exhibit its own work in its own space the same year. From then on and into the period of the First World War, the museum regularly bought examples at the annual exhibitions of Hoffmann's designs in a wide range of materials. Most of them were made by the firms of Johann Lötz, Joseph and Ludwig Lobmeyr, Johann Backhausen & Söhne, J. Ginzkey, Jacob & Josef Kohn, and the Wiener Werkstätte. From 1910, these works were included in what was known as the touring inventory, and they, along with the small pieces in glass, ceramics, and metal, as well as a selection of textile designs, constitute our basic Hoffmann collection today. The special inventory includes all the contemporary arts-and-crafts objects and industrial design products chosen for the specialized crafts schools of the monarchy for touring exhibitions. At the same time, the museum continued its practice of presenting complete interiors, including rooms designed by Josef Hoffmann. At the *Winterausstellung* of 1911/12, a reception room in black and white by Jakob Soulek was shown, and Soulek also produced the black-and-yellow dining room featured in the *Frühjahrsausstellung* (spring exhibition) of 1912. That exhibition marked an important shift in the direction of Viennese interior design. In contrast to Josef Hoffmann's dining room, its furniture still governed by the notion of overall unity, Josef Frank's drawing room consisted of individually conceived components.

When in 1913 the museum organized the exhibition *Österreichische Tapeten-Linkrusta und Linoleum-Industrie* (Austrian Wallpapers, Lincrusta, and Linoleum), Josef Hoffmann not only served as a member of the exhibition committee but also provided most of the lincrusta designs, as well as the design for a "living room of a country house."

For the exhibition of Austrian applied arts in 1913/14, he designed a hall furnished in dark gray stained wood and a ladies' salon that was largely of bent wood stained black, made by the firm of J. & J. Kohn. Its ornamentation was already quite Biedermeier in mood. Some of these works were also part of the Austrian pavilion at the *Deutsche Werkbund-Ausstellung* (German Werkbund Exhibition) in Cologne in 1913/14. The museum made its first purchase of furniture by Hoffmann following the *Kunstgewerbe* exhibition of 1913/14 – three chairs manufactured by the firm of J. & J. Kohn. During the war years of 1915/16, Hoffmann curated the museum's *Mode-Ausstellung* (Fashion Exhibition), which attempted to encourage a fashion independent of international influences.

The First World War brought with it a watershed in the museum's purchases and exhibitions. As president of the 1920 *Kunstschau* exhibition committee, Hoffmann was represented by works in metal and glass and by jewelry, all of which had been made by the Wiener Werkstätte; it was not until 1921 that the policy of designing and making interiors specifically for exhibitions was reinstated. For the exhibition *Vornehme Wohnungseinrichtungen* (Elegant Furnishings),

Reception room for the winter exhibition, 1912

"Lady's Salon" for the *Kunsthandwerk* exhibition, 1923

intended to demonstrate to the Viennese consumer the superior quality of Viennese cabinetry, Hoffmann designed a bedroom in cherry wood that was produced by the workshop of the cabinetmaker Johann Jonasch. At the Austrian *Kunsthandwerk* exhibition in 1923 he presented his "Lady's Salon," entirely veneered in walnut. It was exhibited two years later at the Exposition Internationale des Arts Décoratifs in Paris and finally at Macy's in New York in 1928. In 1924 the Wiener Kunstgewerbeverein (Vienna Applied Arts Association) celebrated its fortieth jubilee with an exhibition of nineteen furnished rooms. Hoffmann presented a living room manufactured by A. Pospischil with paintings by Camilla Birke, as well as a living room in walnut with a matt finish, made by Jakob Soulek. Recalling the success of their legendary *Kunstschau* exhibition of 1908, the museum organized another *Kunstschau-Ausstellung* in 1927, the catalogue of which declared it to be a homage to Josef Hoffmann's creative energies,[2] which were evident not only in his work as a designer (he exhibited one living room by A. Pospischil and designed the Wiener Werkstätte exhibition space) but also in his role as teacher at the Kunstgewerbeschule; the products of both his master class in architecture and his metal and enamel workshop were on view. The school mounted a separate exhibition in 1929 to mark its sixtieth birthday, featuring the work of its entire teaching staff. Other examples of Hoffmann's furniture designs and interiors include a tearoom for the 1928 exhibition *Die neuzeitliche Wohnung* (The Modern Apartment), and a music room for the exhibition *Wiener Raumkünstler* (Viennese Interior Designers) in 1929/30. The 1930 Werkbund exhibition, with its innovative concept, was a highlight in the history of

the Österreichisches Museum. In addition to the usual exhibition spaces, it featured specific examples of modern public spaces, some of which could be used by the visitors (a tearoom, café, and espresso bar). As vice-president of the Werkbund, Hoffmann was responsible for the artistic direction, as well as the entire installation, designing the central exhibition space (fashion and sports) and the café with adjoining terrace.

Regarding the period following the First World War, Hoffmann's active presence in museum exhibitions contrasts with the institution's total abstinence from purchasing any of his works. Only in 1930 did this freeze of more than ten years end, with the acquisition of nearly two hundred of Hoffmann's design drawings, as well as contemporary silver and brass objects by the Wiener Werkstätte. In 1932/33 the Gewerbeförderungsinstitut (an institute dedicated to the promotion of the applied arts) attempted to revitalize the craft and manufacture of upholstery and passementerie through their exhibition *Raum und Mode* (The Room and Fashion), providing the last interior Hoffmann designed for the Österreichisches Museum (a corner hearth for a living room). His last exhibition designs came in 1934 for the fiftieth anniversary of the Wiener Kunstgewerbeverein and

Living room for the *Kunstschau* exhibition, 1927

Tea room for the exhibition *Die neuzeitliche Wohnung*, 1928

Music room for the exhibition *Wiener Raumkünstler*, 1929/30

Café at the Werkbund exhibition, 1930

the exhibition *Das befreite Handwerk* (Crafts Liberated). The latter provided the first opportunity in some time to purchase two pieces of furniture for the collection. Both were made to demonstrate that formal variety and craftsmanship could continue without conflicting with the requirements of modern life and the ideas of the New Objectivity (Neue Sachlichkeit). Such efforts were soon to be eclipsed by economic and political realities. Josef Hoffmann was able to show examples of his work and current production for the last time in 1943 in the exhibition *Deutsche Werkkunst* (German Applied Arts): glasses made by Joseph & Ludwig Lobmeyr and a coffee service by the Wiener Porzellanmanufaktur Augarten.

In 1932 the Wiener Werkstätte went bankrupt, and the auction of its inventory provided a chance to buy textiles and works in metal and leather. In 1947 the museum was able to obtain the large and important archives of the Wiener Werkstätte, although unfortunately they did not survive the war intact. However, among other things, they contain nearly five thousand drawings from every period of Hoffmann's work, spanning a wide range of territory in the applied arts. Another set of designs was acquired from his studio shortly after the end of the war, in 1945, together with a number of wooden boxes and cases, and works in brass and tombac. The objects were made in 1942 in the Entwurfs- und Versuchswerkstätten für das Kunsthandwerk der Gemeinde Wien (Design and Experimental Workshops for the City of Vienna) and in 1950 for the Österreichischen Künstlerwerkstätten (Austrian Artists' Workshops).

The first object to be acquired after the death of Josef Hoffmann in 1956 was his personal writing desk, purchased in 1960 from his widow, Karla Schmatz Hoffmann. In the sixties Austria witnessed the gradual rediscovery of its own artistic production at the turn of the century, and with its exhibition *Wien um 1900* (Vienna around 1900) in 1964 the Historisches Museum der Stadt Wien laid the foundation for a general resurgence of interest in this period. The art world responded quickly and has since been putting new material on the market and arranging sales exhibitions. In 1966, shortly before its major exhibition of the following year, *Die Wiener Werkstätte: Modernes Kunsthandwerk von 1903-1932*, the Österreichisches Museum succeeded in buying a large group of early works by the Wiener Werkstätte that had previously scarcely been represented in its collection. Thus, the museum was able to acquire its first case pieces that had previously furnished the apartment of Hermann Wittgenstein, as well as outstanding work in silver. A purchase of particular importance for the history of

Austrian decorative arts was made in 1967 during the Wiener Werkstätte exhibition, when the museum bought a great variety of silverware made between 1904 and 1908 for Lilly and Fritz Waerndorfer, who had provided the original financial backing for the Wiener Werkstätte.

After this concentrated wave of acquisitions, purchased at extremely favorable rates judging by today's prices, only isolated additions were made to the collection in the seventies. This was probably due to the enormous increase in prices on the international market, a fact which only began to be accepted in the early eighties. A positive side-effect of this increase in price was to create greater public awareness of the value of this part of our cultural heritage. Things that would earlier have been destroyed, their value unrealized or their aesthetic qualities rejected, had a new chance of survival as purely material assets. The new interest also brought the museum major donations. In 1983, for instance, studio furniture that had belonged to Ernst Stöhr, some of the earliest furniture by Josef Hoffmann (1898), was bequeathed to the museum, and some of the furniture designed for Hugo Koller (ca. 1905) was also donated to the collection. All areas of the collection had been greatly augmented by 1987. In the last few years we have concentrated more on individual additions in the most important areas. The metal collection received a lidded goblet made in 1902 by Würbel & Czokally Silberwarenfabrik as part of the Wilhelm Mrazek gift of 1989. It is the earliest work by Hoffmann in silver in the Mrazek group, and it dates prior to the establishment of the Wiener Werkstätte. In 1990 the museum bought a silver pepper-and-paprika caster, set with semiprecious stones, our most recent purchase to date. With its date of 1903 it is one of Hoffmann's earliest and most original examples of Wiener Werkstätte silver work.

Josef Hoffmann's ephemeral exhibition designs are an important part of the identity of the Österreichisches Museum für angewandte Kunst, as are his design drawings and realized works, which it also houses. It is an identity that, like the response to Josef Hoffmann's work, has changed over time and will go on changing. That is necessary if the institution and its collection are to remain a living, essential part of our everyday lives. In both cases this flexibility can provide a creative basis for dialogue. But this will not be achieved by replacing one shortsighted and quick response to the dictates of fashion by another one-sided "truth."

Notes

1 Josef Hoffmann, "Einfache Möbel: Entwürfe und begleitende Worte von Professor Josef Hoffmann," *Das Interieur* 2 (Vienna, 1901): 196-97.
2 See the introduction by Leopold Wolfgang Rochowanski to Österreichisches Museum für Kunst und Industrie, *Kunstschau Wien* 1927 (Vienna 1927): 14: "The artists of the Kunstschau, with the leadership and consultation of Josef Hoffmann, have always been bound by the certainty that they know the way, a certainty nothing will shake or distract."

Catalogue

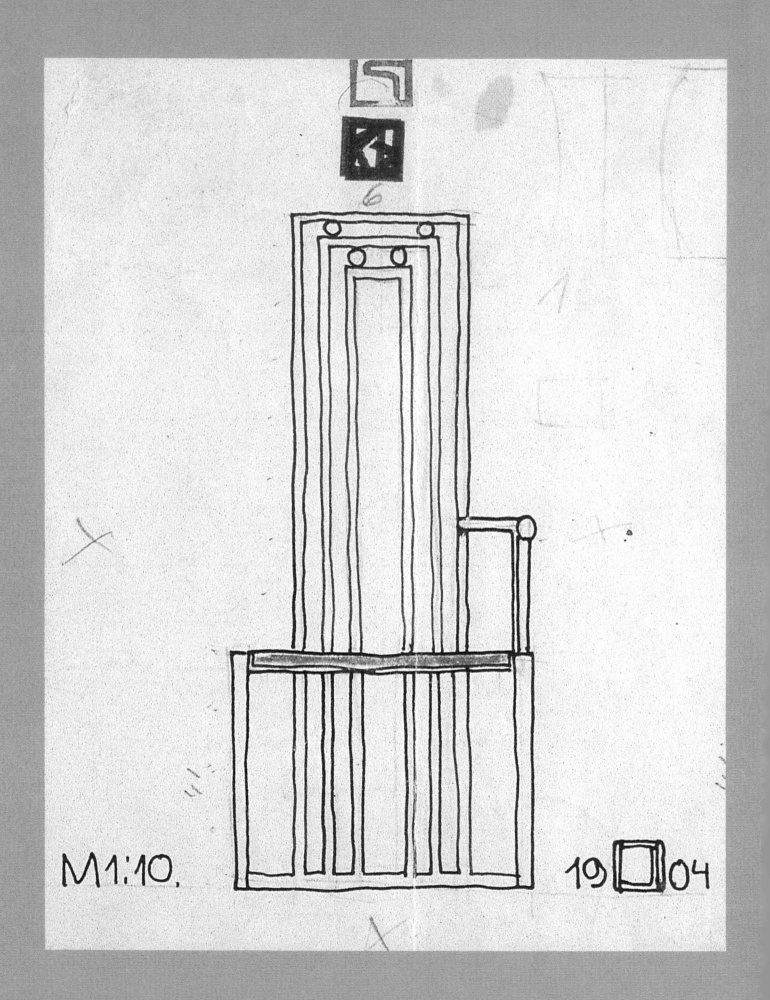

M1:10.

19 04

Furniture and Wooden Objects

To think of Josef Hoffmann and furniture is above all to think of his designs for the bent-wood industry. Most of these were mass-produced chairs, some of which have been in production continuously since that time. The names of the models have given them an independent, communicable identity in the marketplace, such as the Fledermaus chair of 1907, created for the Viennese cabaret of that name, and the *Sitzmaschine* ("Machine for Sitting In"), which was first displayed at the Vienna *Kunstschau* in 1908. These chairs designed by Hoffmann are marketed as modern classics, as timeless components of our culture, part of our heritage.

What is it that still appeals to us in this furniture by Josef Hoffmann? First, certainly, it is the modern appearance, which seems natural today, although the designs were very avant-garde when they first appeared. And then there is Hoffmann's sureness in handling proportion, material, and detail. These elements create a sense of familiarity and distance; they are the raw materials for a tense harmony between the familiar and the new.

Josef Hoffmann and the artists of his generation succeeded in defining values that could serve as points of departure for the development of design in our century. They fought particularly to bring artistic expression, the "creative" element, back into our everyday lives, and they won their battle because they had the courage to break with long-established, conformist values. They recognized that in the course of history, people's basic needs and clear, honest, and dignified solutions to them had been covered over to the point of unrecognizability. They wanted to avoid the moment when "the chain that bound us to the last good old days threatened to break,"[1] and thus tried to work within traditions in which the "old" values still inhered. For them the quality of an object could "not only lie in the work of the artist's hand." It also depended on the clarity of formal expression that results from the integrity of design and production. The furniture of the Biedermeier era provided these artists with unsuspected, highly relevant sources of inspiration.

Equipped with the rediscovery of "first principles," Hoffmann was able to let artistic expression flow back into the everyday object. The naturalness with which this was done is what distinguishes the aesthetic and artistic quality of his work. His accomplishments make all the more incomprehensible today's revival of the tendency to deny that a practical object can be an expressive work of art.

Note

1 Quoted from Josef Hoffmann, "Einfache Möbel," *Das Interieur* (Vienna, 1901): 193ff.

1   Chair, 1904 (detail of cat. no. 9)

2   Interior, 1899

3　Cupboard, 1899

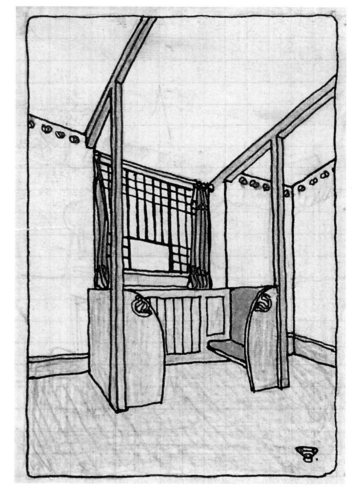

5　High window seat, 1899

4　Hall, 1899

6   Bed arrangement, 1901

7 Bookcase, 1900

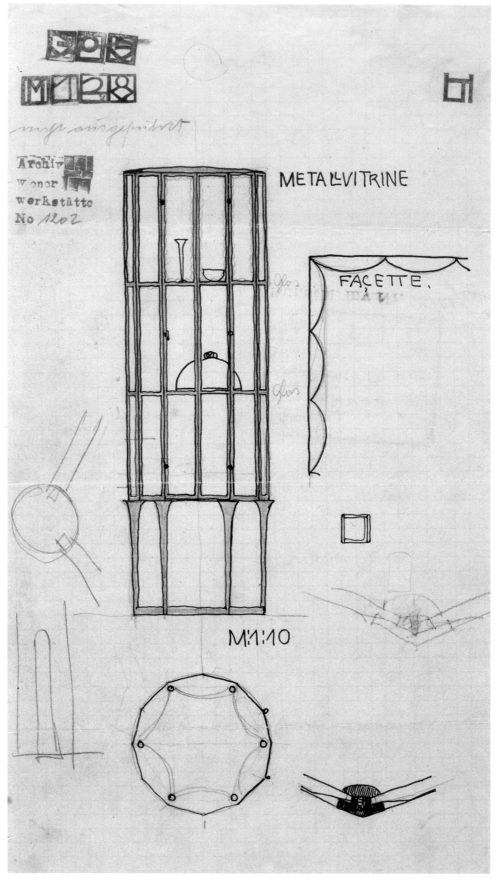

8   Metal vitrine, 1903/4

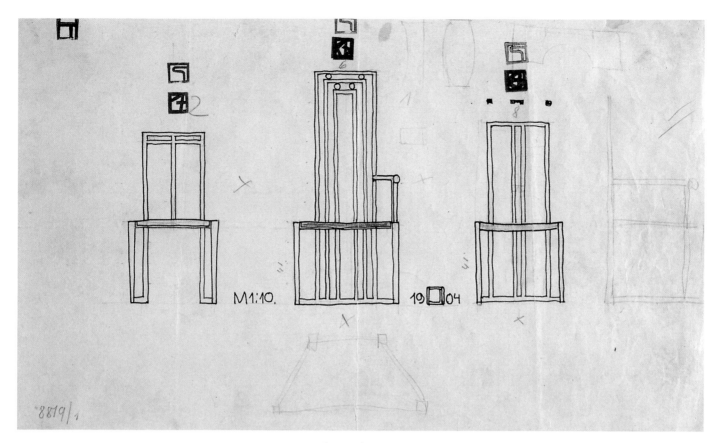

9   Three chairs, 1904

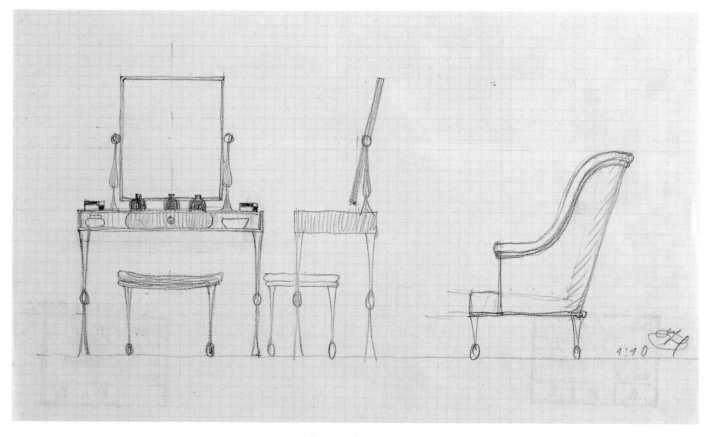

10   Dressing table, stool, and armchair, ca. 1930

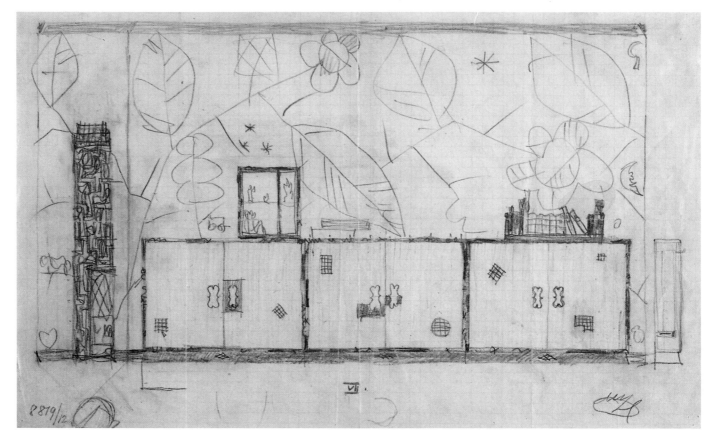

11   Nursery, 1927

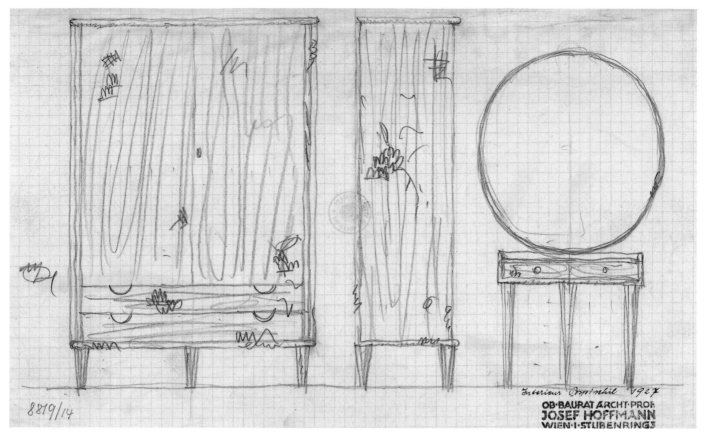

12   Cupboard and a dressing table, 1927

13   Buffet and stove, ca. 1925

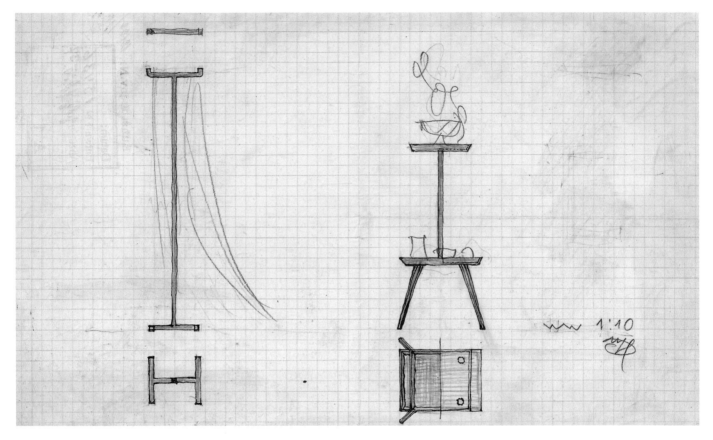

14   Wooden table and stand, ca. 1930

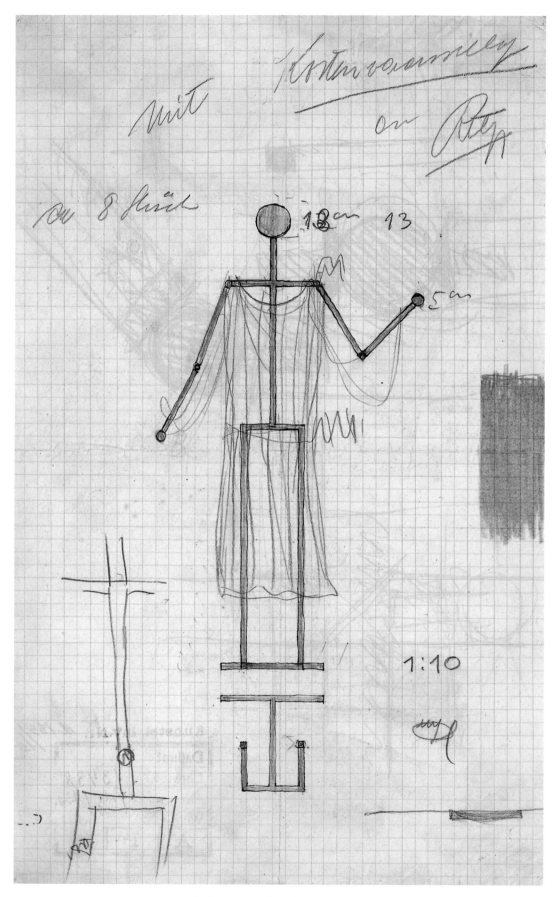

15   Tailor's wooden dummy, ca. 1930

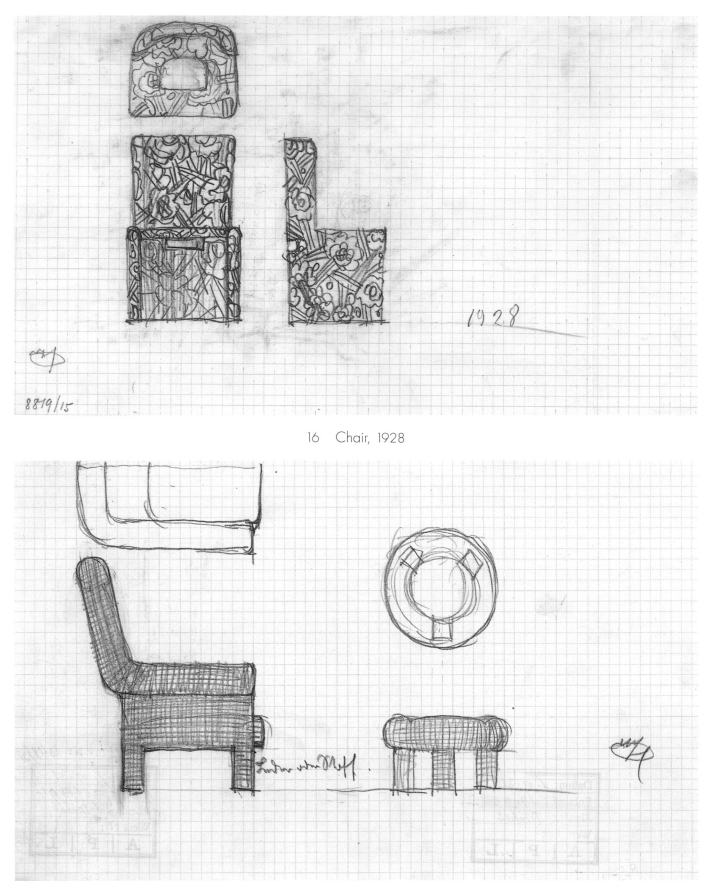

16 Chair, 1928

17 Chair and stool, ca. 1930

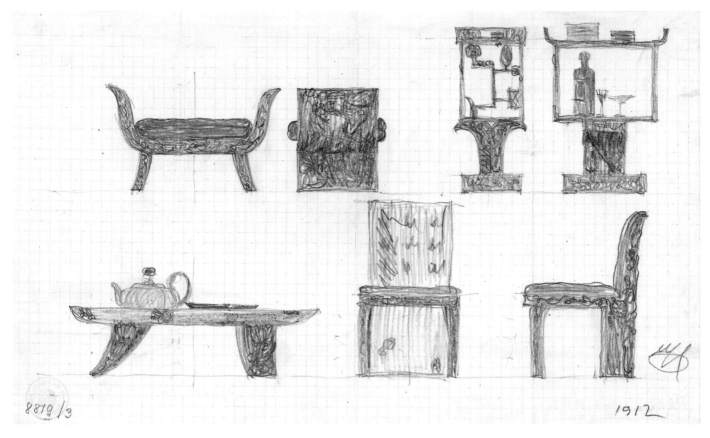

18   Sofa, table, chair, and glass cabinet, 1920/30

8819/13

19   Cabinet, ca. 1930

20   Two chairs and an armchair, 1927

21   Two chairs, 1928

22 Chair, ca. 1898

23 Chair, 1934

24   Chair, 1910

25   Chair, ca. 1907

26   Chair, ca. 1904

27   Armchair, 1903

28 Chair, 1906

29 Chair, 1907/8

30 Chair, 1902

31 Chair, 1930

32 Chair, ca. 1913

33 Chair, ca. 1907

34 Chair, 1930

35 Chair, 1929

36 Piano chair, ca. 1910

37 Piano chair (raised position)

38 Armchair, 1900

39 Armchair, 1910

40 Tea cart, ca. 1908

41 Armchair, 1905

42　Armchair, 1914

43 Armchair, 1907/8

44 Armchair, ca. 1912

45 Stool, 1898

46 Stool, 1937

47   Upholstered chair, 1937

48   Table, 1905

49   Piano stool, ca. 1908

50 Coffee table, 1902

51   Table, 1899

52   Kitchen table, 1905

53   Table, 1907/8

54　Table, ca. 1898

55　Washstand, ca. 1898

56　Cabinet, ca. 1898

57　Dressing table, ca. 1898

58   Lady's desk, 1905

59   Desk, 1909

60   Desk, ca. 1910

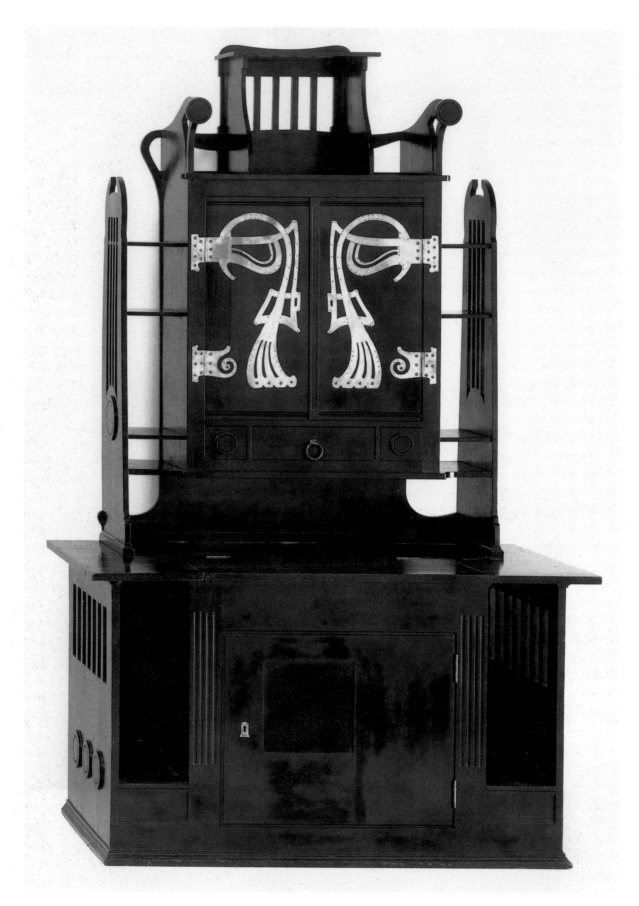

61   Cabinet, 1898

62 Buffet, 1899

63   Cabinet, ca. 1898

64   Cupboard, ca. 1898

65 Cupboard, ca. 1898

66 Cupboard with mirrored door, ca. 1898

67   Cupboard, 1903

68   China cabinet, 1909

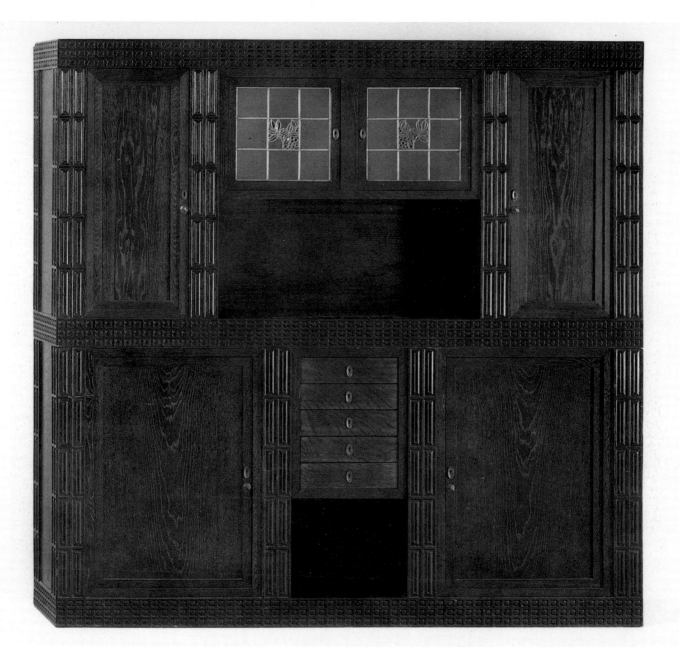

69   Buffet, 1908/9

70   Broom cupboard, 1906

71   Desk and shelf arrangement, ca. 1914

72 Cupboard, 1906

73 Cupboards, 1906

74   Wardrobe, 1906

75 Etagère, ca. 1898

76 Longcase clock, 1908/9

77 Shelves, ca. 1914

78   Bed, chest, and two night tables, ca. 1898

79   Bed, 1903

80 Bed, ca. 1905

81 Bed, ca. 1905

82 Stool, 1899

83 Stool, 1907/8

84 Night table, ca. 1905

85   Night table, 1903

86   Sewing table, 1905

87   Liquor cabinet, 1908/9

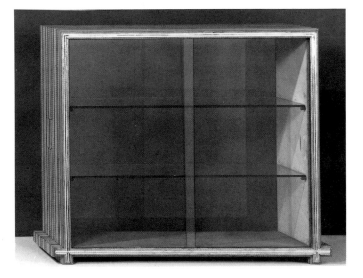

88   Vitrine, 1934

89   Vitrine, 1934

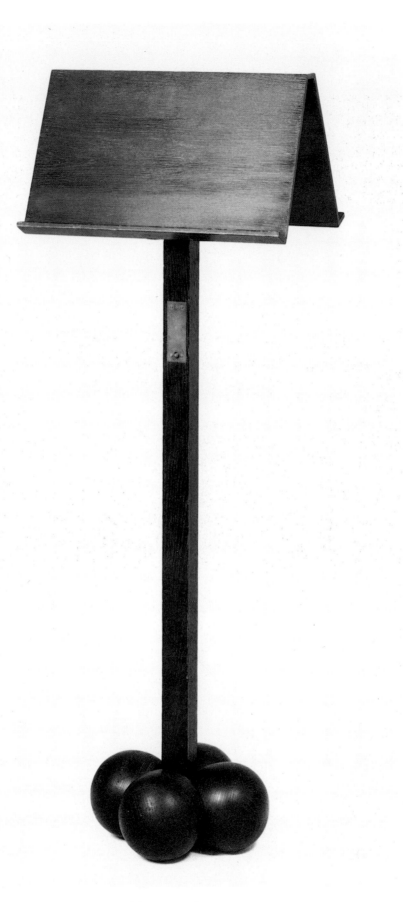

90   Music stand, ca. 1908

91   Box, 1950

92   Box, 1940 (?)

93   Cigarette box, ca. 1910

94   Cigarette case, 1923

95   Bonbonnière, 1942

96   Easter egg, ca. 1906

97   Box, 1943

98   Jewel box, before 1904

99   Box, 1950

100   Box, 1950

101   Box, 1950

102   Cigarette case, 1950

103   Box, 1943

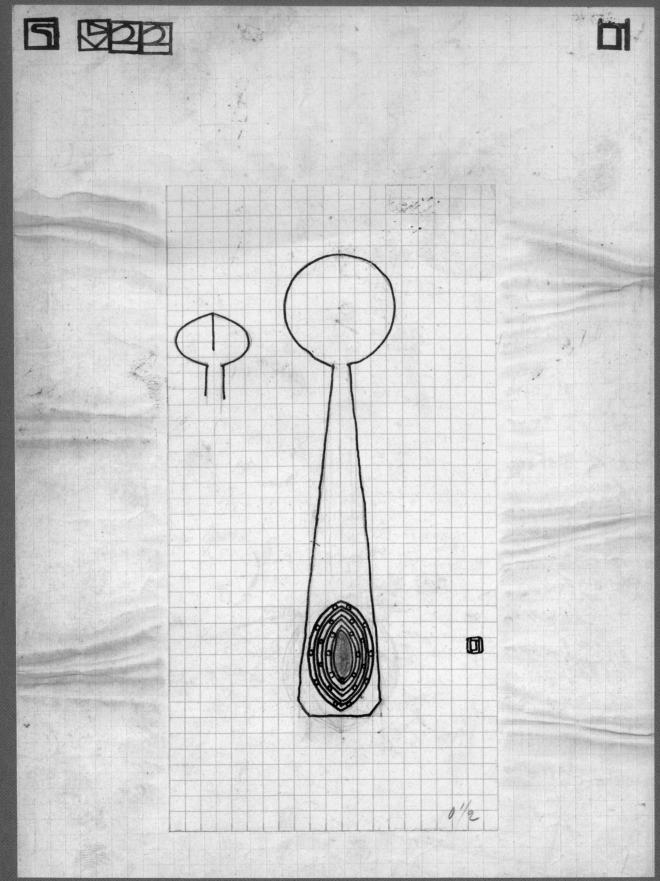

0½

Metal Objects

In a catalogue raisonné of the work of Josef Hoffmann, metal objects would account for the largest section. Was he attracted by the surface of metals, which could be polished smooth, hammered, or punched to provide a field for embellishment with spare or voluptuous designs, or was it simply that, in Hoffmann's time, the demand for practical objects in precious and nonprecious metals had increased so much? No doubt both factors played a role. Certainly, the metal objects show most directly the stylistic changes in his work.

Shortly before the turn of the century, Hoffmann's affinity to the Viennese version of Jugendstil, with its reduced floral and zoomorphic elements, became evident. Around 1900 he turned to geometric forms. In 1903 he began to design simple tableware made by the Viennese goldsmiths Alexander Sturm and Würbel & Czokally. Most of the objects were tall, lidded goblets of geometric design, corresponding in form to vessels in wooden holders that Hoffmann had been sketching the year before. His first designs for metalwork produced by the Wiener Werkstätte followed almost immediately. About 1904 Josef Hoffmann and Koloman Moser reached an extreme form of simplicity and geometric abstraction in their work, leading toward a pure reduction to elementary forms. At times this reduction was carried so far that it was no longer possible to surmise the use of an object from its appearance. To counter the criticism that they were impractical, the artists displayed photographs of the objects in use. Such pieces were either one-of-a-kind or editions of up to five pieces. The perforated-wire vessels in lacquered iron (used to hold glass vases, or as baskets), the dressing tables and writing desk sets, and the trays and tableware were produced for much larger distribution. From about 1905/6 these objects were also made in silver to harmonize with luxurious interiors. It was then that Hoffmann turned more to floral ornamentation; stylized leaves, flowers and vines were used as a frieze or covered an entire object. In some cases the same object was offered with different decorations, such as vine leaves or rose patterns. However, the geometric outline was always retained, and only around 1915 did more Baroque forms begin to appear. The walls of vessels had vertical fluting or convex or concave stopping towards the top.

Josef Hoffmann's designs influenced the metalwork of the Wiener Werkstätte and of other designers to such an extent that his oeuvre became exemplary for a brief epoch in the history of applied art.

104   Spoon, 1905

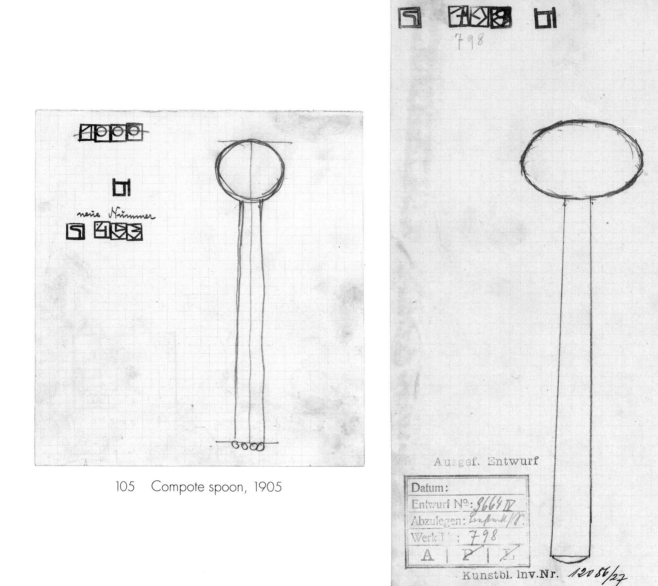

105   Compote spoon, 1905

106   Spoon, 1907

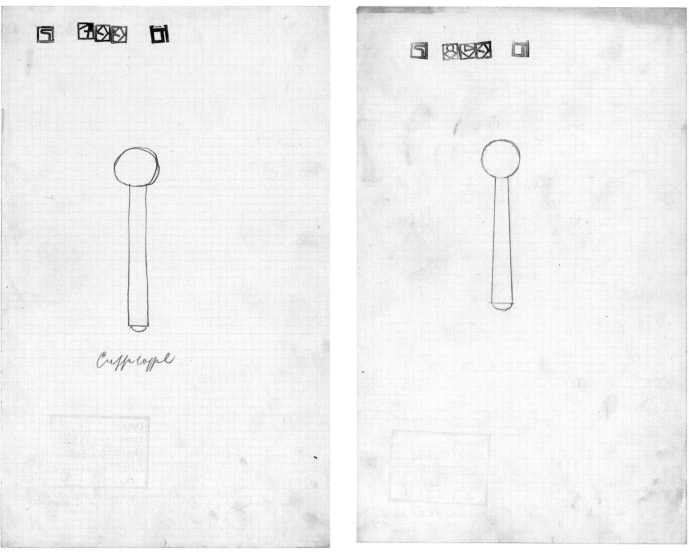

Cupscople

107   Coffee spoon, 1906

108   Demitasse spoon, 1907

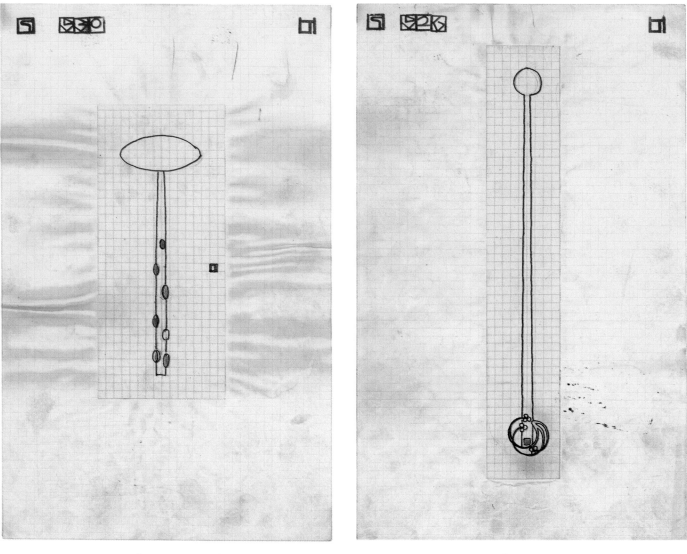

109   Spoon, ca. 1905

110   Spoon, 1905

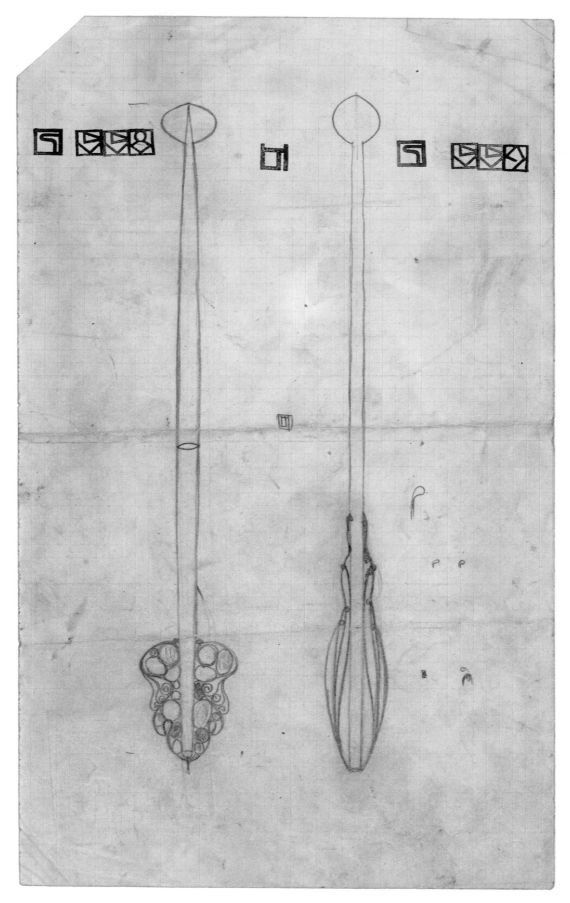

111　Two spoons, 1905

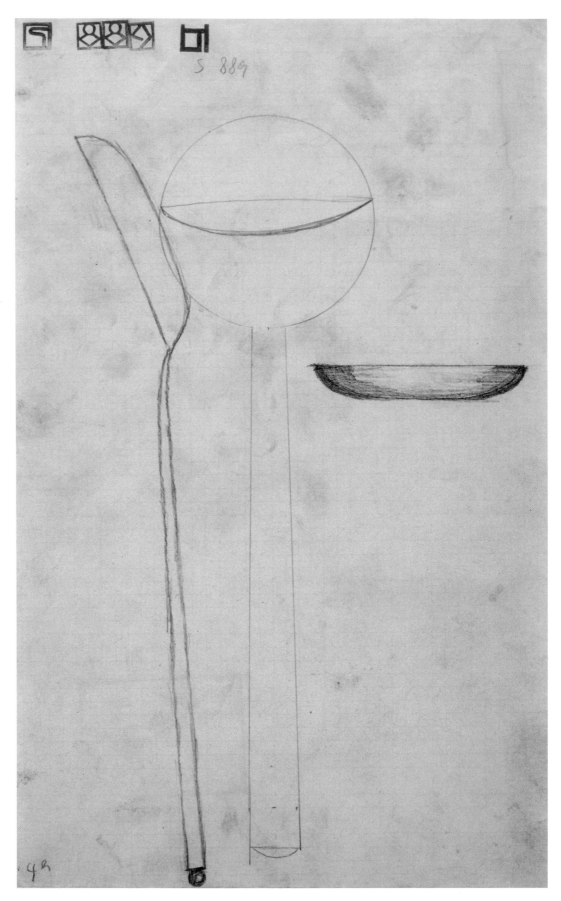

112   Cutlery, date unknown

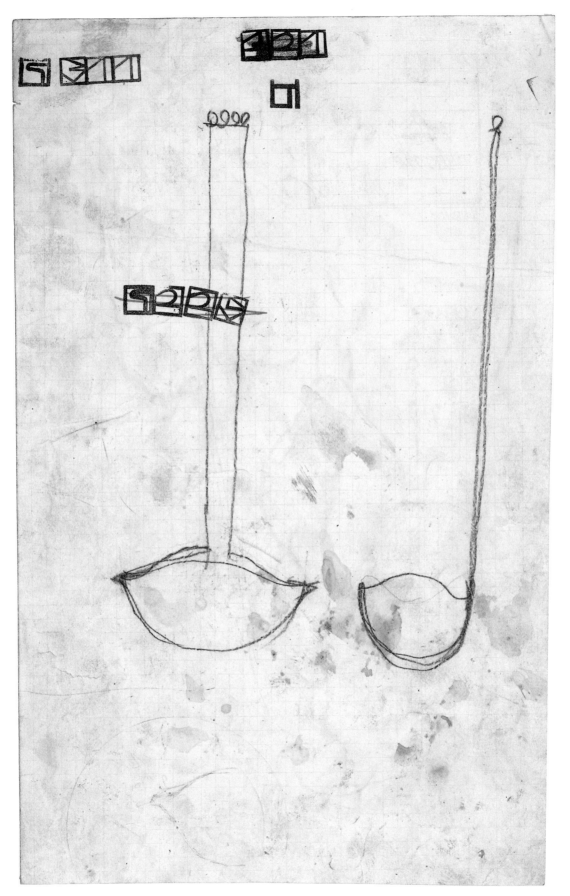

113   Ladle, 1904

114   Dessert cutlery, date unknown

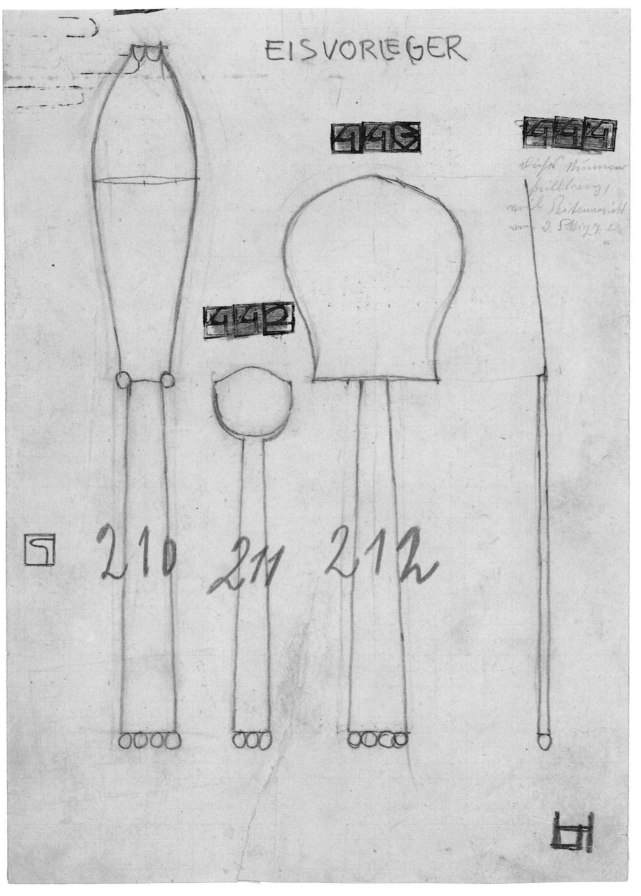

EISVORLEGER

115   Ice cream servers, 1904

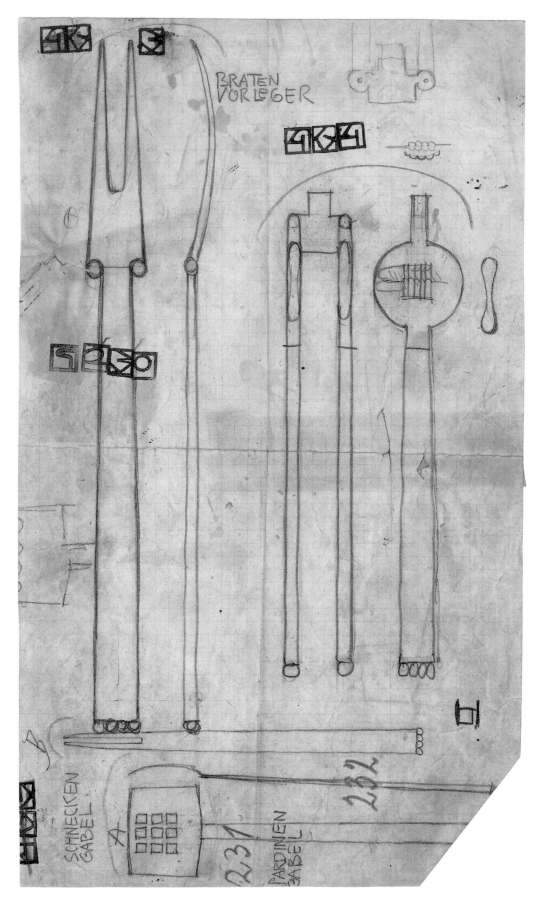

BRATEN VORLEGER

SCHNECKEN GABEL

SARDINEN GABEL

116   Carving, sardine, and escargot forks, 1904

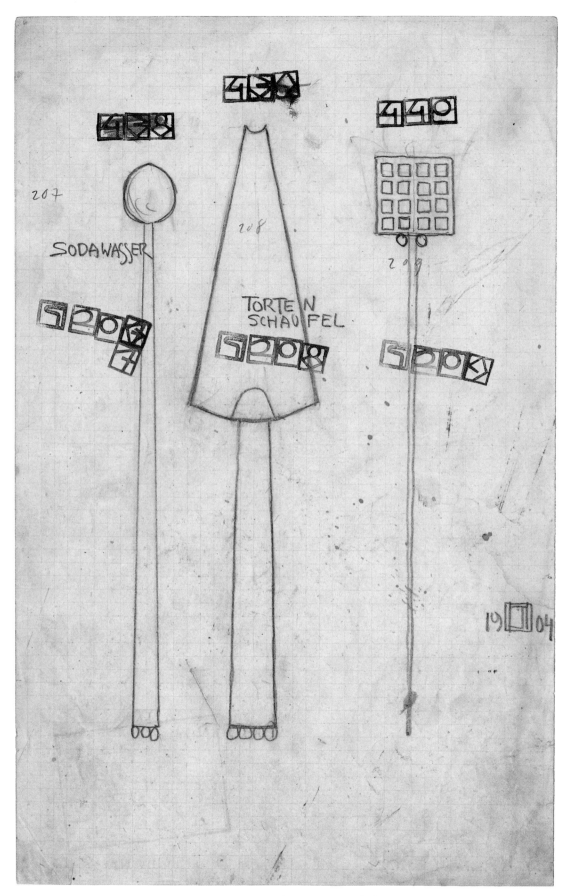

117   Soda water stirrer, cake server, and skewer, 1904

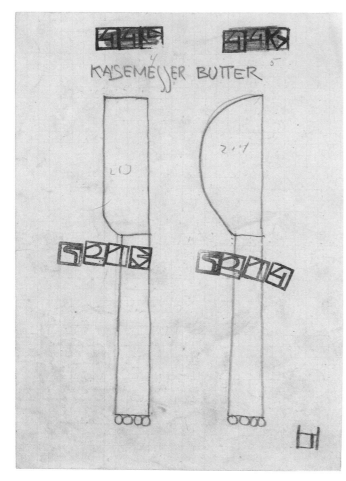

118   Cheese and butter knives, 1904

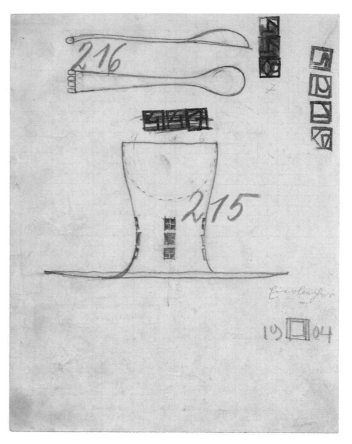

119   Spoon and eggcup, 1904

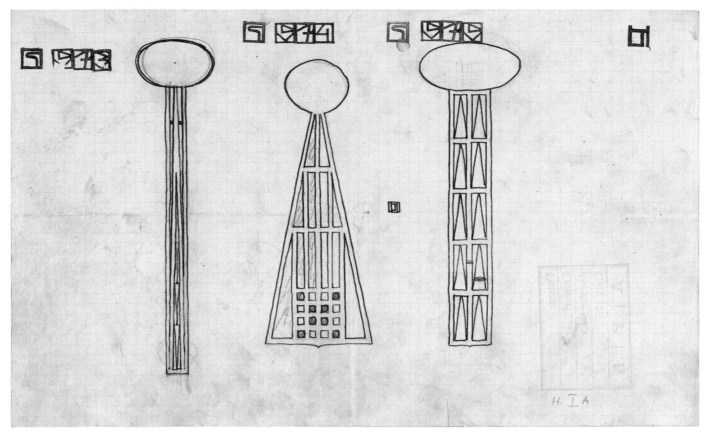

120   Three spoons, 1905

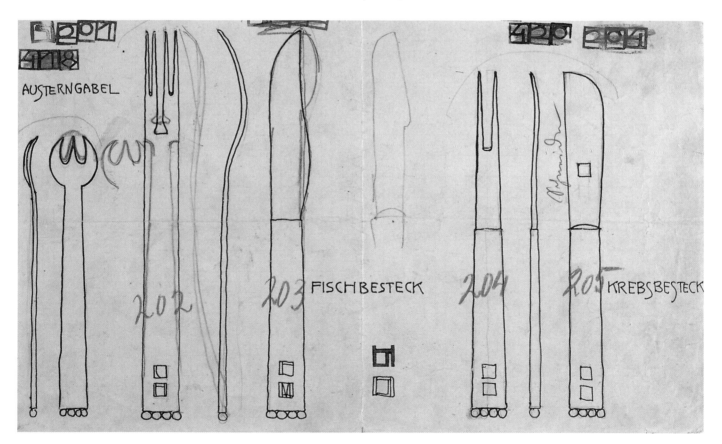

121   Oyster fork, cutlery for fish and for crab, date unknown

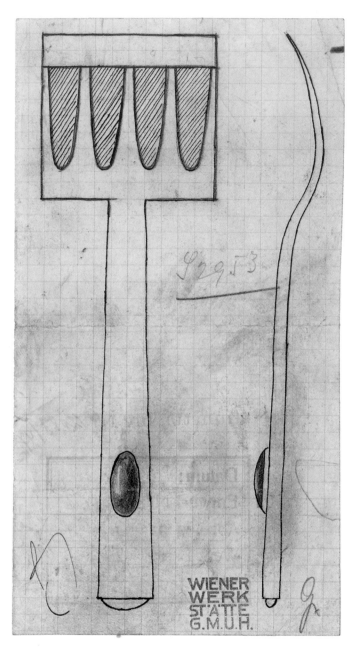

122   Sandwich server, 1912

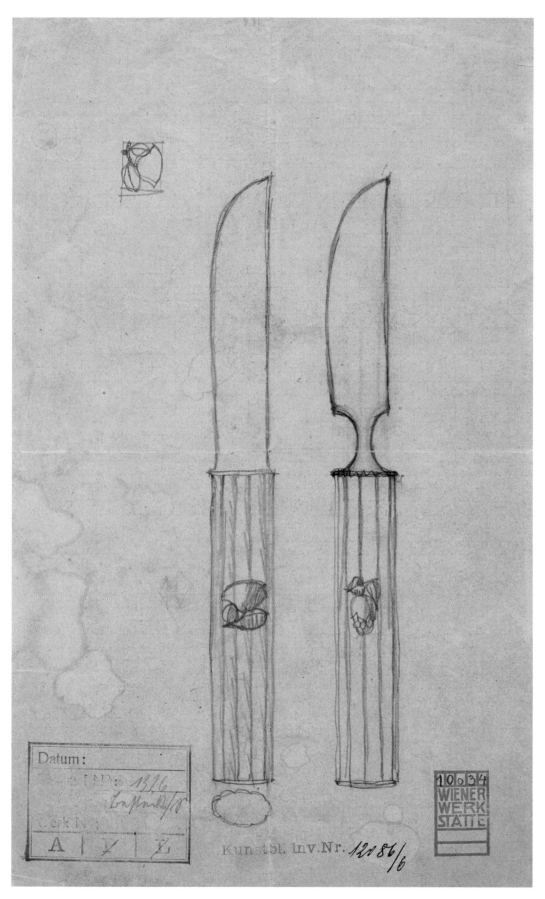

123   Fish knife and fish fork, 1904

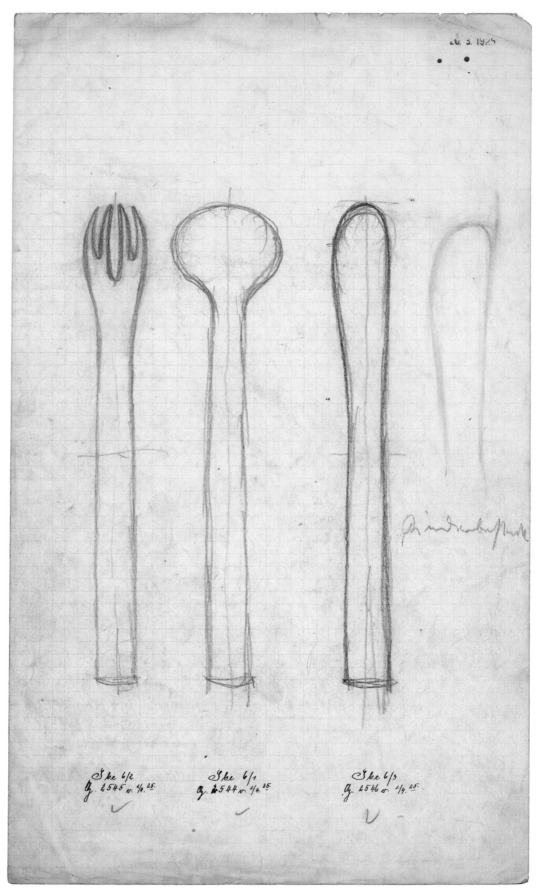

124   Children's cutlery, 1925

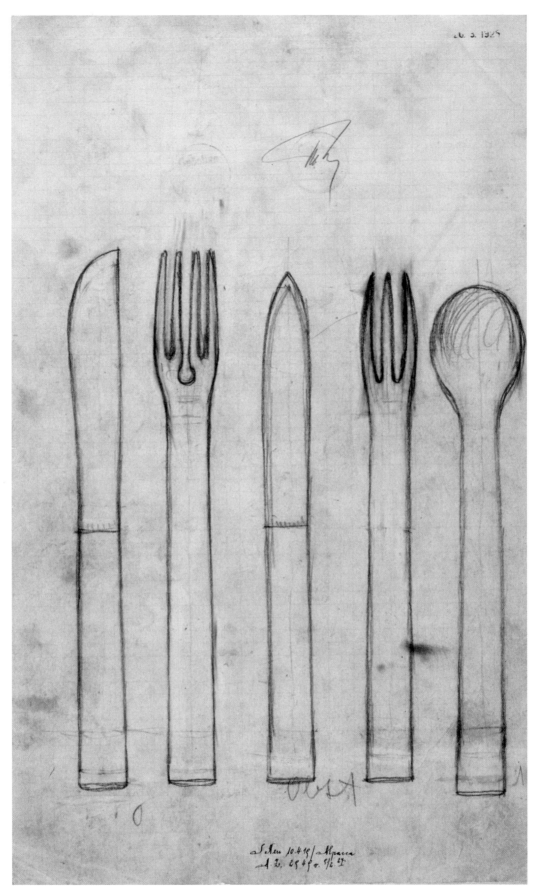

125   Cutlery for fish and for fruit, 1927

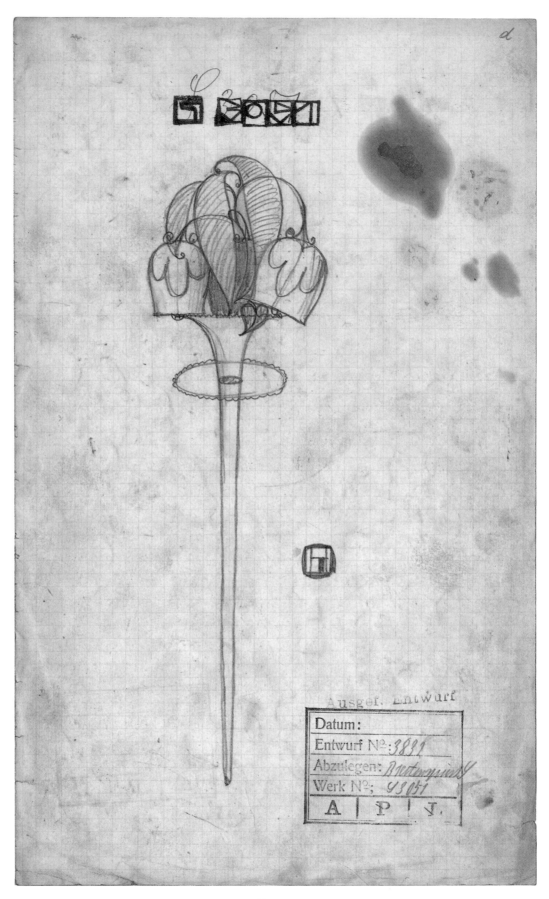

126   Skewer, 1913

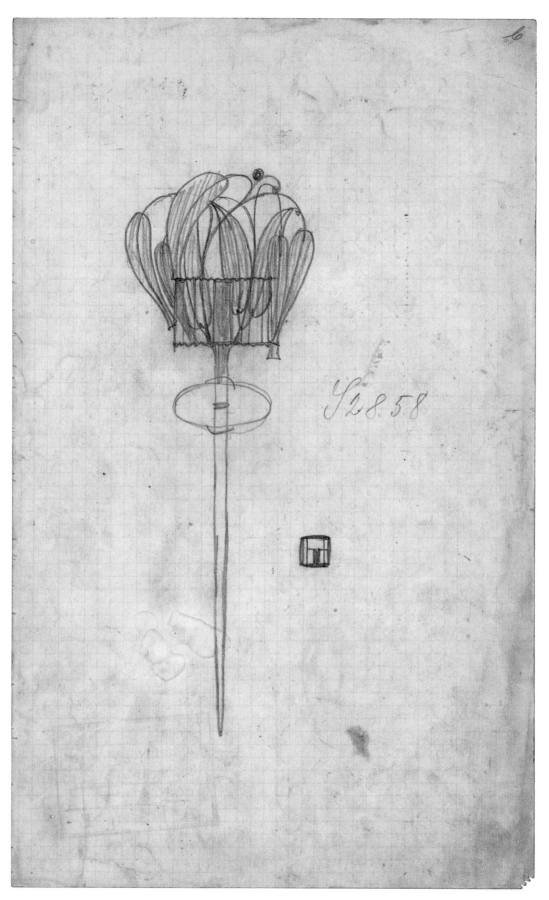

127   Skewer, ca. 1911

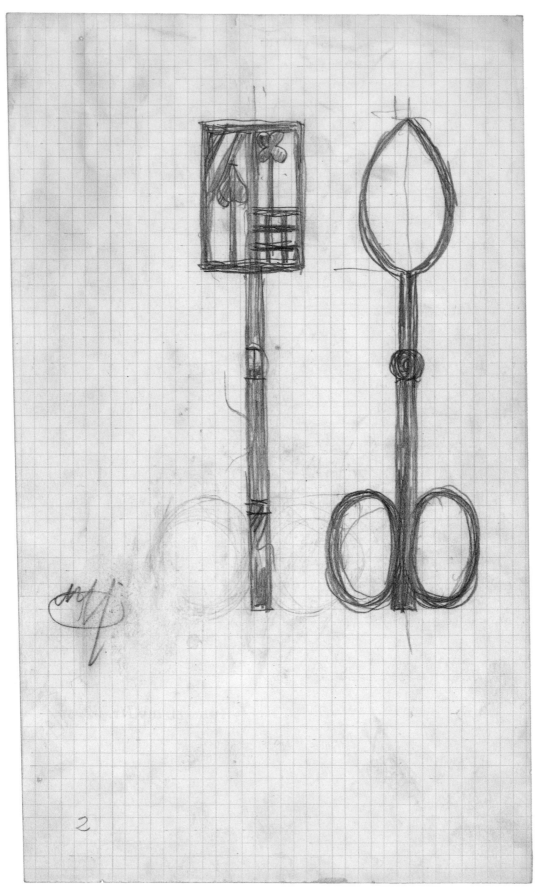

128   Sandwich server, after 1918 (?)

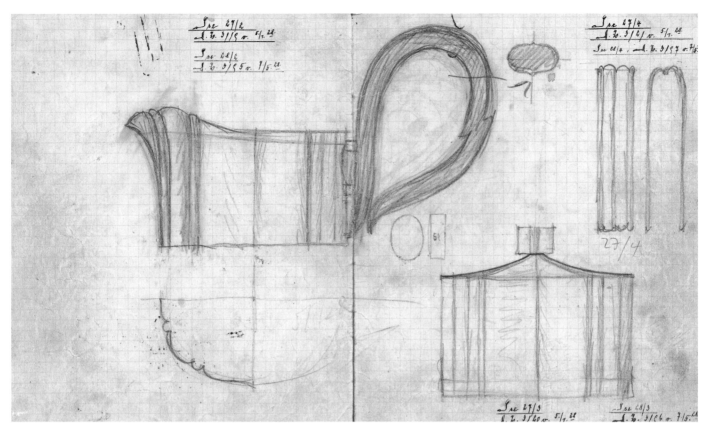

129   Milk pitcher, sugar bowl, and sugar tongs, ca. 1927

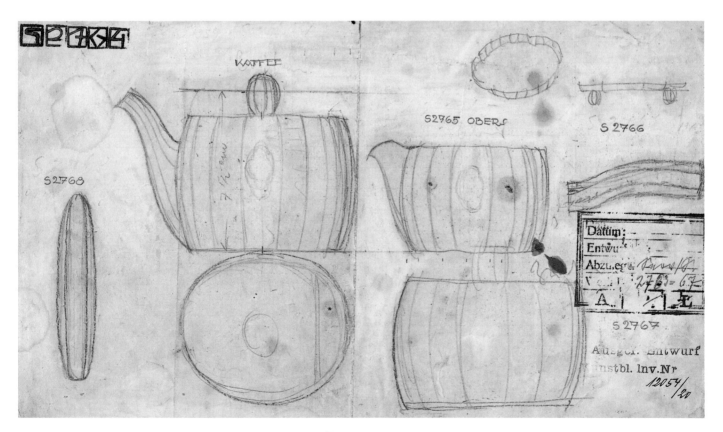

130   Tea service, 1912

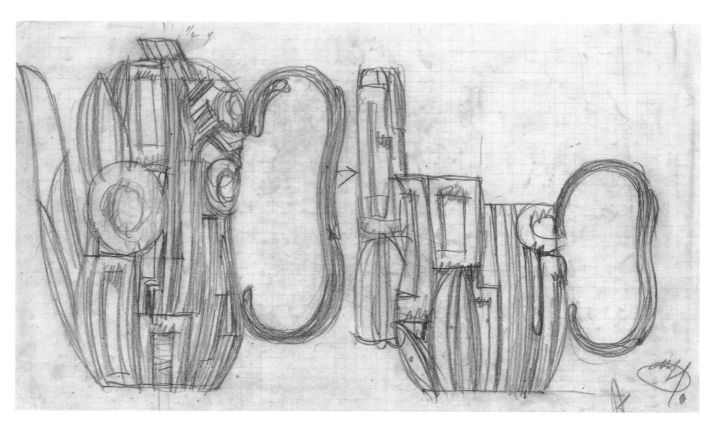

131   Coffeepot and milk pitcher, 1925/30

132   Sugar bowl, cup and saucer, 1925/30

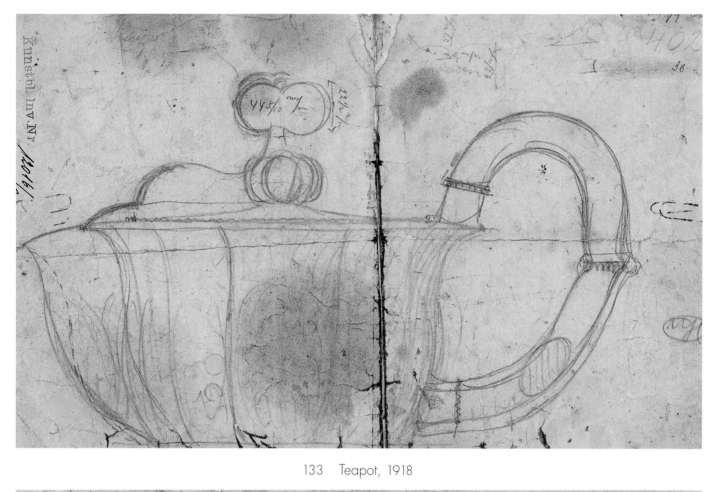

133   Teapot, 1918

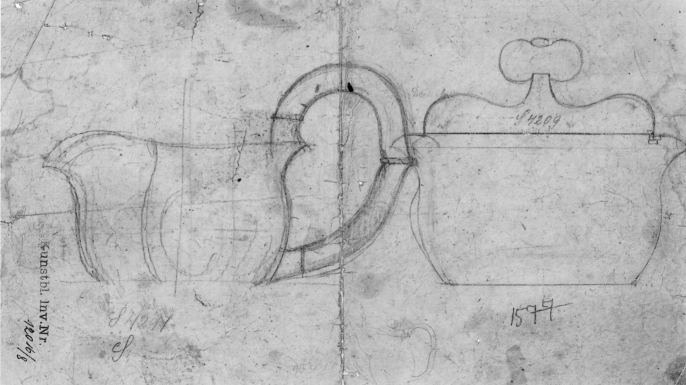

134   Sugar bowl and creamer, 1918

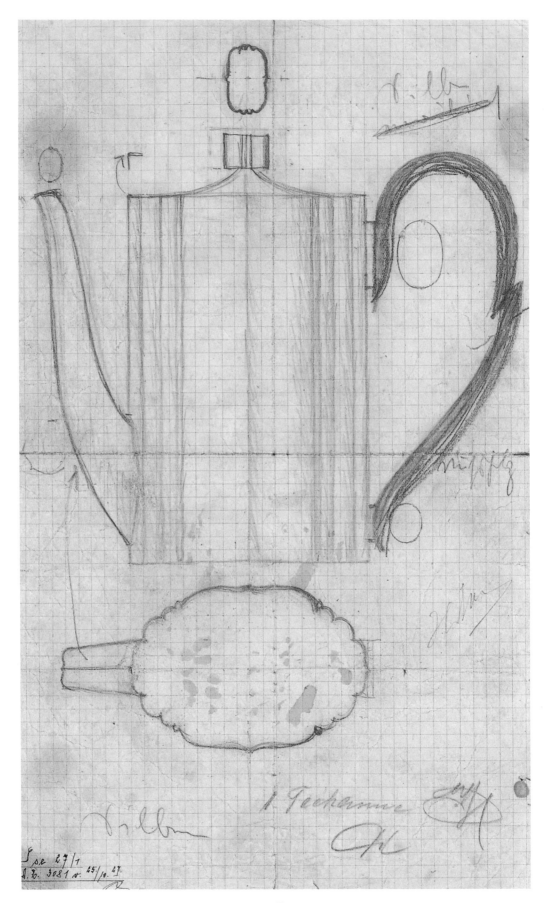

135   Tea- or coffepot, ca. 1927

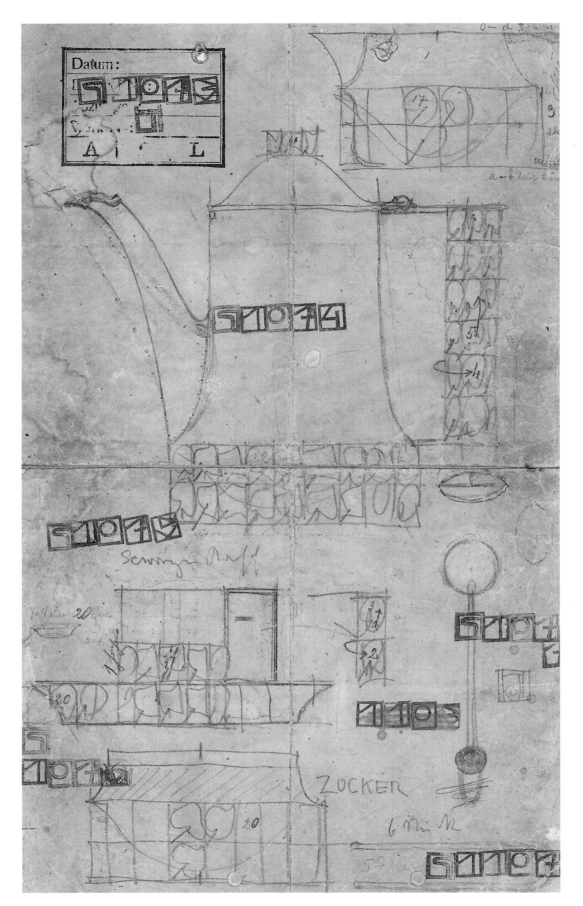

136   Coffee service, ca. 1907

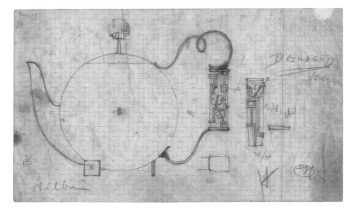

137 Teapot, ca. 1928

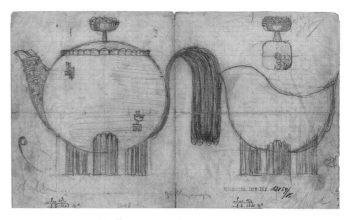

138 Coffeepot and creamer, ca. 1928

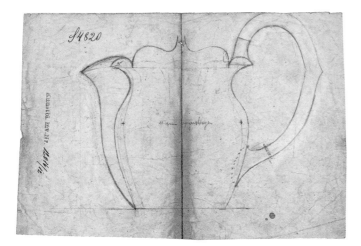

139 Milk pitcher, 1923

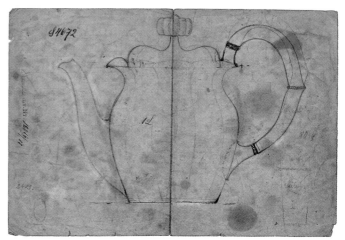

140 Coffeepot, 1923

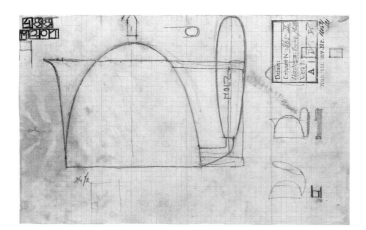

141 Teapot, 1904

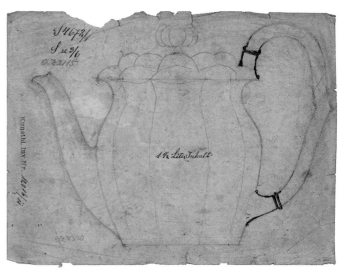

142 Coffeepot, 1923

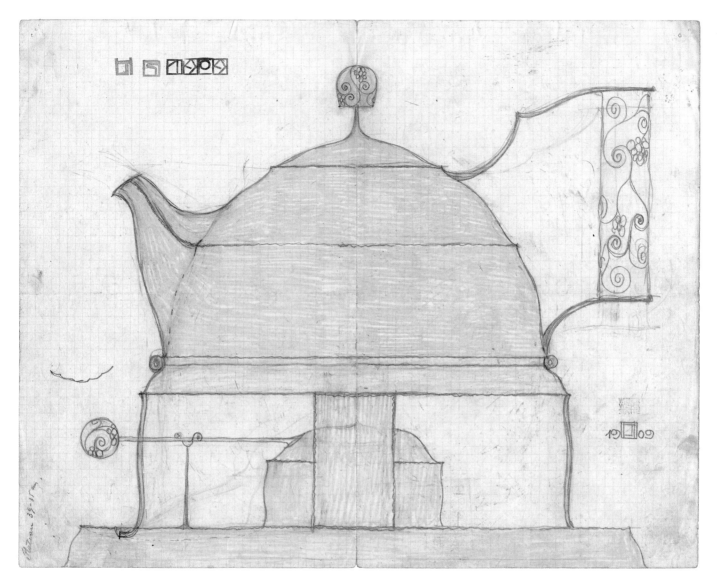

143   Teakettle, 1909

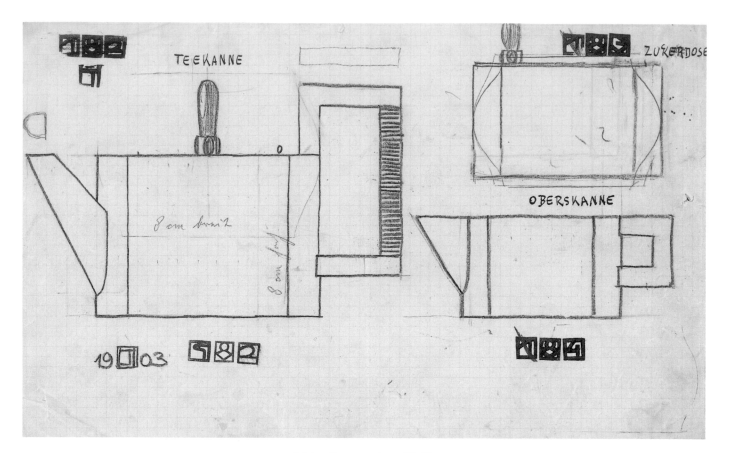

144   Tea service, 1903

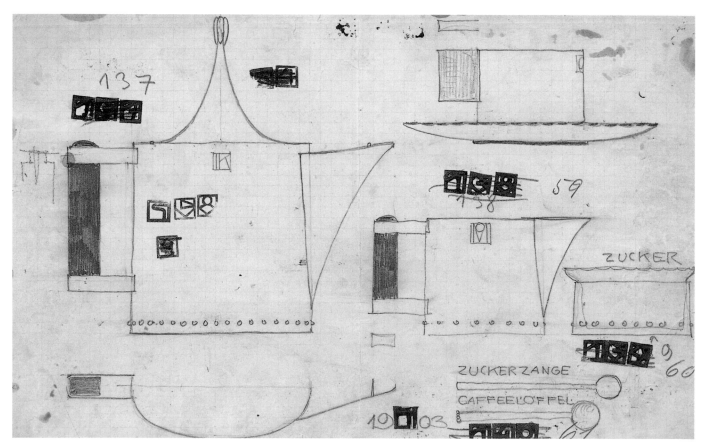

145   Tea service, 1903

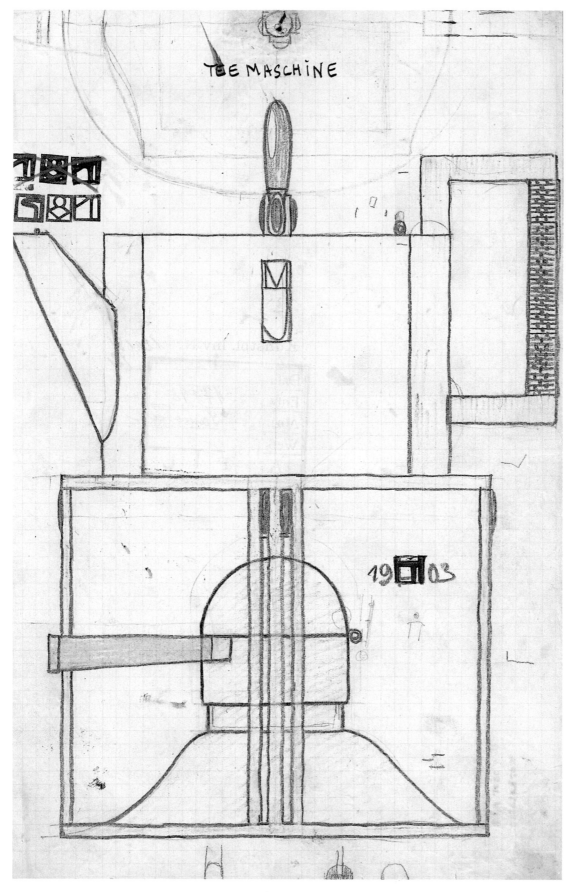

TEE MASCHINE

146   Samovar, 1903

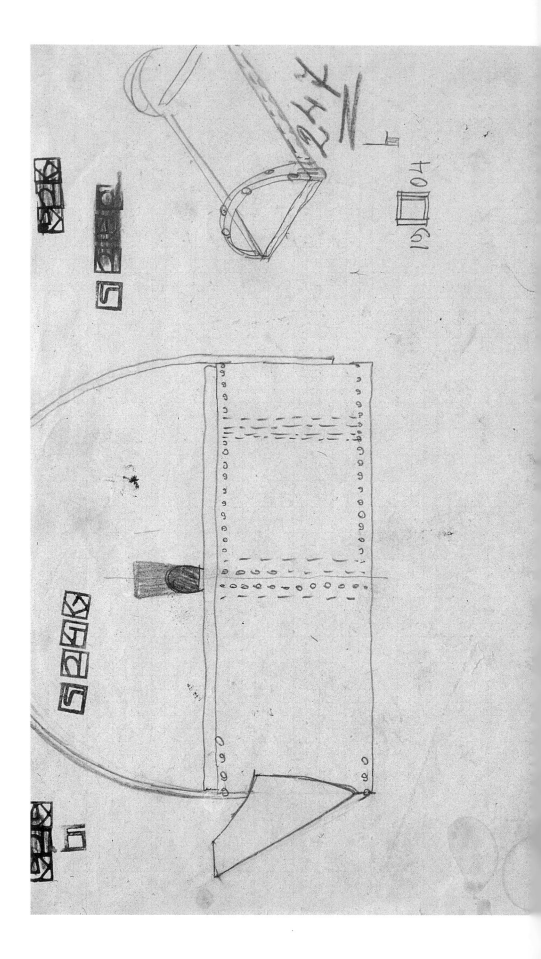

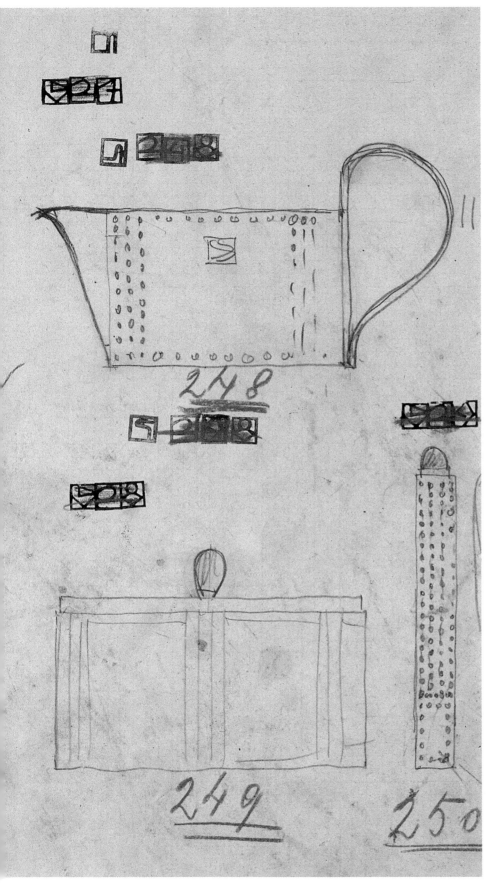

147   Tea service, 1904

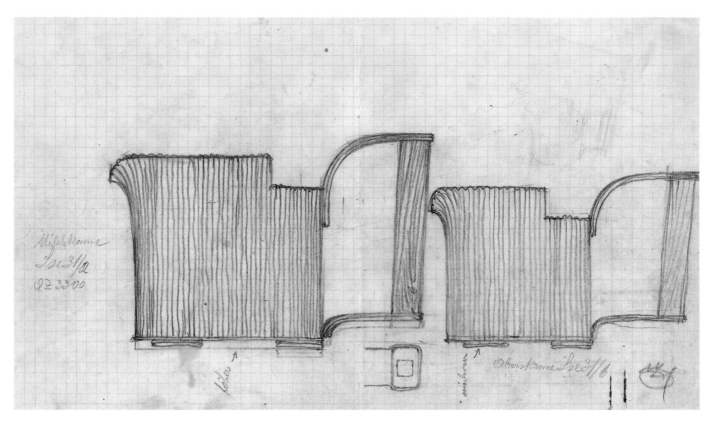

148   Milk pitcher and creamer, 1928/29

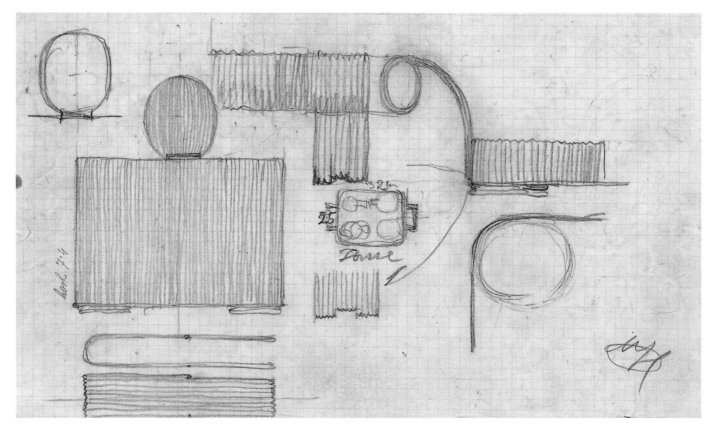

149   Sugar bowl, sugar tongs, and cup, 1928/29

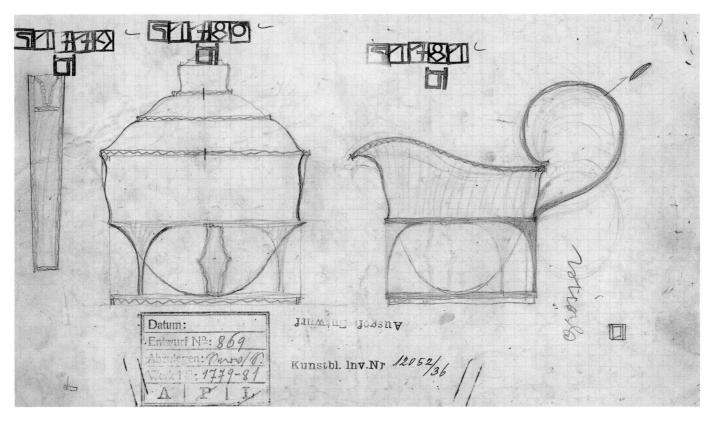

150 Sugar tongs, sugar bowl, and creamer, 1909

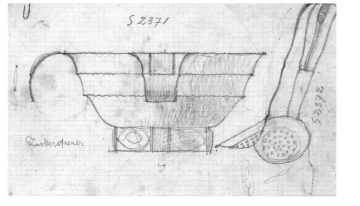

151 Sugar bowl and spoon, ca. 1910

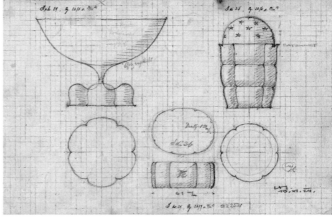

152 Bonbonnière, sugar caster, and napkin ring,
ca. 1924

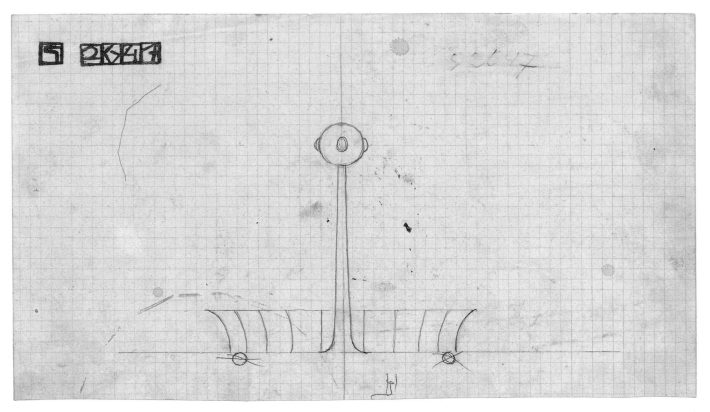

153   Centerpiece (bonbonnière), 1912

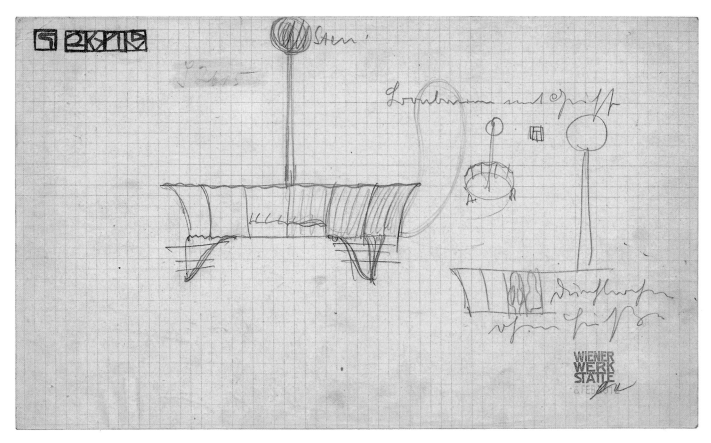

154   Silver centerpiece (bonbonnière), 1912

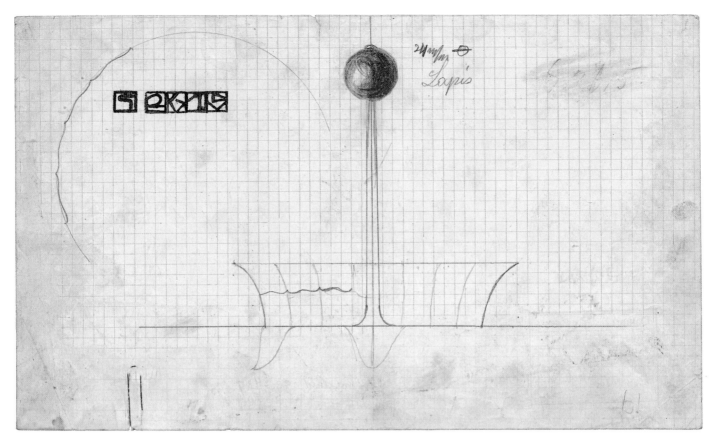

155   Silver centerpiece (bonbonnière), 1912

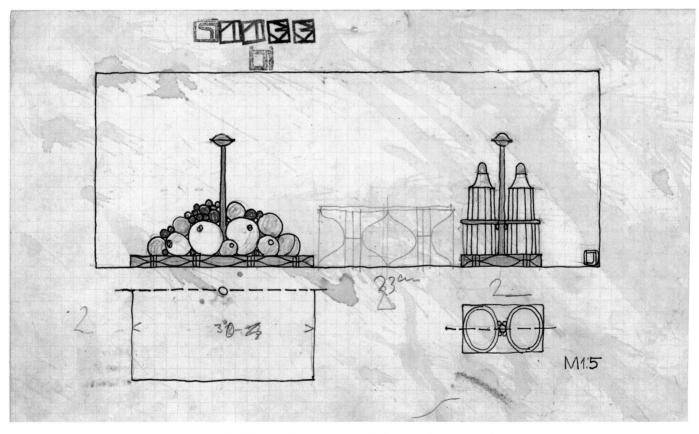

156   Centerpiece for fruit, and vinegar and oil cruets from a tableware set, 1908

157   Centerpiece, 1924/25

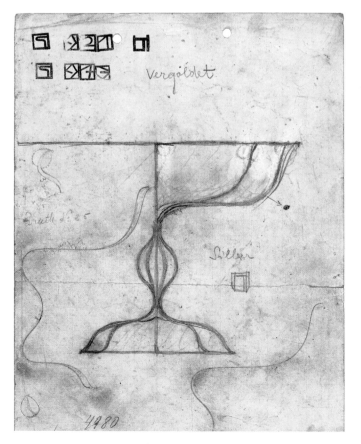

158   Centerpiece, 1907

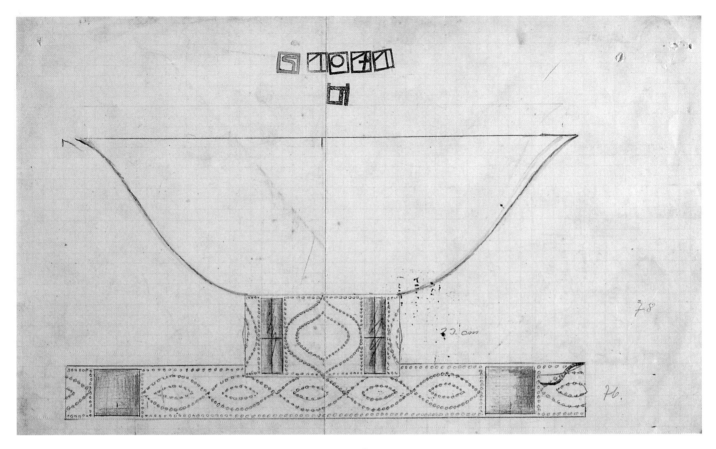

159   Sauceboat, 1908

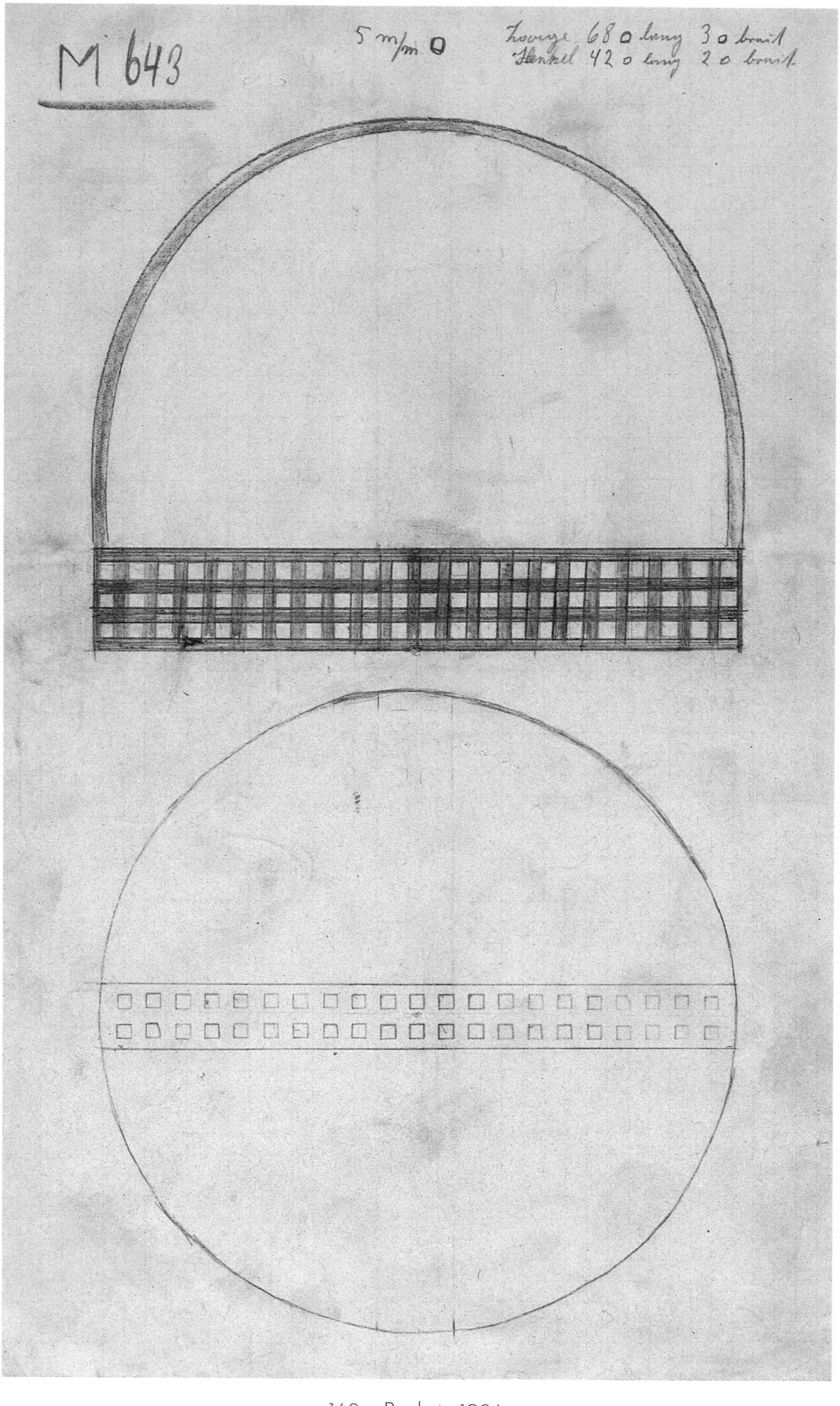

M 643

5 m/m ⌀   Bouege 68 ⌀ lang 3 ⌀ breit
            Henkel 42 ⌀ lang 2 ⌀ breit.

160   Basket, 1906

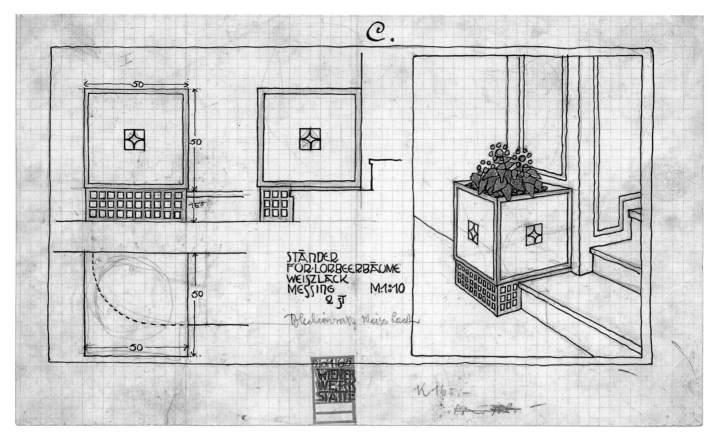

161 Jardinière for laurel, ca. 1907

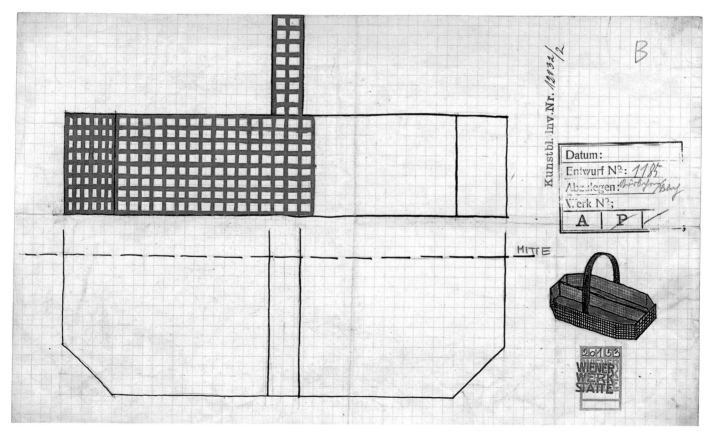

162 Basket, 1906/10

163 Jardinière, 1905

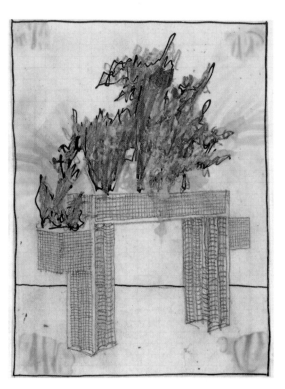

164 Jardinière, 1905

165 Jardinière, 1905

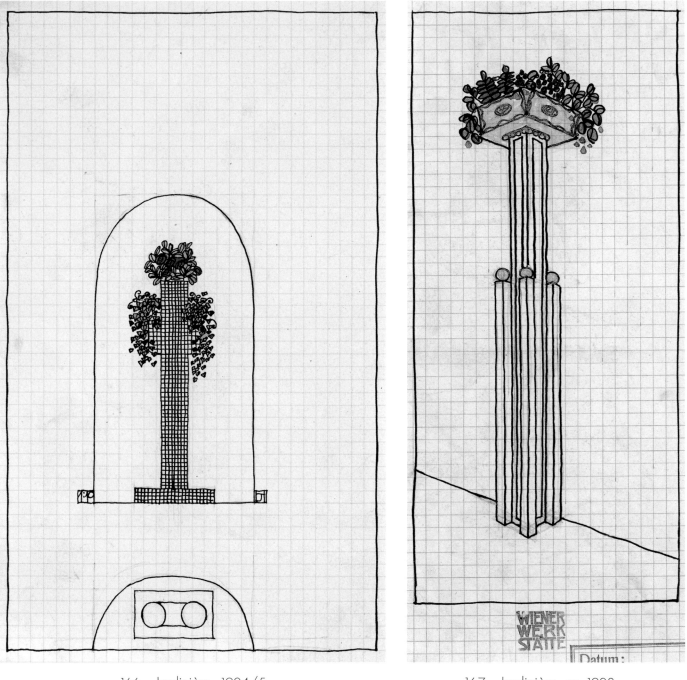

166   Jardinière, 1904/5   167   Jardinière, ca. 1908

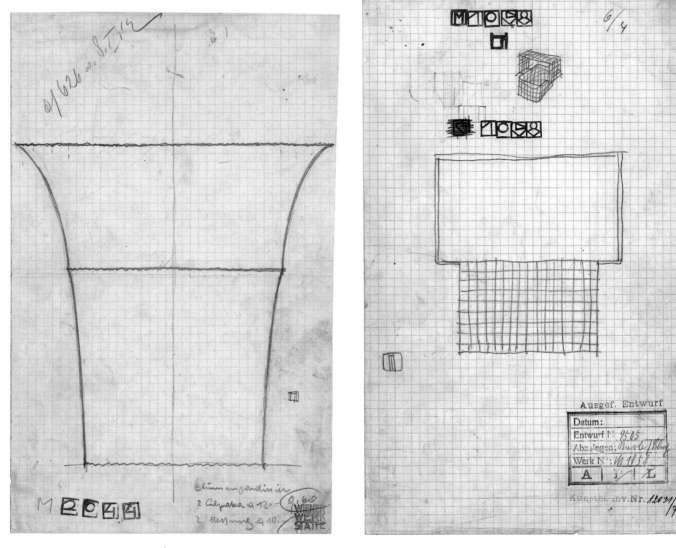

168   Jardinière, 1912   169   Basket, ca. 1909

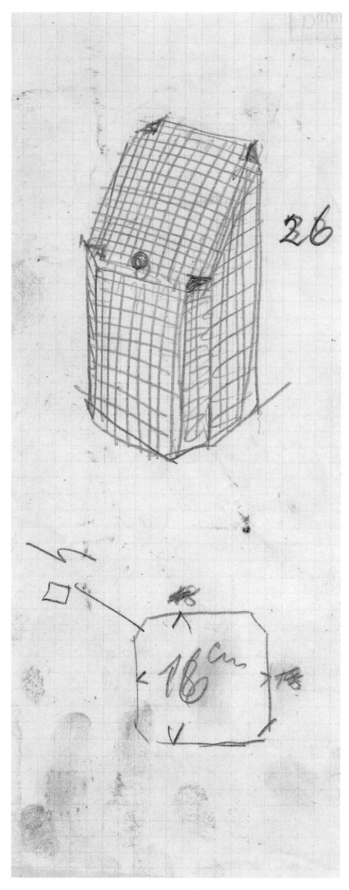

170 Wastepaper basket, 1906

171 Basket, 1907

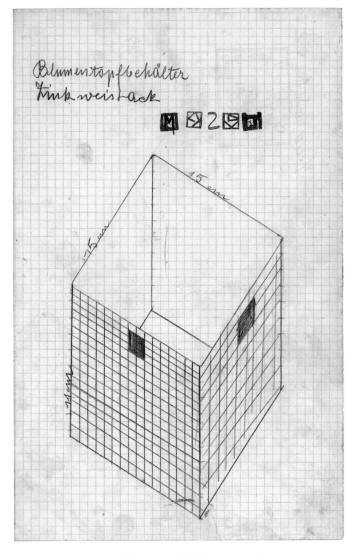

172 Flowerpot holder, 1907/8

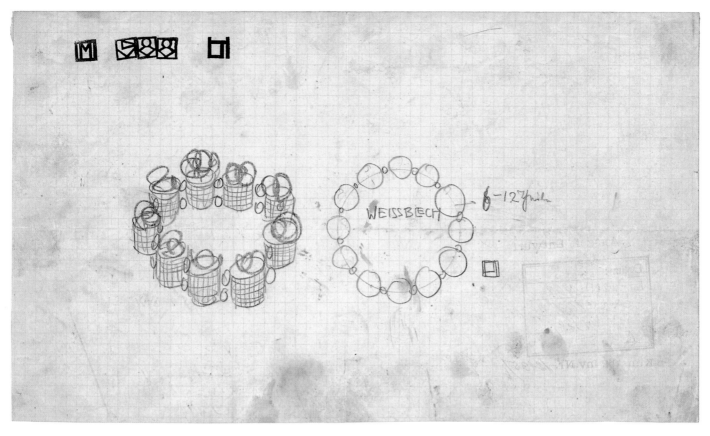

173   Flower basket, 1906

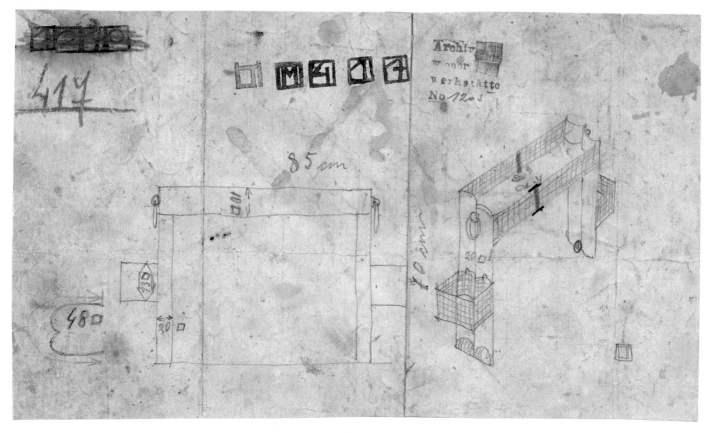

174   Jardinière, 1905

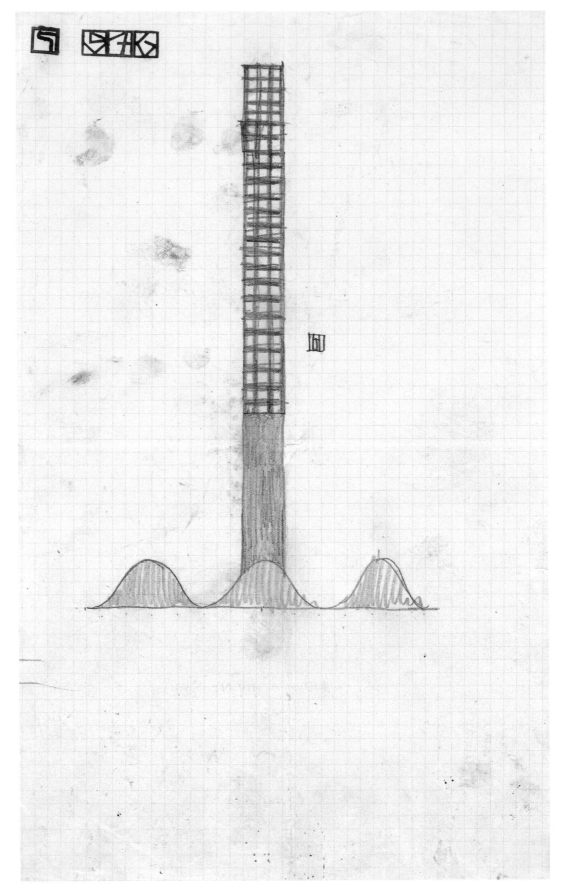

175   Candlestick, 1905

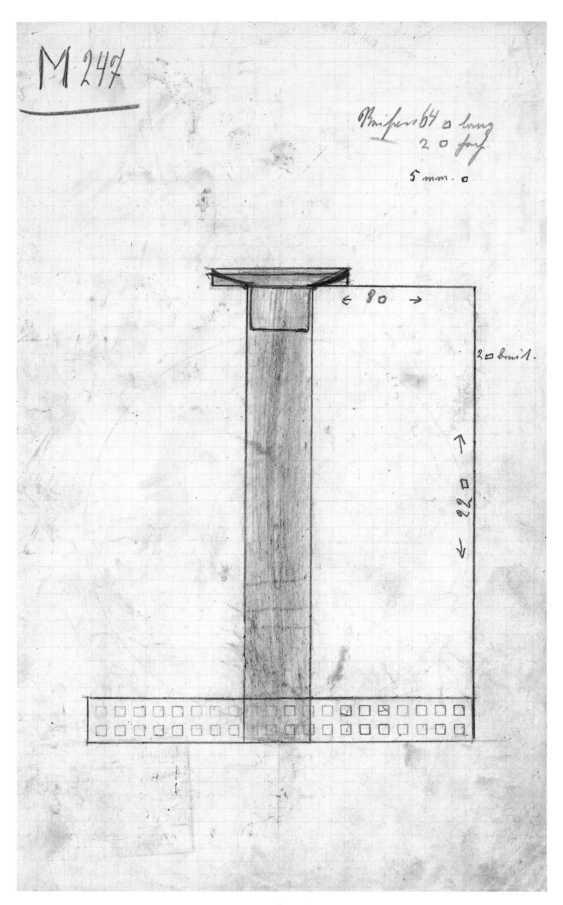

176 Candlestick, 1904

177   Candelabrum, ca. 1905

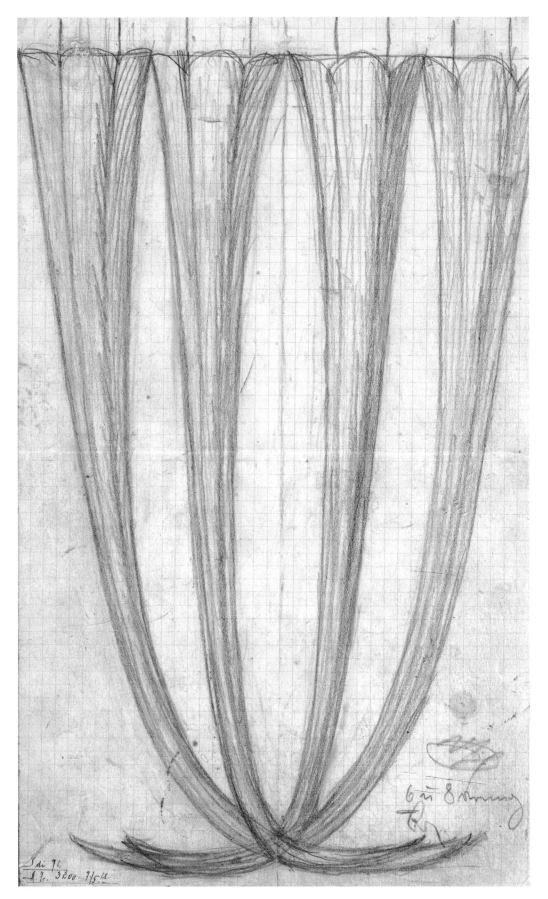

178   Candelabrum, 1928

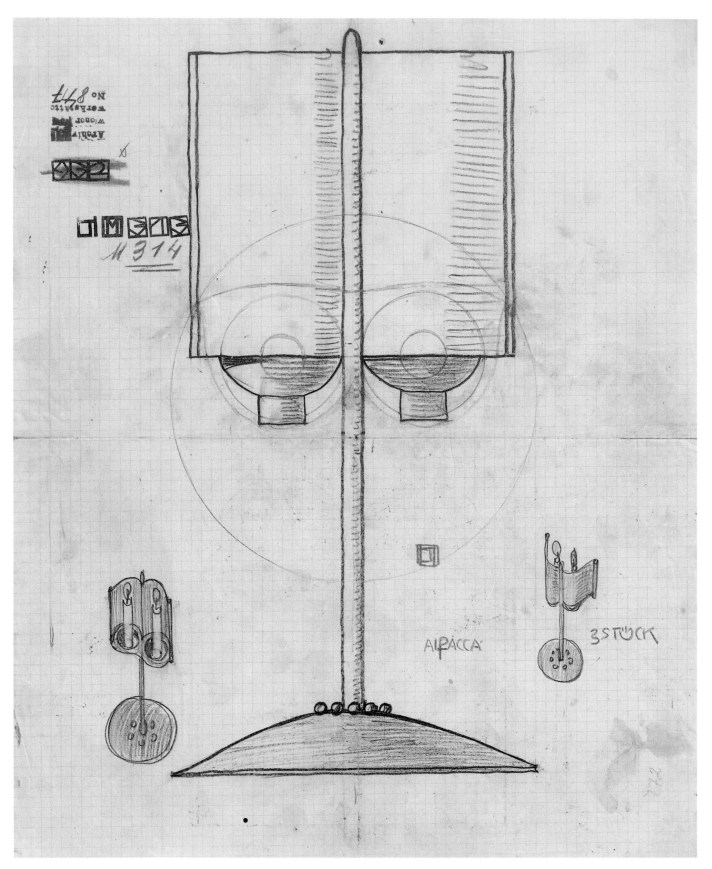

179 Candlestick, 1904

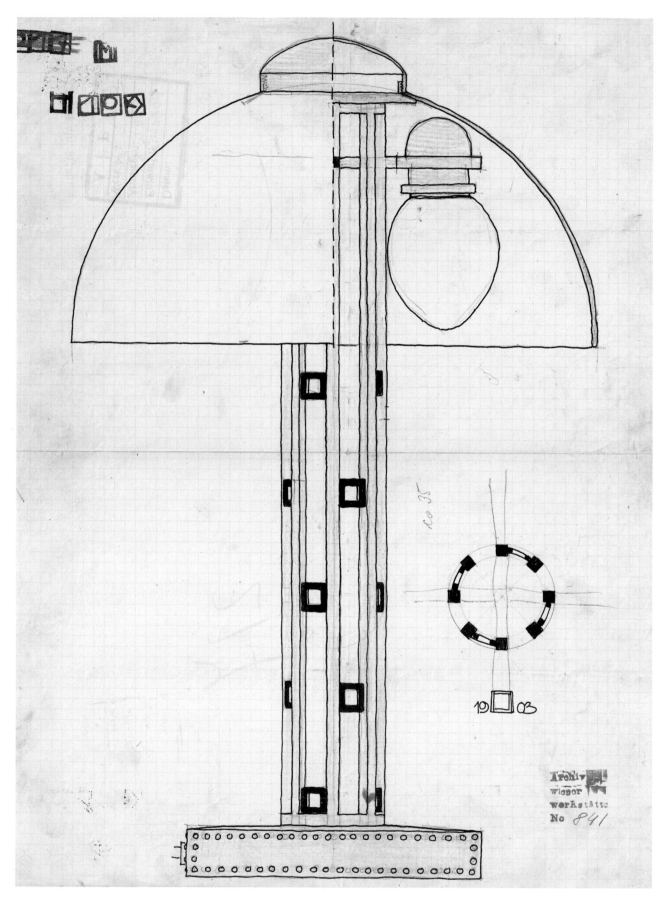

180   Lamp, 1903

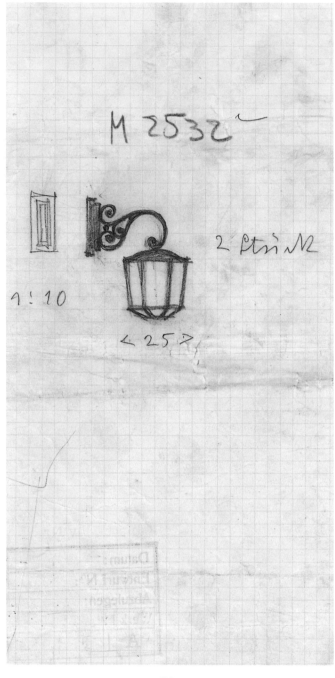

181   Wall lamp, 1914

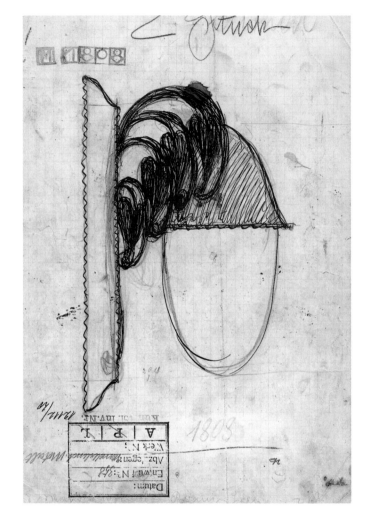

182   Wall lamp, 1911

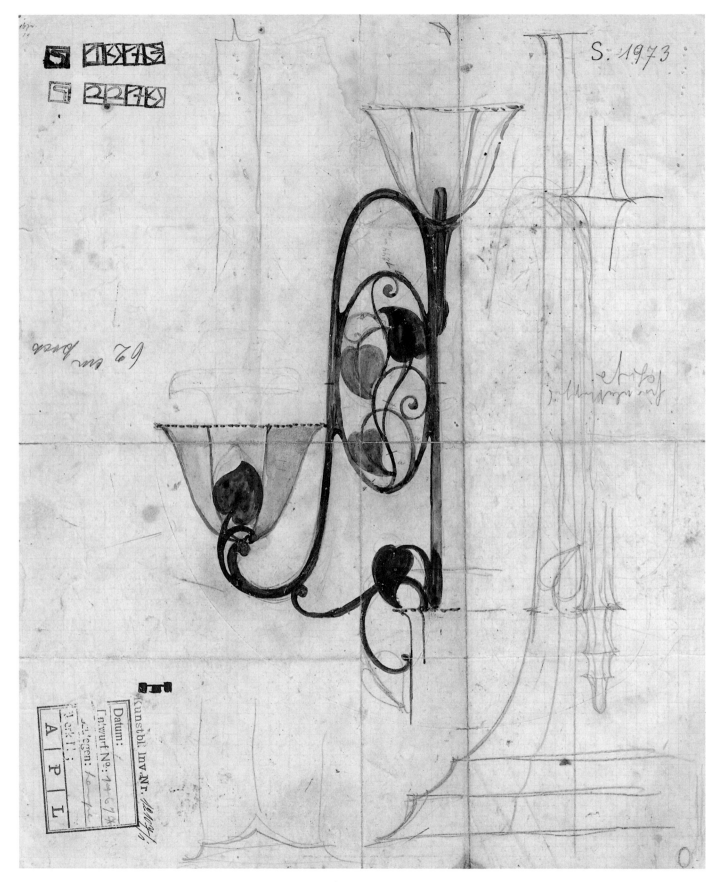

S. 1973

183   Lamp, ca. 1909

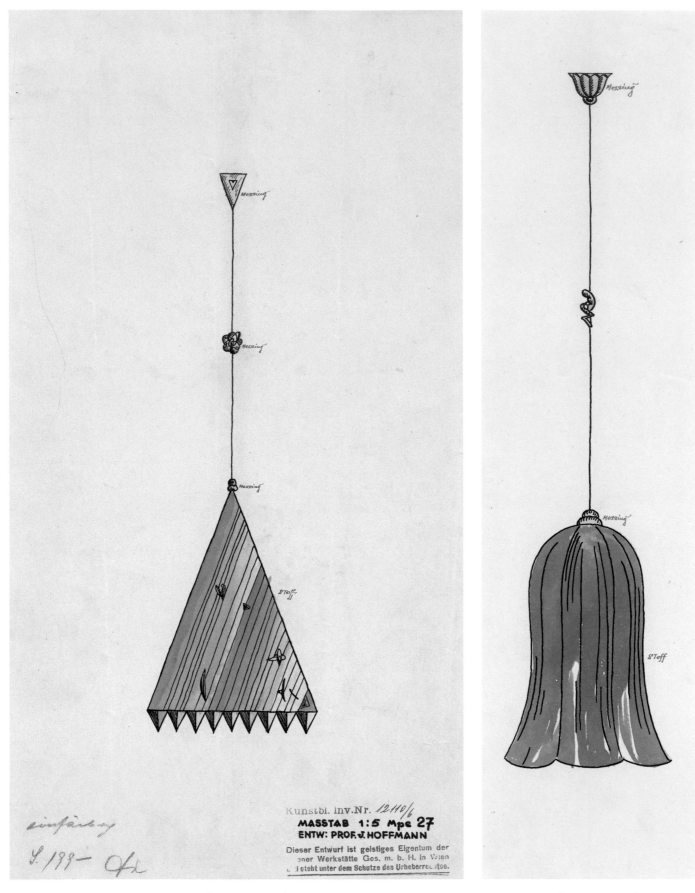

184 Lamp, 1925/28

185 Lamp, 1927/29

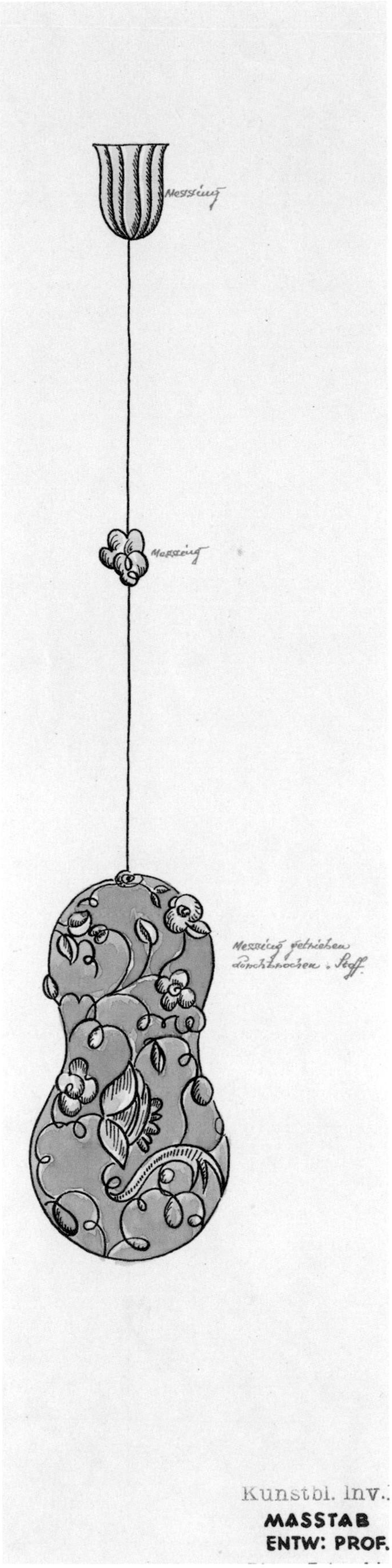

186 Lamp, 1925/28

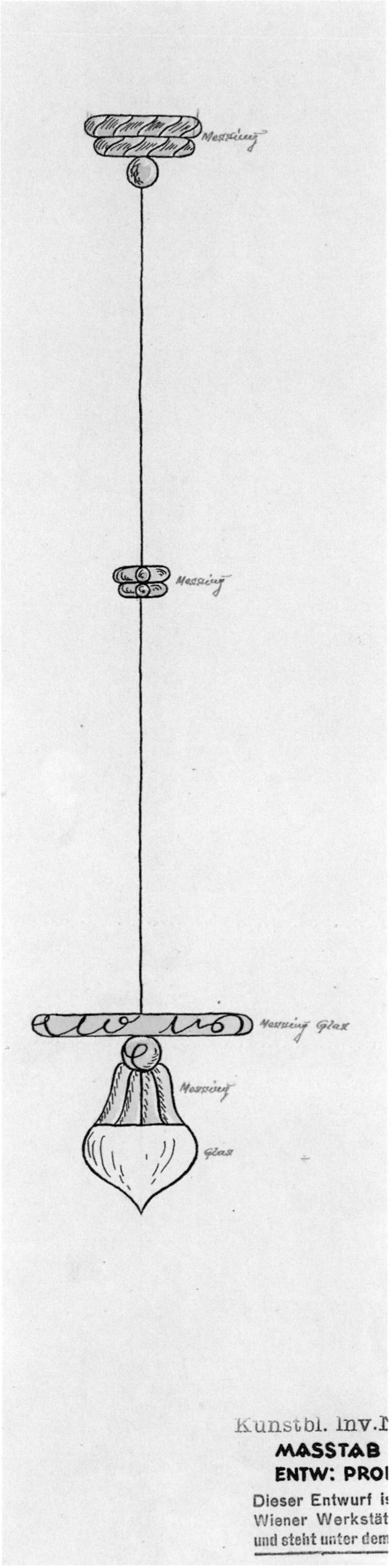

187 Lamp, 1927/29

188 Lamp, 1925/28

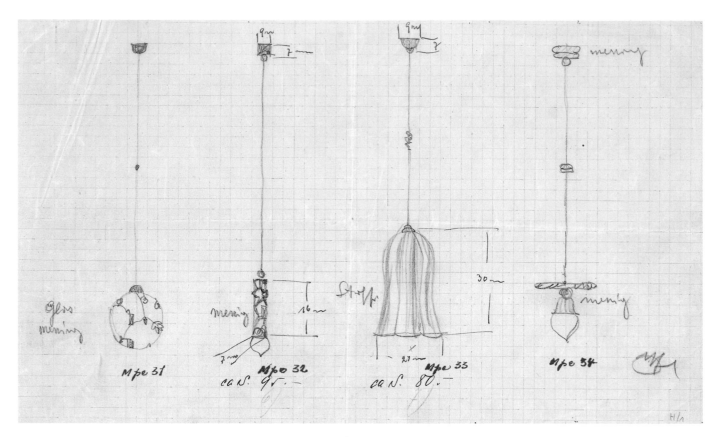

189   Four lamps, 1927/29

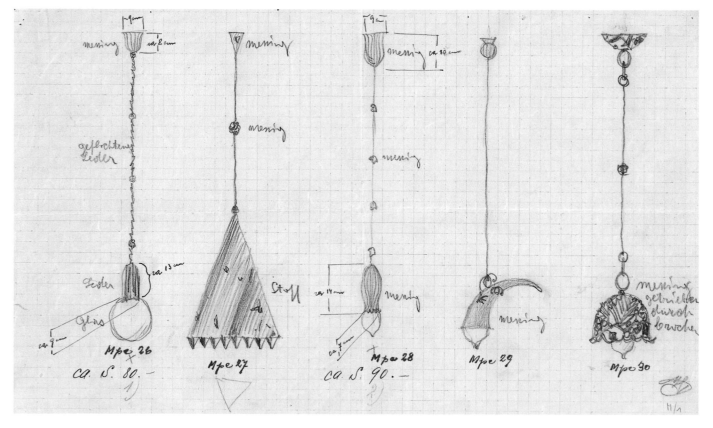

190   Five lamps, 1925/28

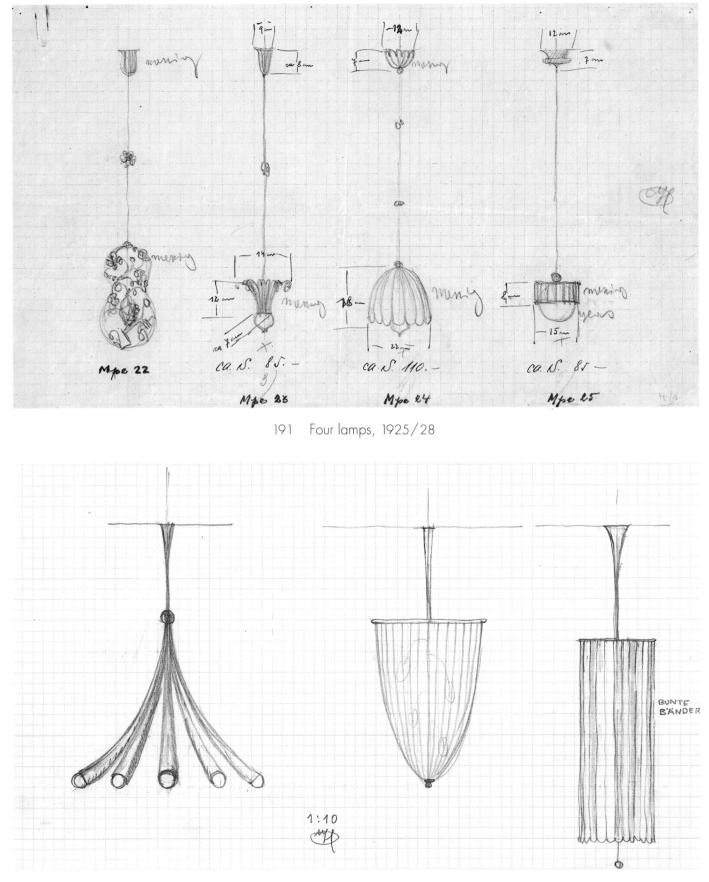

191   Four lamps, 1925/28

192   Three ceiling lamps, ca. 1931

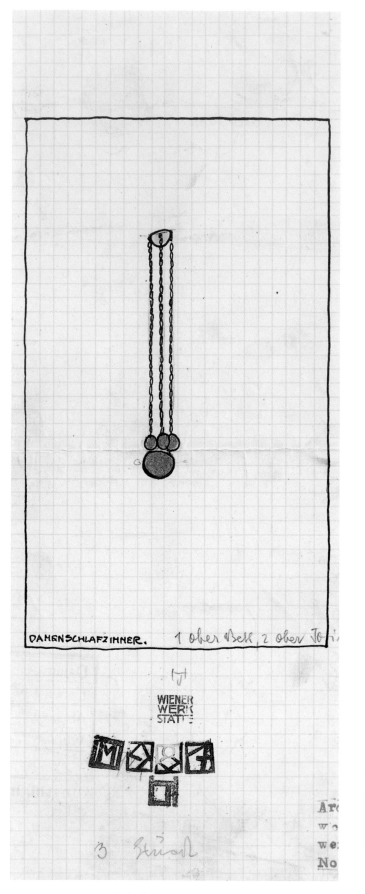

193   Droplight for a lady's bedroom, 1908

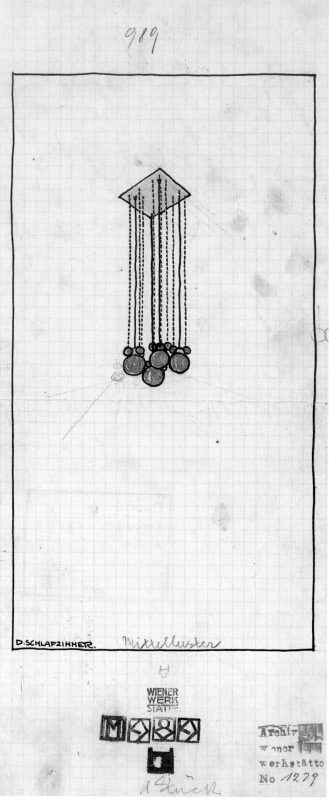

194   Luster for a lady's bedroom, 1908

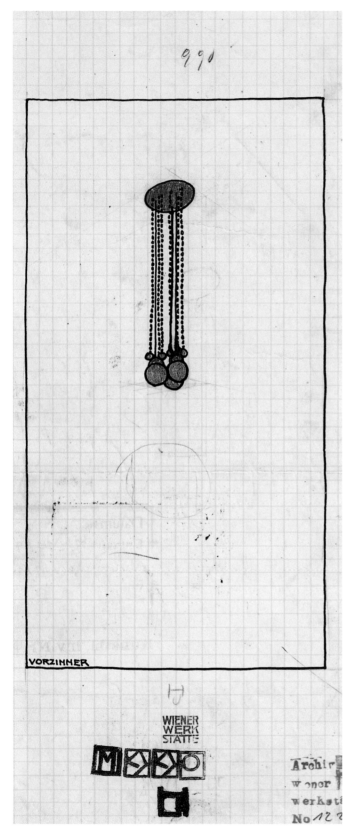

195   Luster for an antechamber, 1908

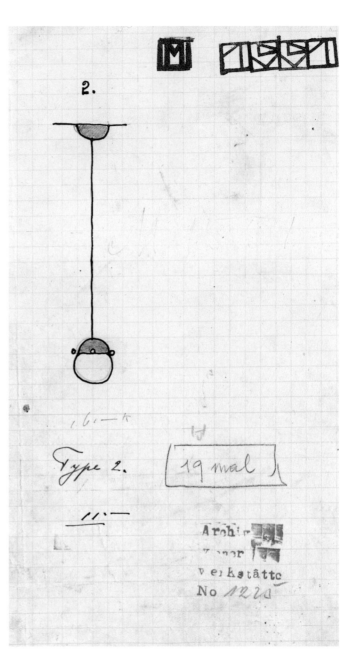

196   Droplight, 1910 / 15

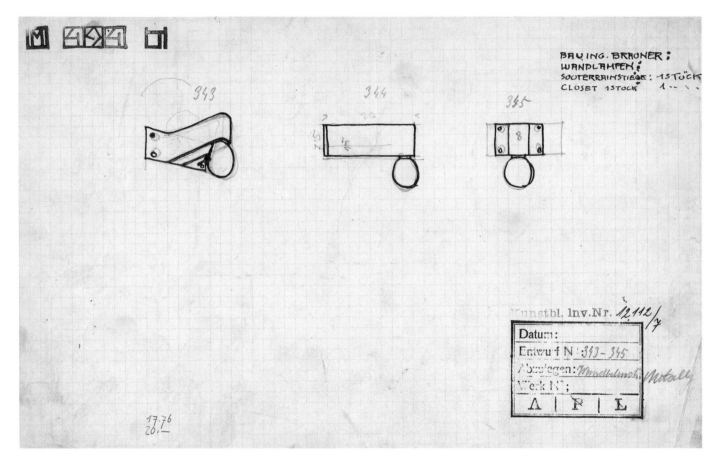

197   Wall lamp, 1906

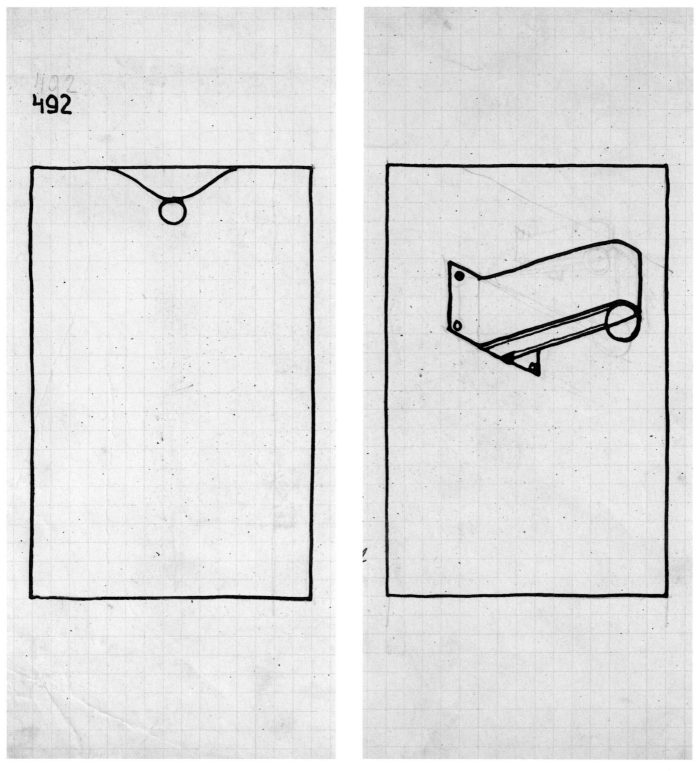

198   Ceiling lamp, 1906

199   Wall lamp, 1906

200   Casket, 1919

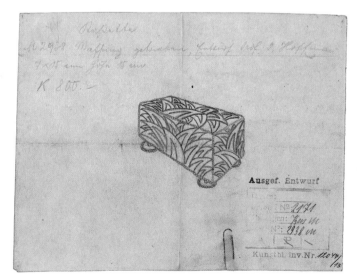

201   Casket, 1919

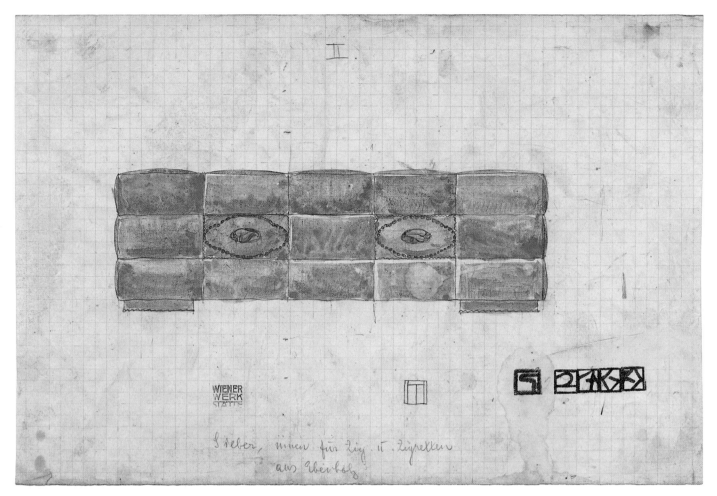

202　Casket, 1912

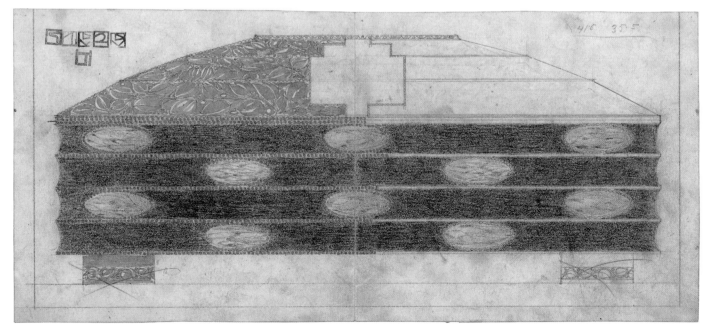

203　Casket, 1909

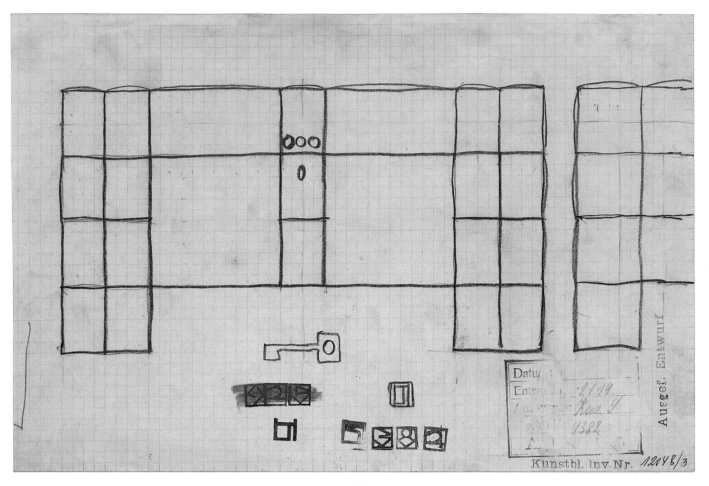

204   Jewel box, 1905

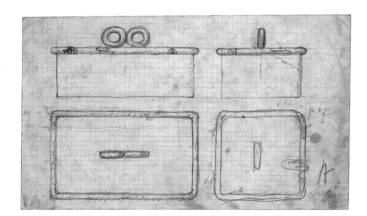

205   Cigar box, 1930

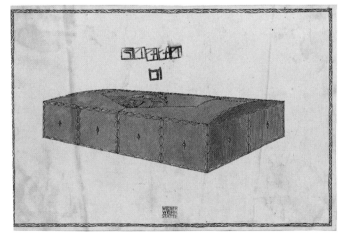

206   Casket, 1909

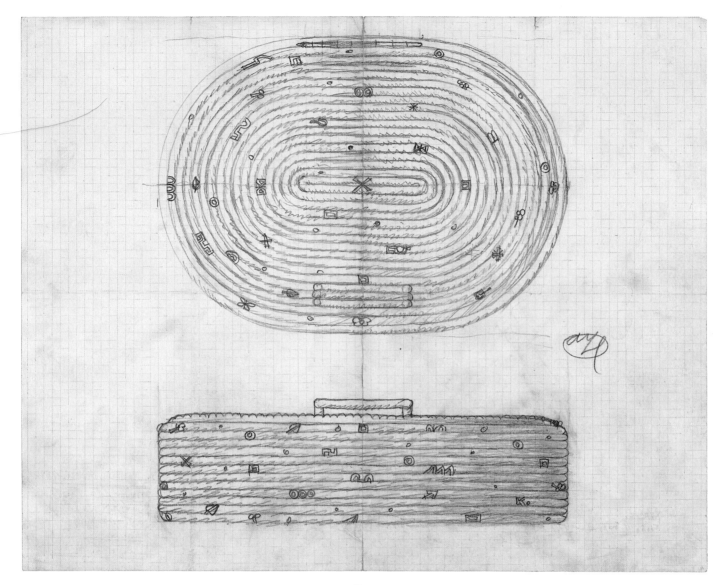

207 Box, 1931

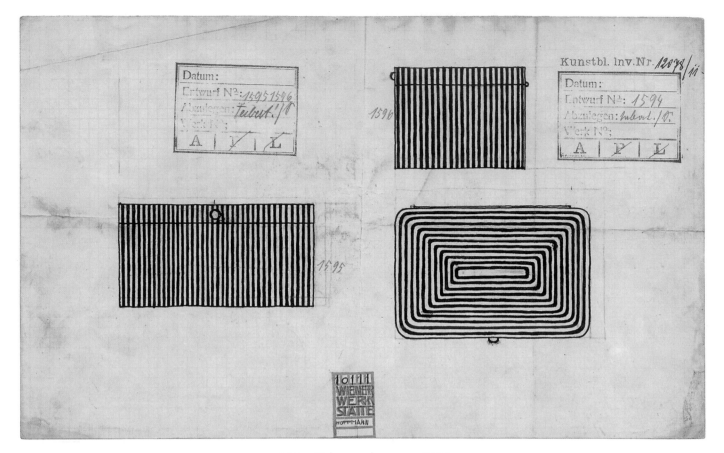

208   Tobacco box, ca. 1905

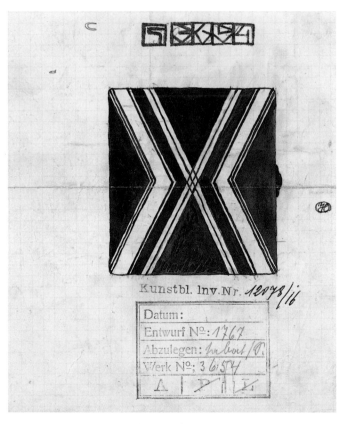

209   Tobacco box, ca. 1915

210   Box, ca. 1904

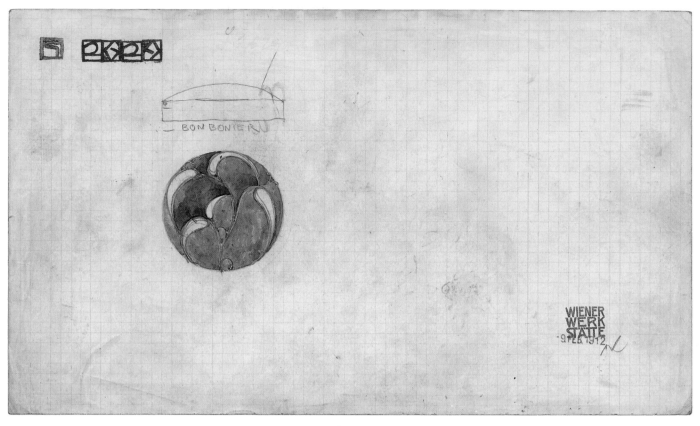

211   Bonbonnière, 1912

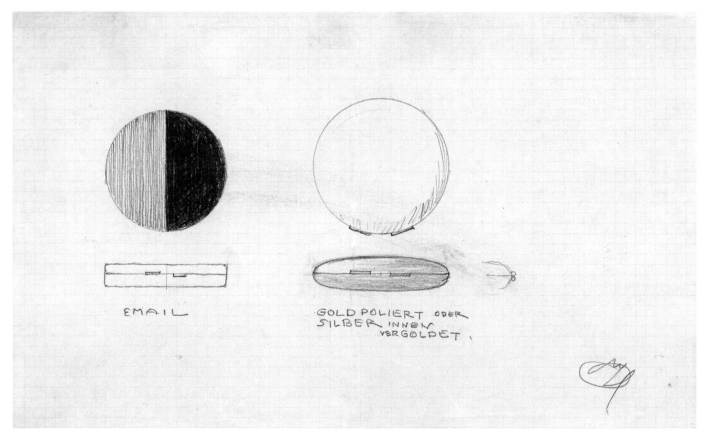

212   Silver and enamel box, ca. 1920 (?)

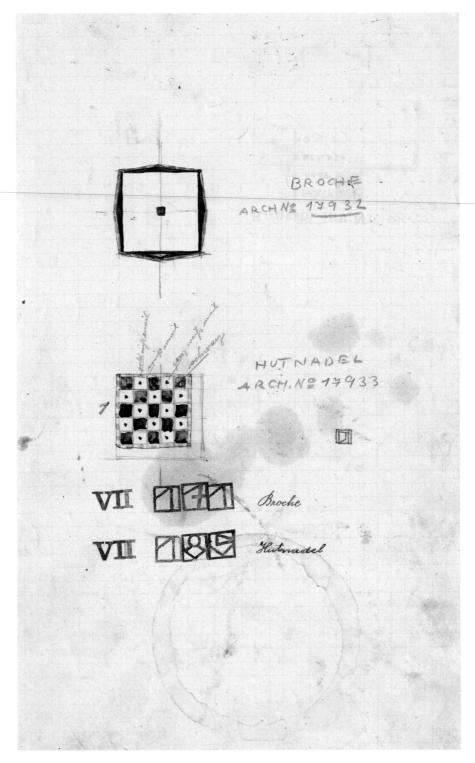

213   Brooch and hatpin, 1905/10

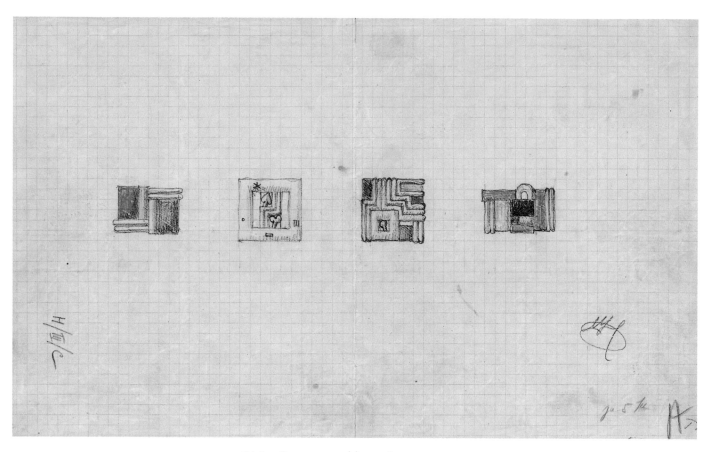

214   Four enamel brooches, ca. 1929

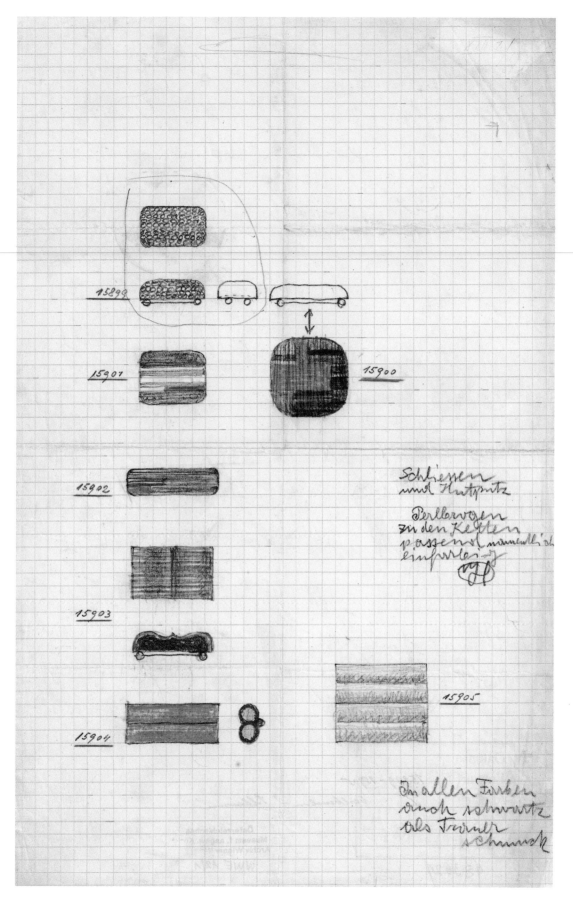

215   Pearl brooch and clasps, 1929

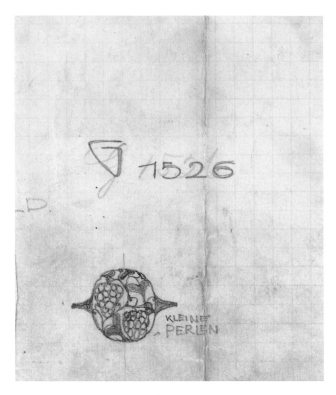

216   Ring, 1912

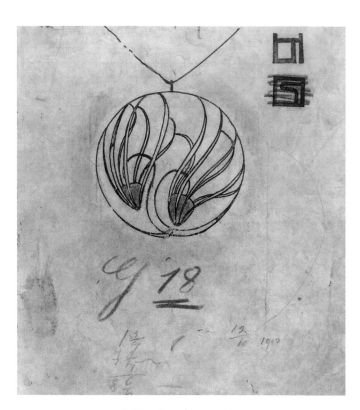

217   Pendant, 1903

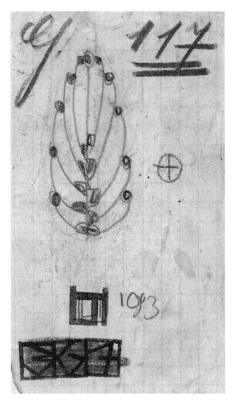

218   Pendant, 1903

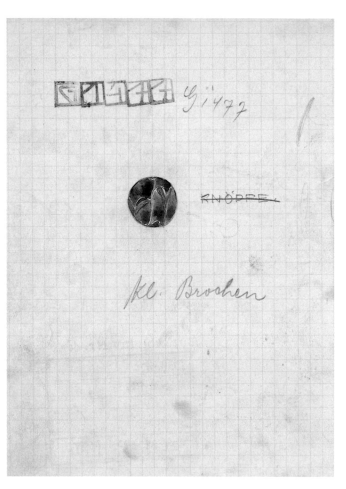

219   Brooch, 1912

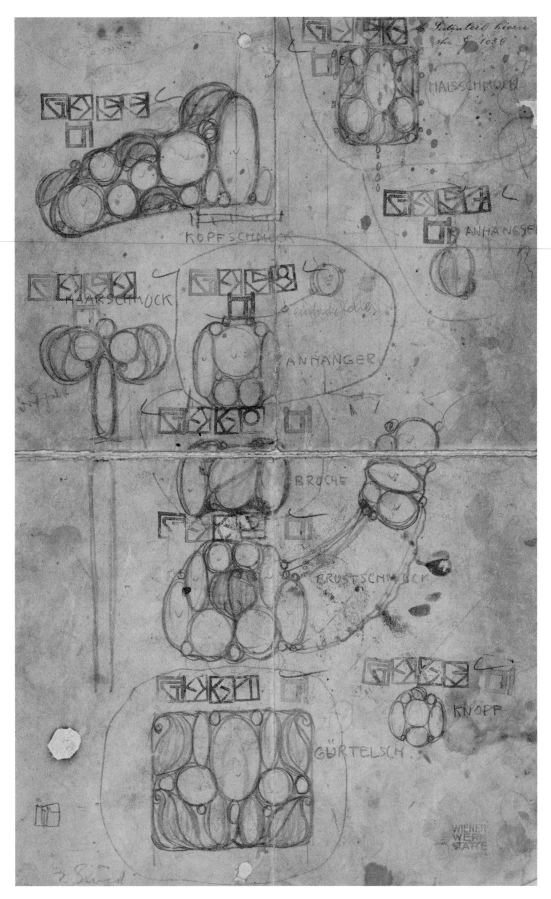

220 Jewelry set, 1909

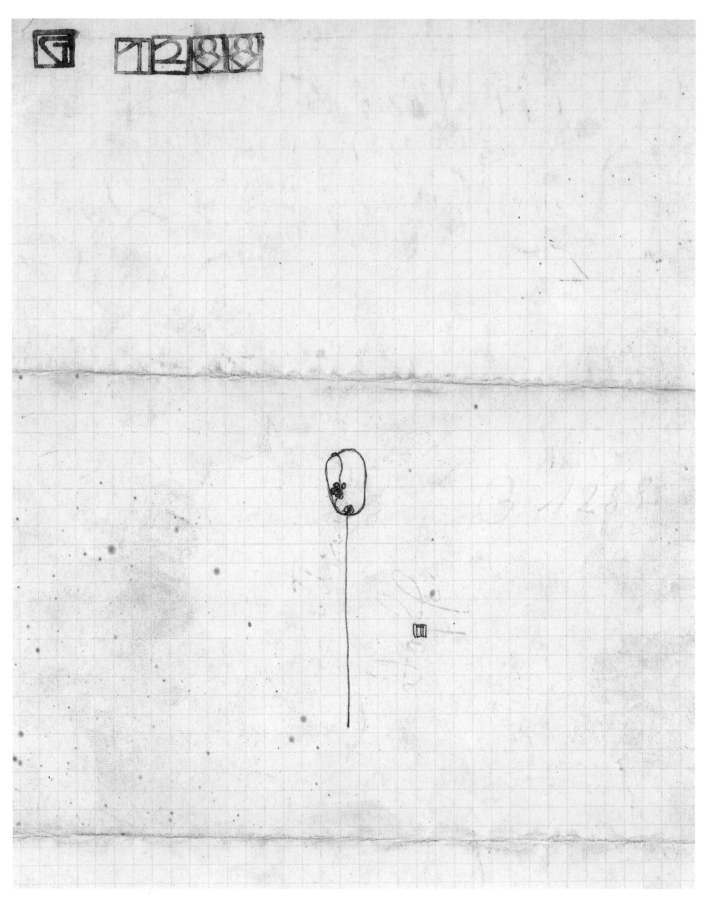

221   Tiepin, 1911

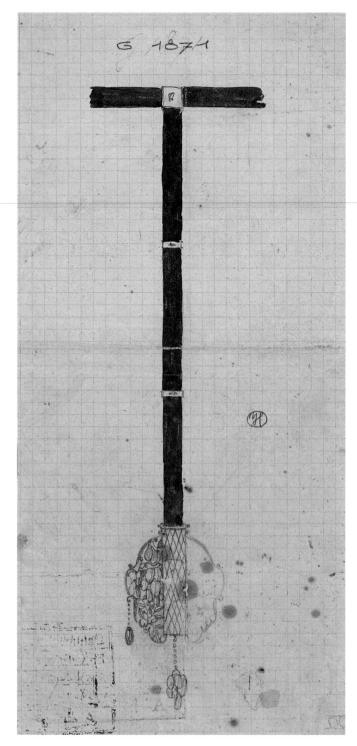

222   Pendant, 1915

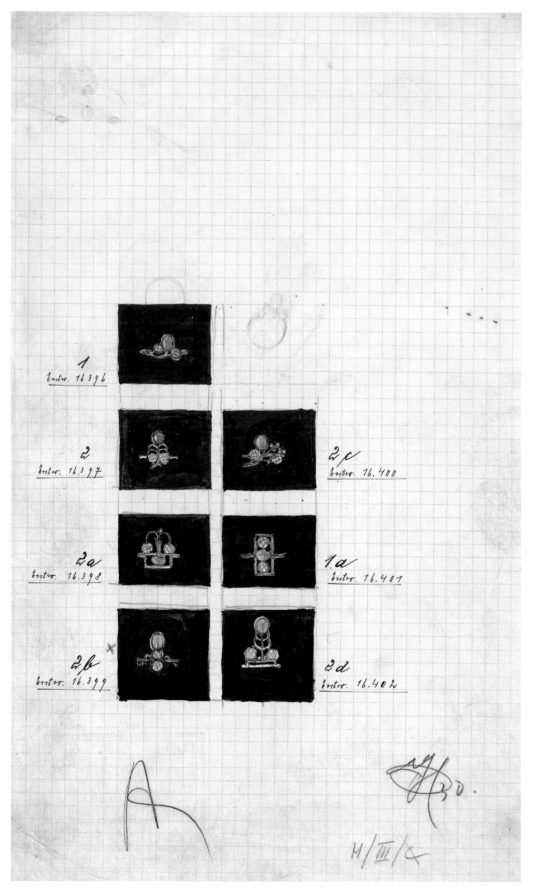

223　Gold ring, 1930

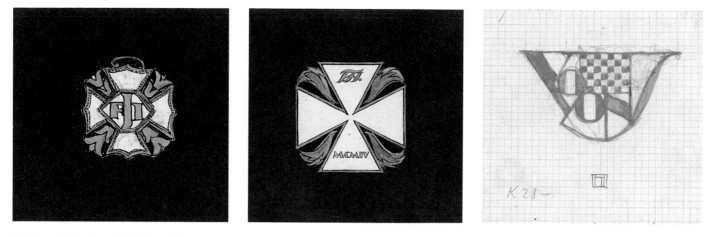

224 Medal, ca. 1904   225 Medal, ca. 1904   226 Monogram, date unknown

227 Medal, ca. 1904   228 Medal, ca. 1904   229 Monogram, 1912

230 Monogram, 1922 (?)

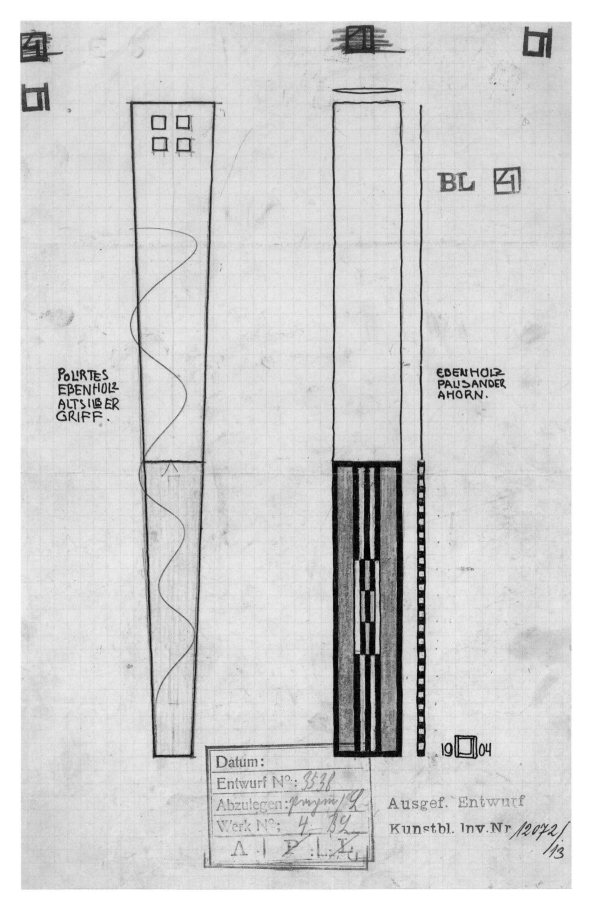

231   Paper knife, 1904

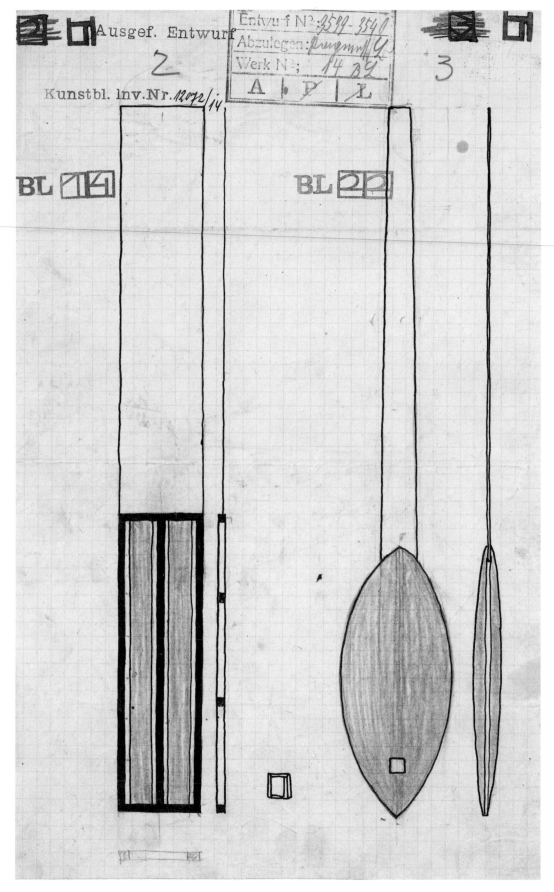

232   Paper knife, ca. 1904

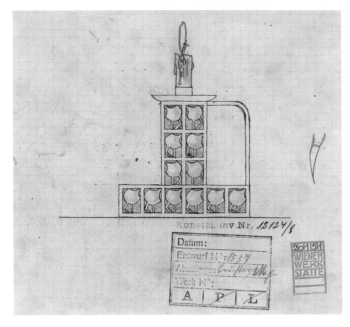

233 Candlestick, 1912

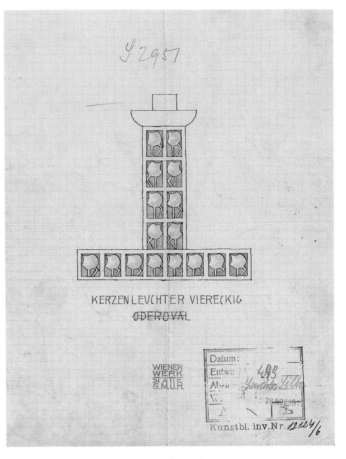

234 Candlestick, 1912

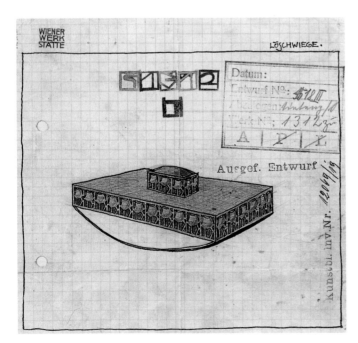

235 Ink blotter, 1908/9

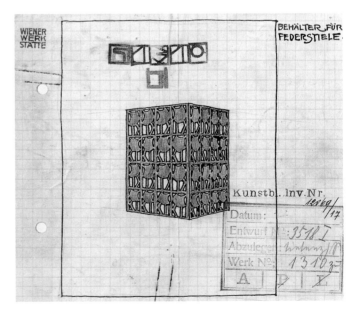

236 Feather duster container, 1908/9

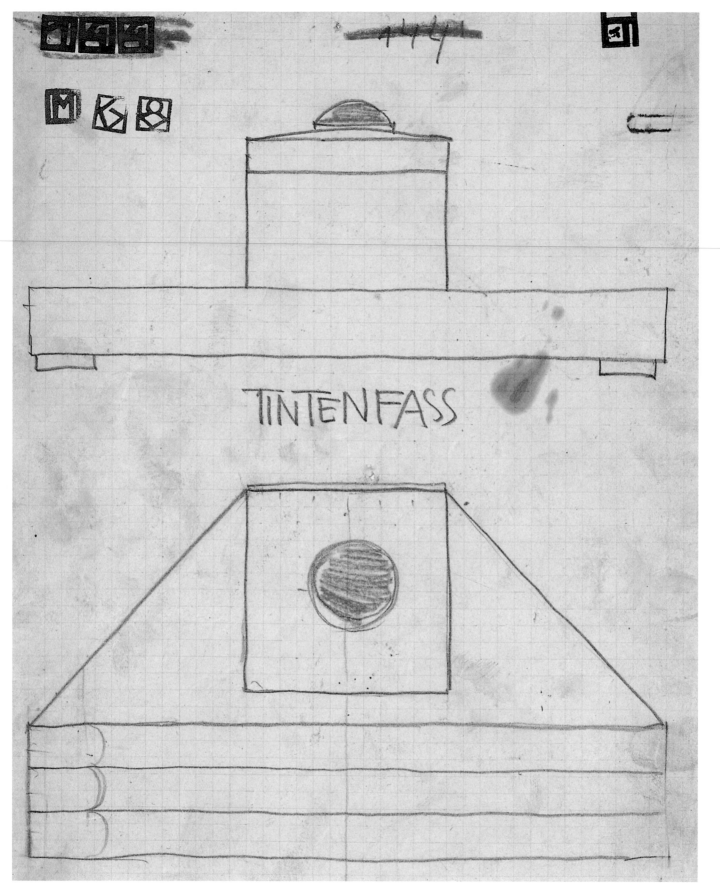

TINTENFASS

237   Inkwell, 1903

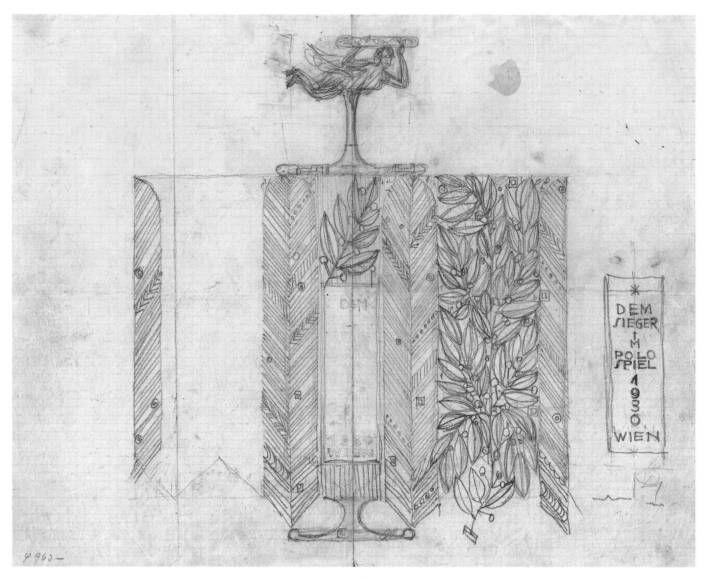

238 Trophy, 1930

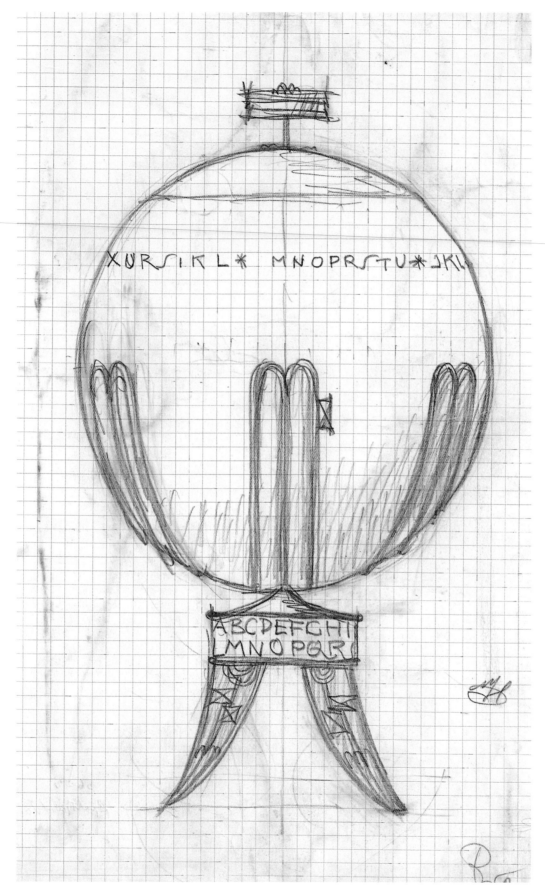

239   Trophy, 1925/30

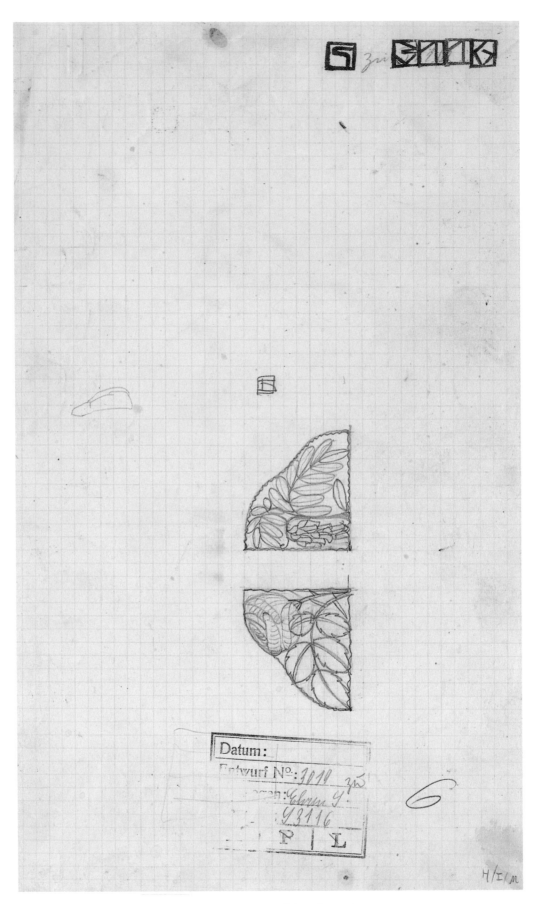

240　Hammer (detail), 1913

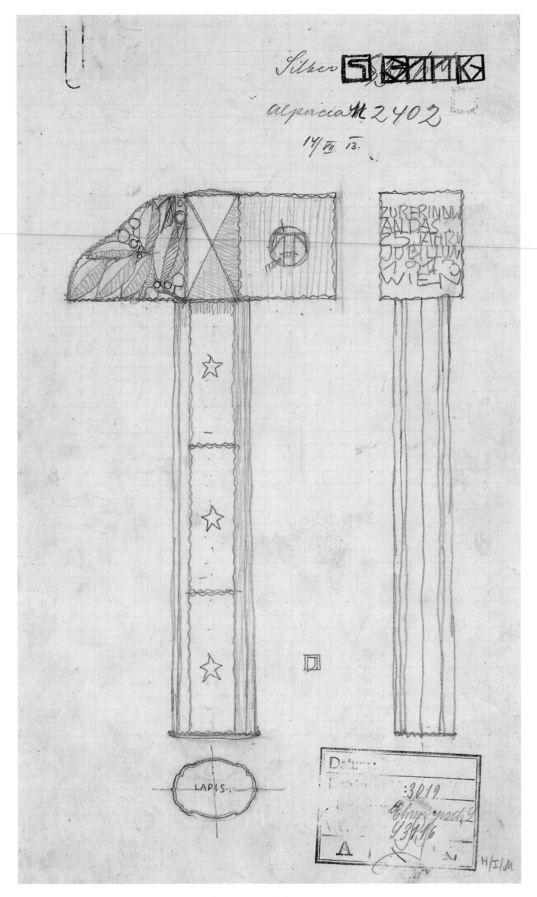

241   Freemason's hammer, 1913

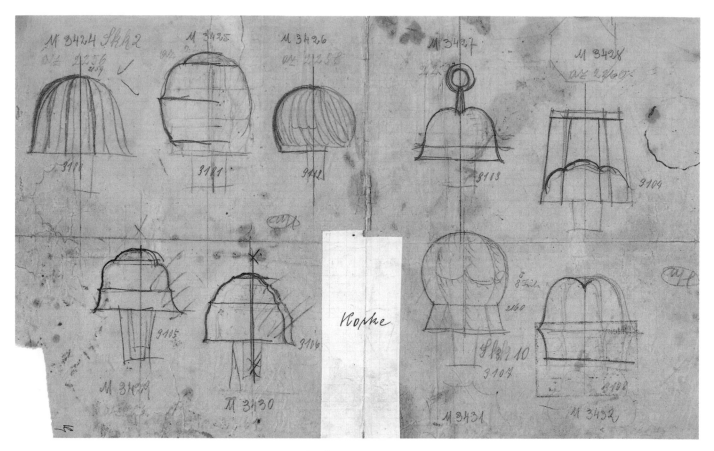

242   Bottle stoppers, ca. 1924

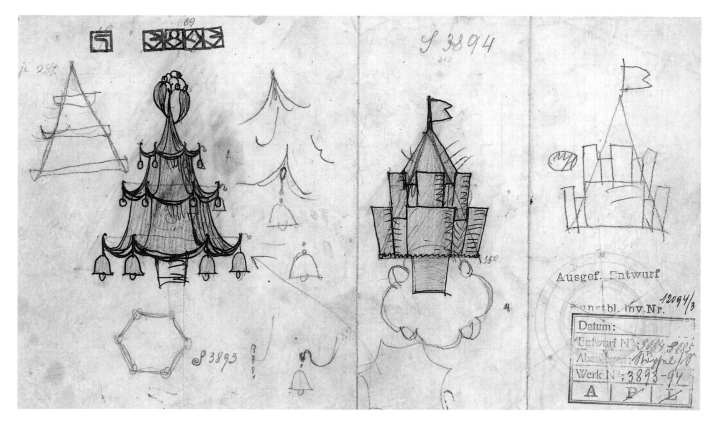

243   Bottle stoppers, 1917

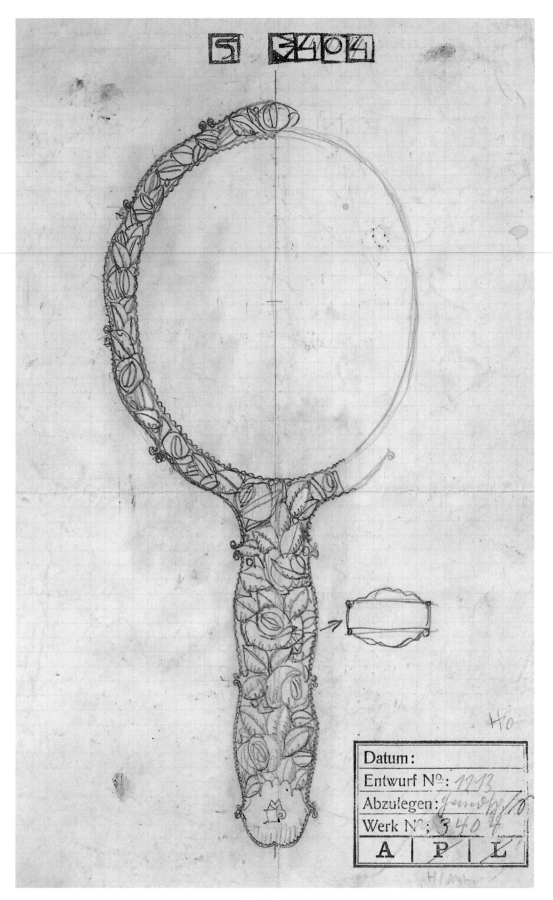

244 Hand mirror, 1914

245   Pieces from a 106-part cutlery set for 12 people, 1904/8

246   Fish knife and fish fork from a 106-part cutlery
set for 12 people, 1904/8

247   Butter knife and cheese knife from a 106-part
cutlery set for 12 people, 1904/8

248   Pieces from a 106-part cutlery set for 12 people, 1904/8

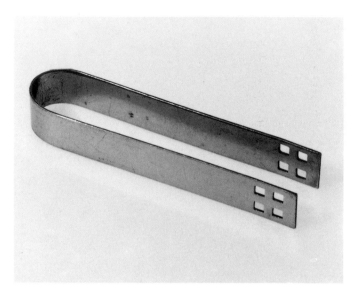

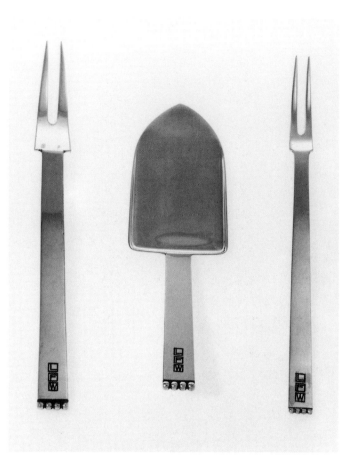

249 Sugar tongs from a 106-part cutlery set for 12 people, 1904/8

250 Serving forks and cake server from a 106-part cutlery set for 12 people, 1904/8

251 Eggcup with spoon, 1904

252 Pieces from a 14-part cutlery set, 1907/12

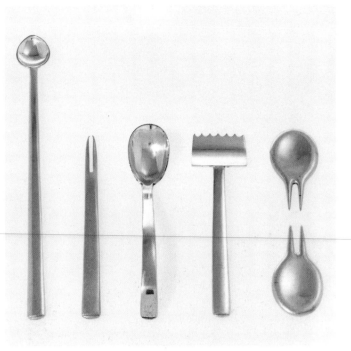

253 Pieces from a 14-part cutlery set, 1907/12

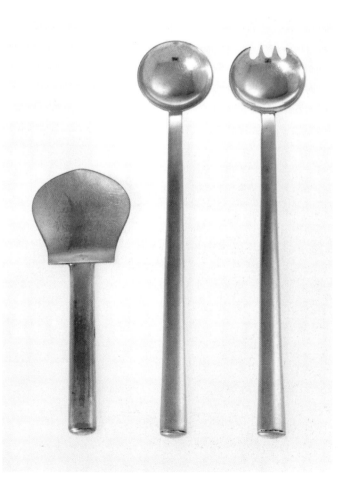

254 Ice cream server, salad spoon, and salad fork
     from a 14-part cutlery set, 1907/12

255 Fish knife and fish fork, 1916

256 Tea service, 1903

257 Tea service, 1912

258   Samovar, 1909

259   Tea service, 1923

260   Sugar caster, 1924

261   Coffee and tea service with samovar, 1918/25

262   Tea service, 1928

263   Coffee service, ca. 1927

264 Centerpiece, 1908/9

265 Centerpiece, 1910

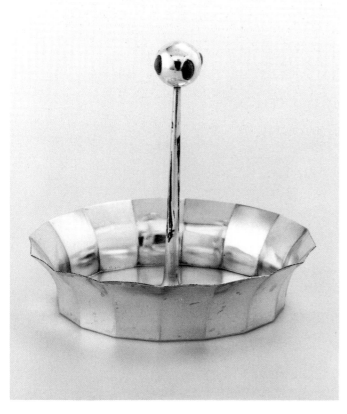

266 Bonbonnière, 1912

267 Centerpiece, 1905

Metal Objects 171

268   Centerpiece, 1924/25

269   Centerpiece, 1907

270   Centerpiece, 1940/42

271   Goblet, 1940/42

272   Vase, 1940/42

273   Bottle cooler, 1919

274   Tumbler, 1940/42

275   Goblet, 1940/42

276   Vase, 1911

277   Vase, 1909

278   Vase, 1940/42

279   Jardinière, 1912

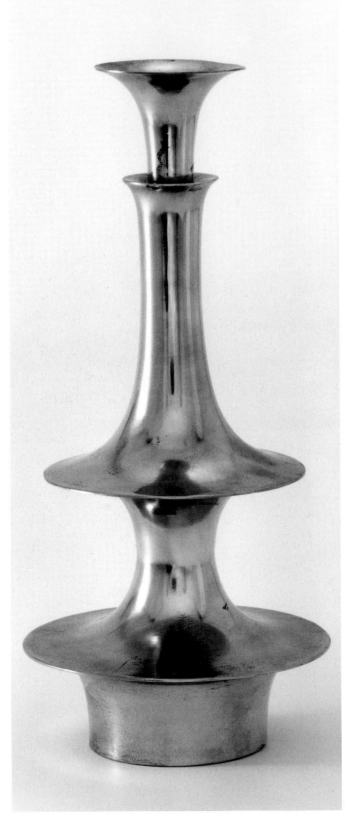

280   Candlestick, 1912

281   Candlestick, 1912

282   Vase, 1912

283 Box, 1919

284 Bowl, date unknown

285   Jardinière, 1907

286   Bowl, 1918

287   Vase with handle, 1905/6

288   Basket, 1906

289 Candelabrum, 1928

290   Table lamp, 1925

291   Table lamp, 1904

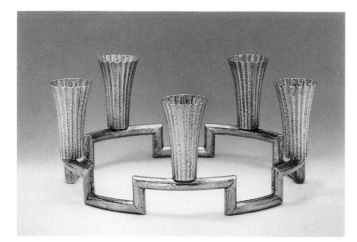

292 Candelabrum, 1930

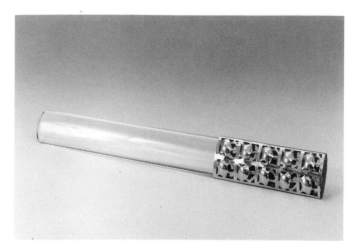

293 Paper knife, 1908

294 Box, 1930

295 Box, 1908

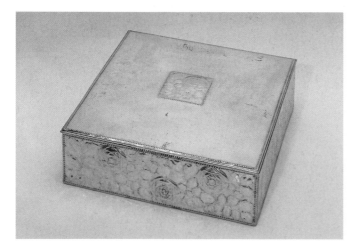

296 Casket, 1910

297 Casket, 1928/29

298   Wall lamp, 1912

299   Toiletry set, 1908

300   Carnet de ball, 1909

301   Bottle stoppers, ca. 1910

302   Trophy, 1930

303   Lidded cup, 1911

304   Goblet, 1940/42

305   Necklace, 1916

306   Necklace, 1916 (detail)

307   Necklace, 1916 (detail)

308 Ring, 1912

309 Brooch, after 1910

310 Brooch, 1910

311 Pendant, 1907

312 Pendant, 1912

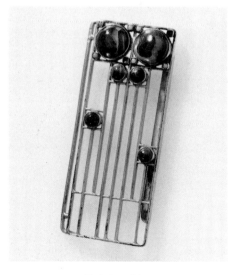

313 Belt buckle, 1905

Textiles, Leather Objects, and Fashion Accessories

In Vienna around 1900 the desire to shape the human environment according to the much-touted idea of a *"Gesamtkunstwerk"* (total work of art) elevated textile design to the realm of art. The interest in surface, pattern, and new types of ornament derived from a contemporary stylistic sensibility, which strove for flatness, stylization of natural forms, and, finally, abstraction in general. Particularly Viennese artists of this period began to move away from natural forms, ultimately rejecting stylization and the principles of floral Jugendstil as such. Small, primarily abstract-geometric surface patterns were created first by Koloman Moser and Josef Hoffmann, and the manufacturers were found who were open to their ideas. In Vienna it was above all the renowned firm of Johann Backhausen & Söhne that performed pioneering work, producing fabrics for interior furnishings and both machine-woven and hand-knotted carpets. The archives of the firm have survived almost intact, giving an exact picture of their innovative textile production.

Josef Hoffmann began to work for Backhausen in 1901. In 1904 the textiles *Notschrei* (Cry of Distress) and *Sehnsucht* (Longing) were made, designed no doubt for the Purkersdorf Sanatorium near Vienna. Hoffmann used his fabric *Streber* (Striver) here as well. The patterns reveal the current tendency toward simplification and small design, with a basic structure of straight lines, squares, and arrows.

Hoffmann's designs for the textile department of the Wiener Werkstätte, which was set up around 1910, form a stylistic and personal continuum that set its stamp on the organization as a whole. Altogether Hoffmann designed about seventy-five textiles for the Wiener Werkstätte, and they vividly trace the development of design over twenty eventful years. All the textile designs are documented in the MAK's collection: drawings, printed silks or cotton fabrics, and material from the Wiener Werkstätte archives. The early years clearly predominate both in terms of quantity and quality. Hoffmann's creative power, his receptive capacity, and his almost obsessive preoccupation with inventing ornament and pattern predestined him both to absorb influences and to exert influences himself. He was able to take the most innovative trend or personality of the time as a model and transform the stimulus into ideas of his own; only thus could so wide a range of trends coexist in his own work. Clearly beyond all envy, Hoffmann frequently used fabrics designed by other Wiener Werkstätte artists for the decoration of his interiors. His lively interest in formal innovation and imaginative talent shaped the style and work of the Wiener Werkstätte in textile design, but his later tendency to cling to outmoded programs and production methods finally brought them to an end.

The many drawings by Hoffmann that have survived are eloquent testimony to the fact that his work on ornament and design was a creative intellectual exercise; but it was also nothing less than a compulsion. That he had an inexhaustible imagination is even confirmed, though not regarded positively, by his most embittered opponent, Adolf Loos. Every form becomes an ornament in Hoffmann's free drawings, and ornament is an integral part of every object. Once certain decorative forms had been invented, he could vary them endlessly, repeating them in a wide variety of contexts until new line formations captured his attention. This compositional principle is most evident in his textile designs: here we find small elements predominating, with the larger motifs only occurring occasionally around 1910. Hoffmann's textiles are often restrained and neutral; indeed, in comparison with the designs by other Wiener Werkstätte artists, they can be banal. For Hoffmann there does not appear to have been a conflict between good, meaningful form and ornament. The fundamental interrelationship between the two is evident in the ornamental character of his formal inventions and the compulsion with which he decorated form. Motifs and forms always correspond to the *Zeitgeist*, but they are never in advance of their time.

314　Block print of "Serpentin" fabric design, 1910/15

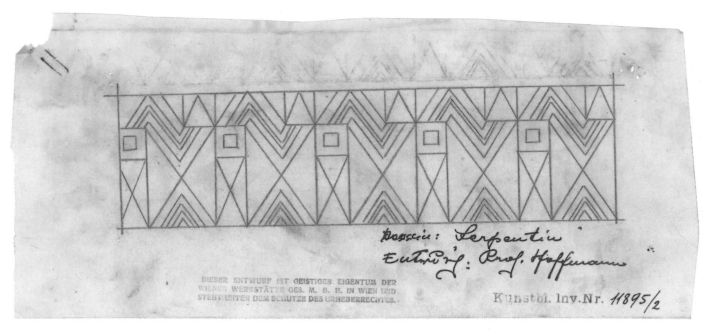

315 "Serpentin" fabric design, 1910/15

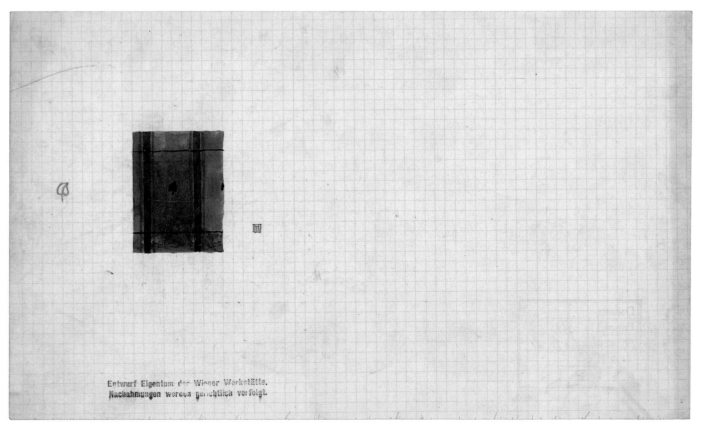

316 Fabric design, 1905/10

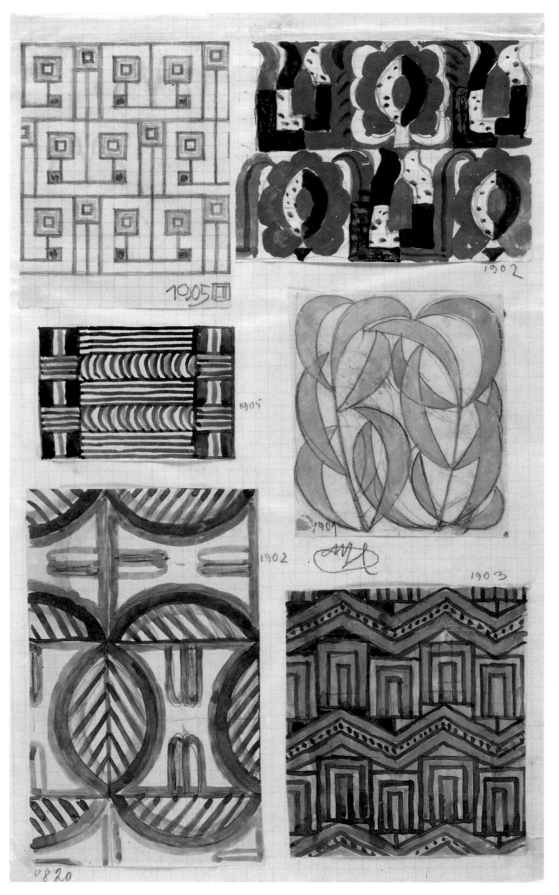

317   Six fabric designs, 1901/5

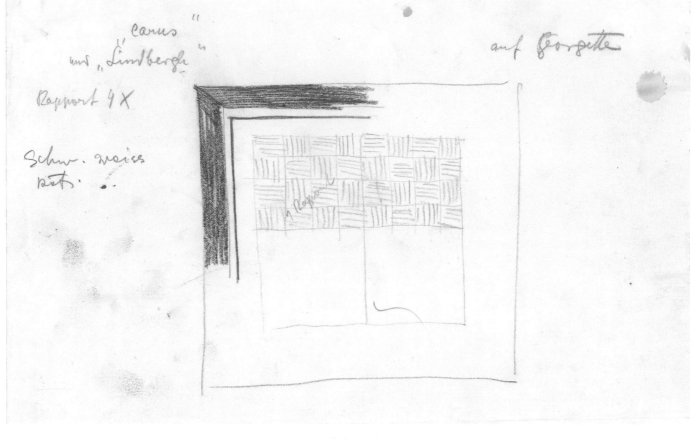

318 "Carus" fabric design, 1929

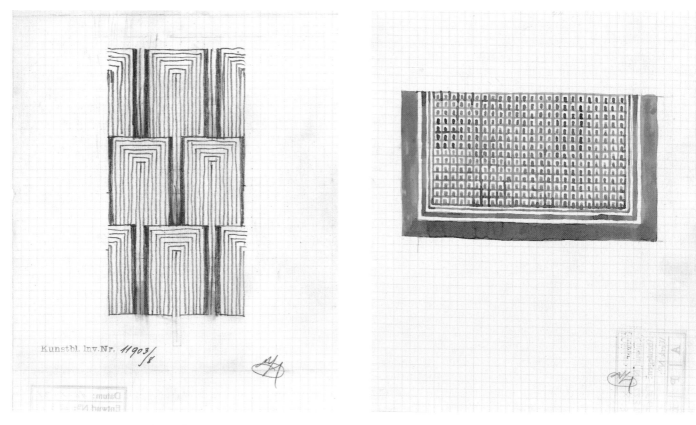

319 Fabric design, 1931   320 Fabric design, 1931

196 Textiles, Leather Objects, and Fashion Accessories

321   "Carus" fabric design, 1929

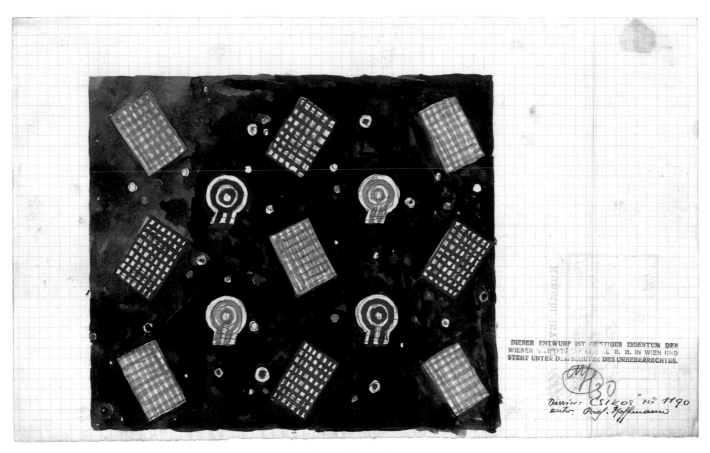

322   "Csikos" fabric design, 1930

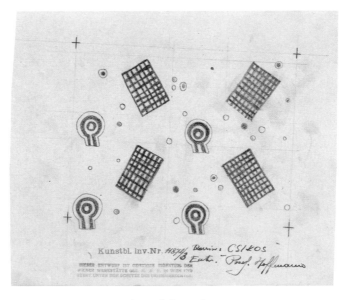

323   "Csikos" fabric design, 1930

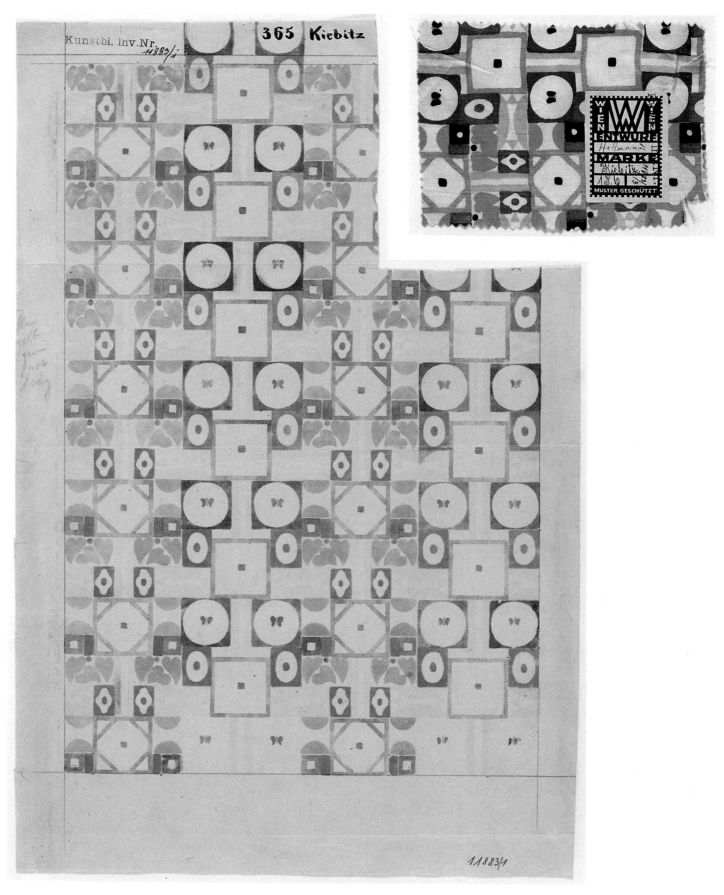

324 Block print and "Kiebitz" fabric sample, 1910/15

325   "Jordan" fabric design, 1928

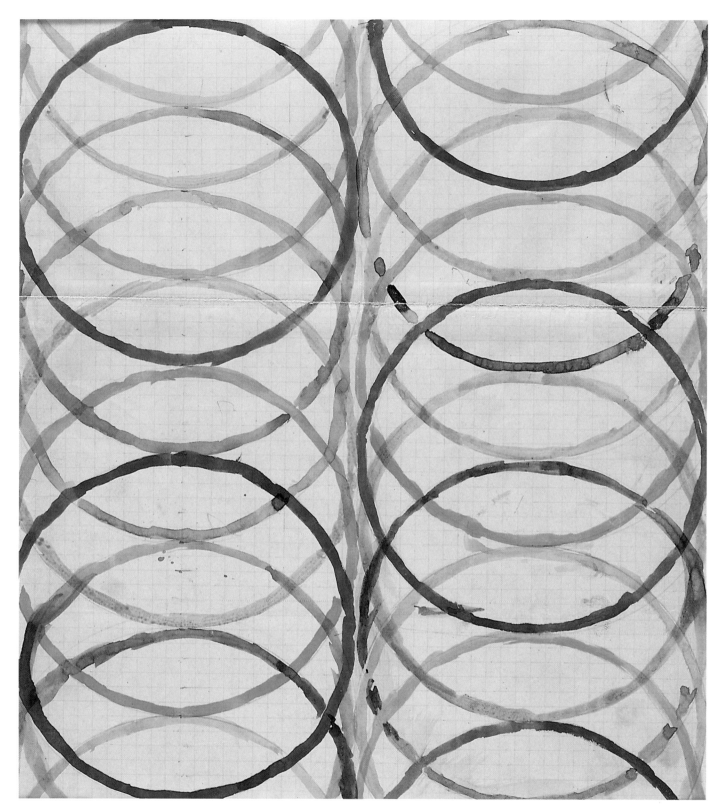

326 "Reifen" fabric design, 1928

327　"Athos" fabric design, 1928

328   Fabric design, ca. 1928

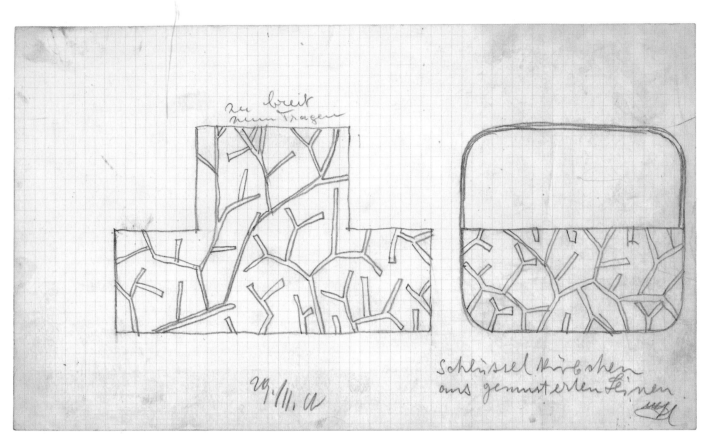

336   Linen basket, 1927

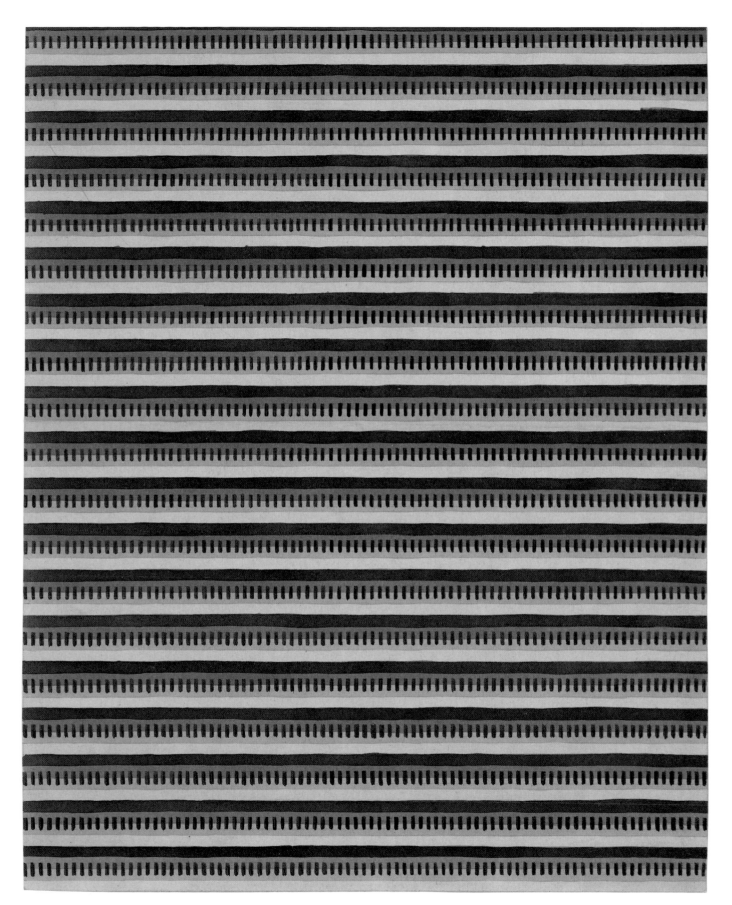

337 Fabric design, 1925/30

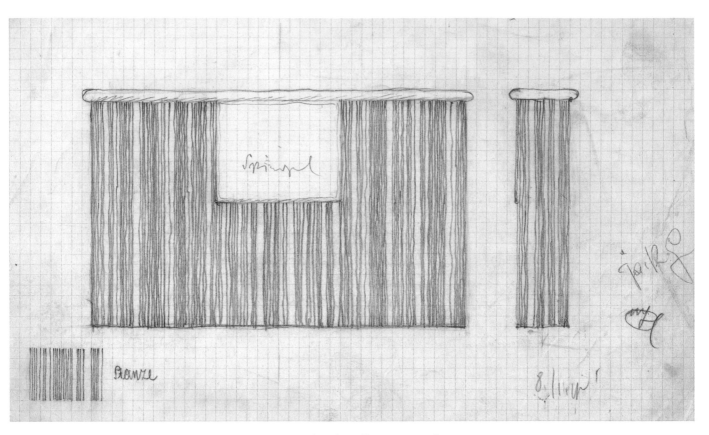

338   Leather handbag, 1925/29

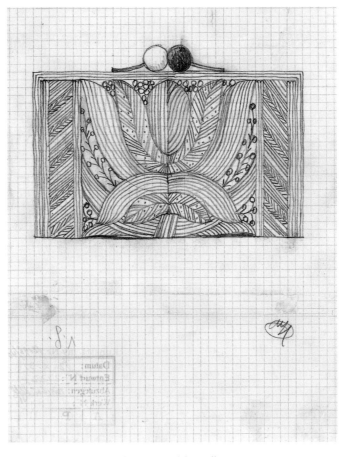

339   Embroidered handbag, 1931

340   Embroidered handbag, 1931

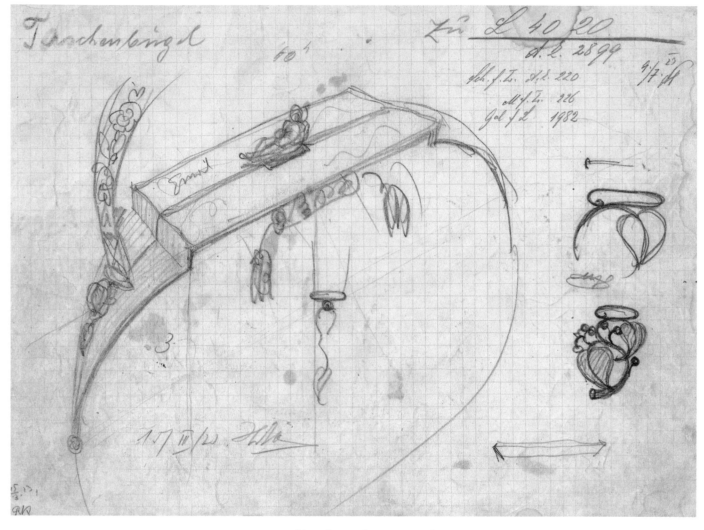

341   Handbag clasp, 1920/23

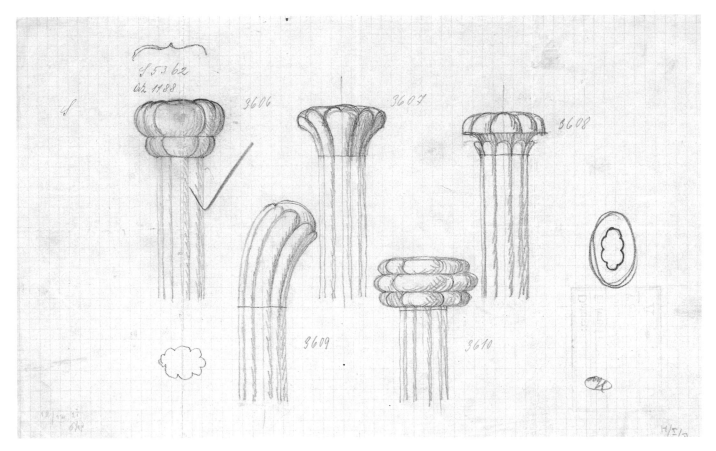

342 Knobs for walking sticks and umbrellas, ca. 1920

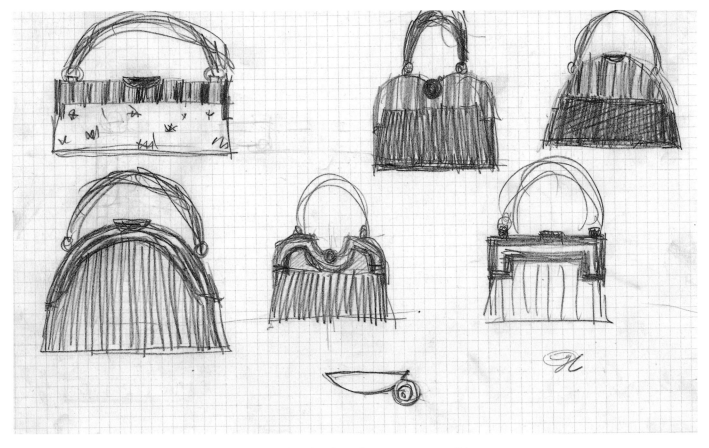

343 Leather handbags, ca. 1925 (?)

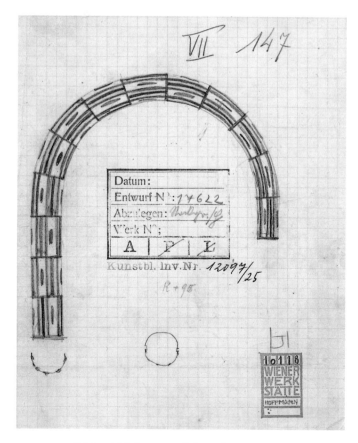

344   Umbrella knobs, ca. 1925

345   Walking stick handle, ca. 1910

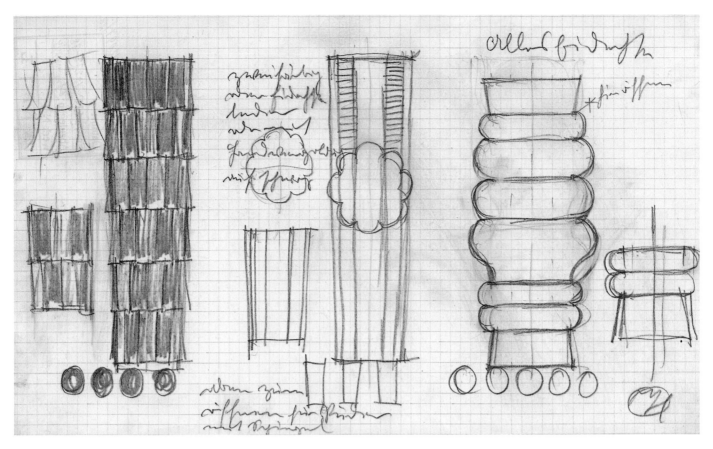

346   Umbrella knobs, ca. 1925

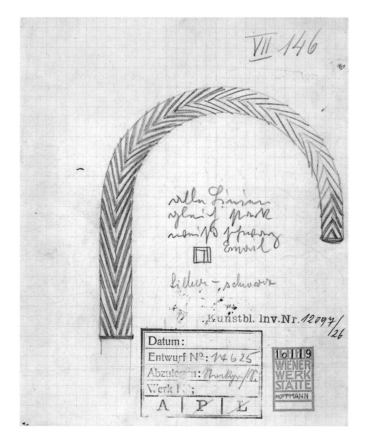

347   Walking stick handle, ca. 1910 (?)

Textiles, Leather Objects, and Fashion Accessories   213

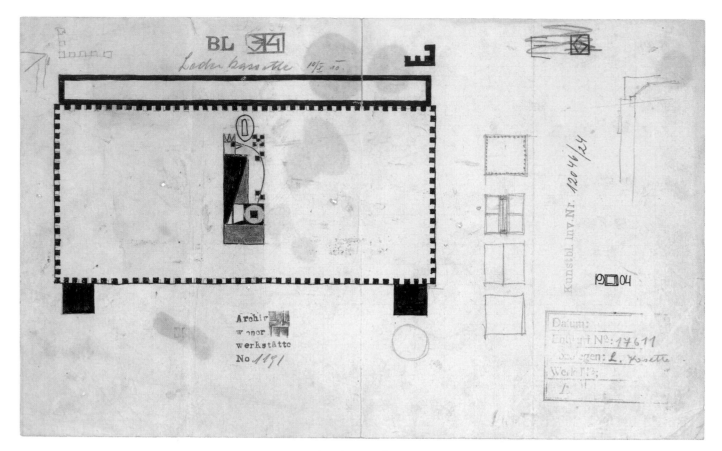

348   Leather casket, 1904

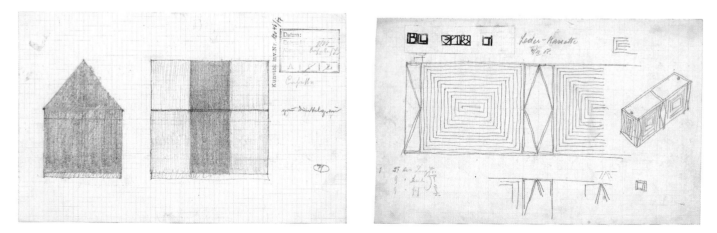

349   Leather casket, 1905/10

350   Leather casket, 1905

351 Book cover for Gerhart Hauptmann's *Hanneles Himmelfahrt,* date unknown

Textiles, Leather Objects, and Fashion Accessories   215

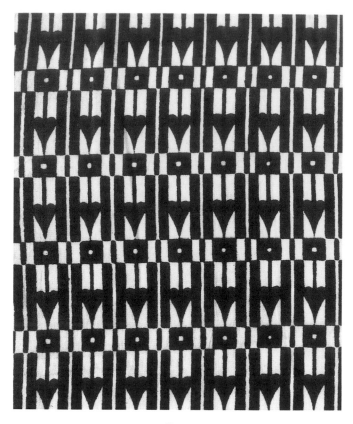

352 "Adler," 1910/12

353 "Herzblatt," 1910 / 15

354 Fabric sample, 1909

355 "Ozon," 1923

356 "Cypern," 1910/15

357 "Luchs," 1910/12

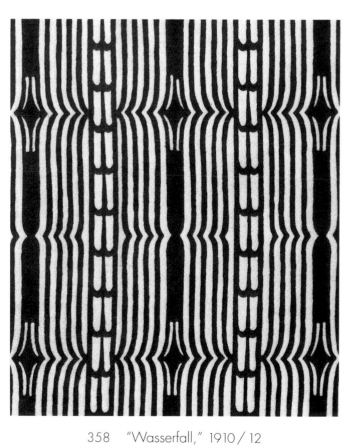

358 "Wasserfall," 1910/12

359 "Miramar," 1910/15

Textiles, Leather Objects, and Fashion Accessories 217

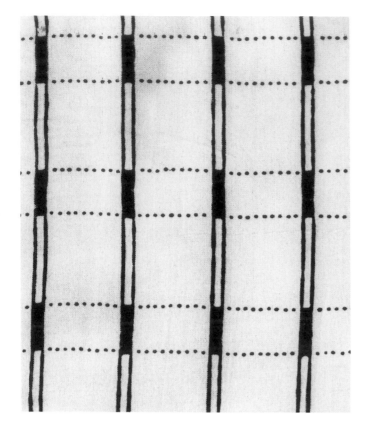

360   "Martha," 1910 / 15   361   "Jordan," 1928

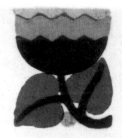

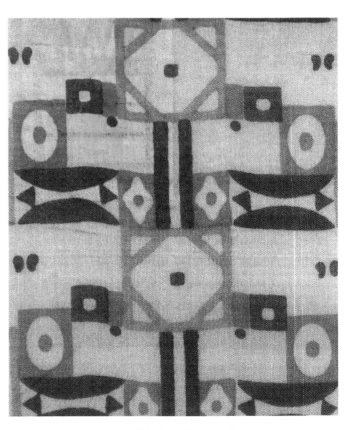

362   "Erlenzeisig," 1910 / 11   363   "Kiebitz," 1910 / 15

364 "Lerche," 1910/11

365 "Oder," 1928

366 "Ibera," 1928

367 Fabric sample, 1909/10

Textiles, Leather Objects, and Fashion Accessories   219

368 "Montezuma," 1910 / 12

369 "Refrain," 1929

370 "Tulpe," 1910 / 15

371 "Mira," 1929

372 "Gotemba," 1925

373 "Triangel," 1910/13

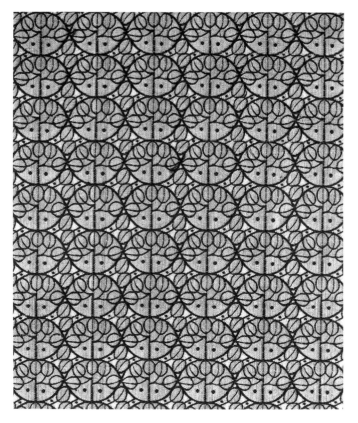

374 Fabric sample, 1909/10

375 "Schwarzblatt," 1910/12

Textiles, Leather Objects, and Fashion Accessories **221**

376 "Kohleule," 1910 / 15

377 "Biene," 1910 / 11

378 "Nil," 1910 / 17

379 "Hirschenzunge," 1910 / 12

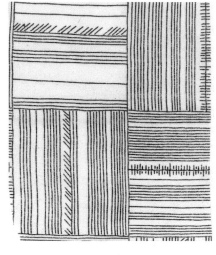

380 "Guido," 1929

381 Book cover, 1907

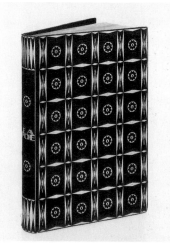

382 Book cover, 1910 / 14

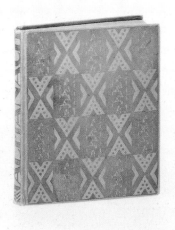

383 Book cover, 1911

384 Book cover, ca. 1915

385   "Ragusa," 1910 / 12

386   "Bremen," 1928

387   "Tenor," 1928

388   Calling card etui, 1925/29

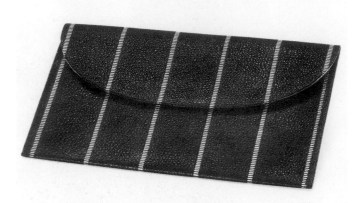

389   Calling card etui, 1925/29

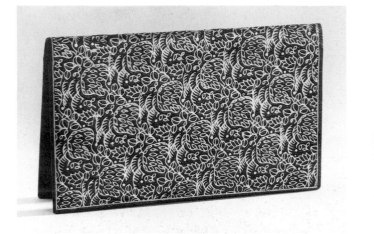

390   Wallet, ca. 1920

391   Handbag, 1930

392   Handbag, 1909/10

393   Calling card etui, 1929/31

394   Writing case, 1927/29

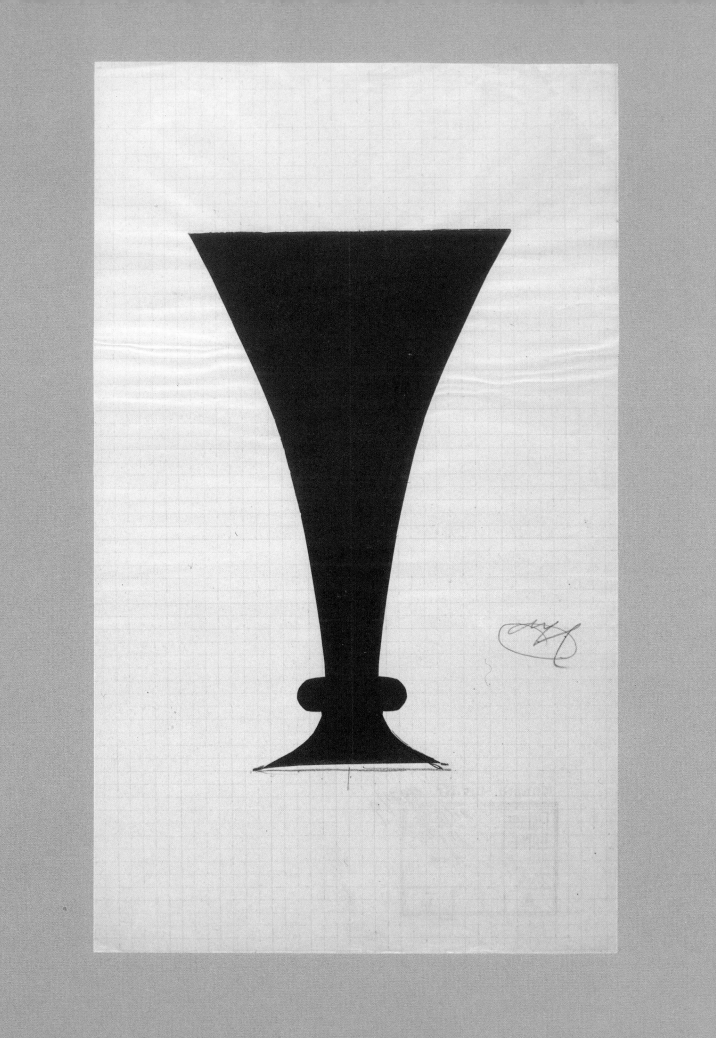

Glass and Ceramics

Glass and ceramics must have had a particular attraction for Josef Hoffmann. His first designs in these mediums appear at the very beginning of his artistic career, and the last only a short time before his death. There was hardly a year in which Hoffmann did not produce a large number of designs for glassware or ceramics, and they all display the characteristic features of his artistic phases.

The glass and ceramic collection of the MAK – Austrian Museum of Applied Arts – does not include work representative of all Hoffmann's creative periods, unlike the collections containing his furniture and metalwork. It begins with works from around 1911 and ends with designs from the early thirties.

During this period Hoffmann designed glass and ceramics for a number of clients. Outstanding in this regard was the Wiener Werkstätte, which not only made the objects to his designs but – and this applies particularly to his ceramics – had the designs altered and developed by other craftsmen. Although the exact basis of Josef Hoffmann's relations with the Wiener Werkstätte has never been fully clarified, it is evident that throughout these years he always endeavored to cooperate with them, give them preferential treatment, and not to compete with them. Thus he only designed glass and ceramics for other manufacturers if this did not affect the Wiener Werkstätte. His designs for publishers and manufacturers, such as E. Bakalowitz Söhne or J. & L. Lobmeyr, are therefore hardly comparable with those for the Wiener Werkstätte, whether judged on the basis of their form, decoration, or, particularly, their technique. Hoffmann rarely worked directly for other firms. Apart from the Wiener Werkstätte, he gave his designs only to the Österreichisches Museum für Kunst und Industrie (which later changed its name to Österreichisches Museum für angewandte Kunst, or MAK), the Verein des Österreichischen Werkbundes (of which he was president for a time), and J. & L. Lobmeyr. Under what conditions this was done is not known, but Hoffmann was evidently very careless with his copyrights.

Although the MAK has no glass or ceramics from Hoffmann's early periods – that is, from 1899 to 1910 – nor from his late period, after the collapse of the Wiener Werkstätte in 1932, its collections do provide impressive evidence of how much Hoffmann determined contemporary style in the form and decoration of his glassware and ceramics. They demonstrate his ability to adopt, transmute, and fuse the predominant styles of his time. This is evident in his adaptation of Biedermeier elements to modern demands, both in designs made by the Wiener Werkstätte (cat. no. 423) and by Lötz, which was entirely in the style of the Werkbund (cat. no. 446). In his ceramics work, it is manifest in the designs executed by Augarten Porcelain.

How far Hoffmann was ahead of his time is clear from his designs. Many were never produced, not so much because of technical difficulties – particularly the designs made for the Wiener Werkstätte – as the concern that the objects would not be saleable.

395 Vase, 1928

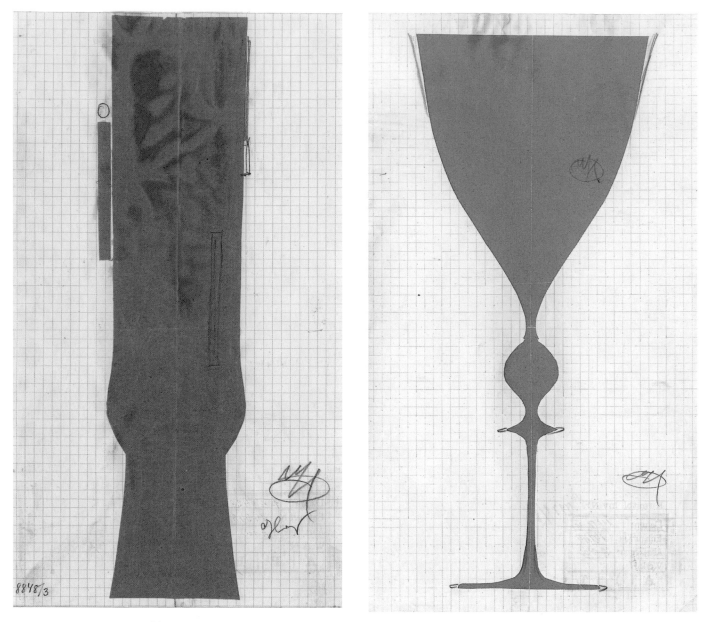

396　Vase, ca. 1928

397　Glass goblet, ca. 1928

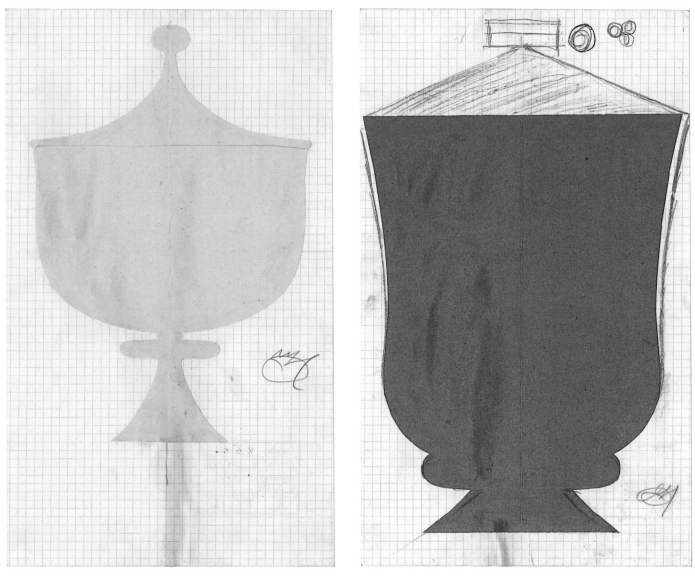

398   Lidded glass goblet, ca. 1928

399   Lidded glass goblet, ca. 1928

400   Three glasses, 1920/24(?)

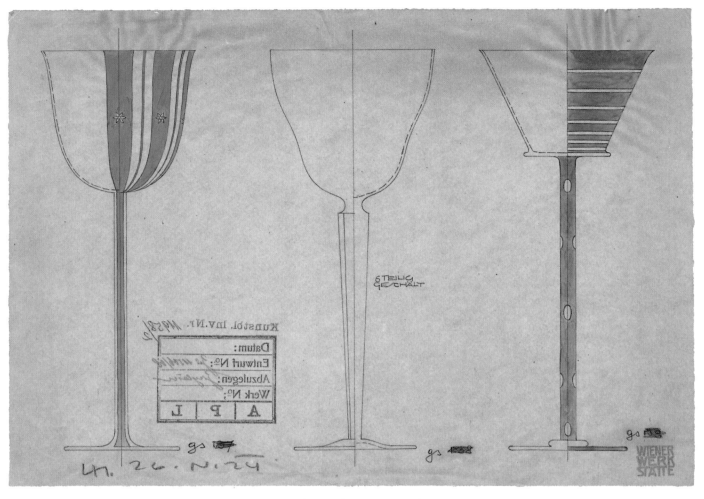

401   Three glasses, 1920/2(?)

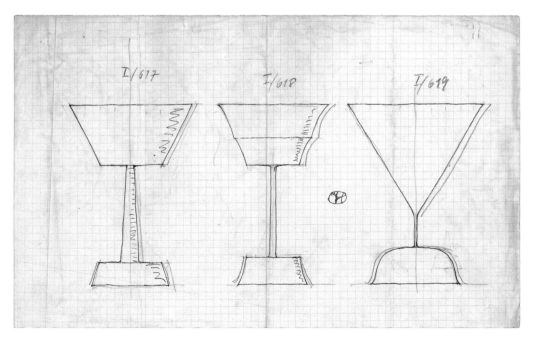

402   Three glasses, 1915

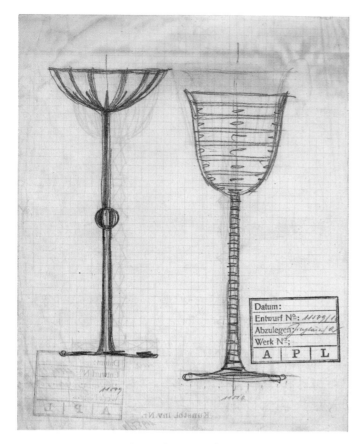

403   Two glasses, date unknown

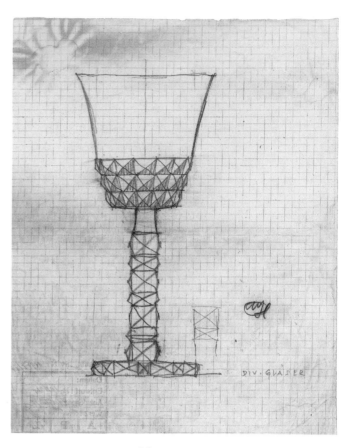

404   Glass, date unknown

405   Teacup, date unknown

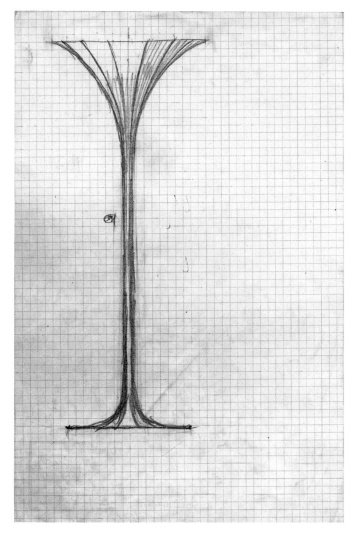

406 Glass, date unknown

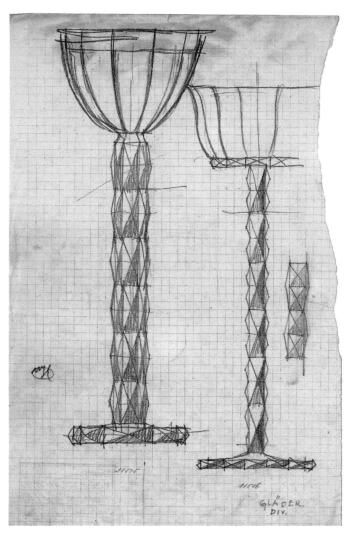

407 Two glasses, date unknown

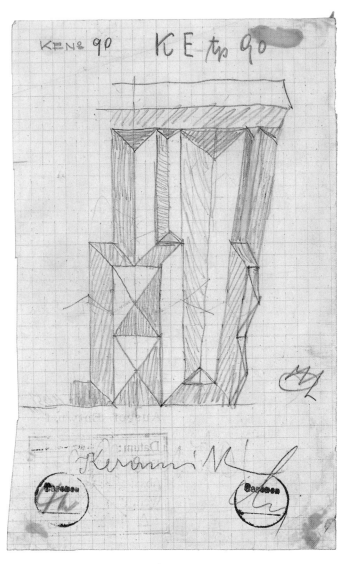

408   Jardinière, ca. 1927

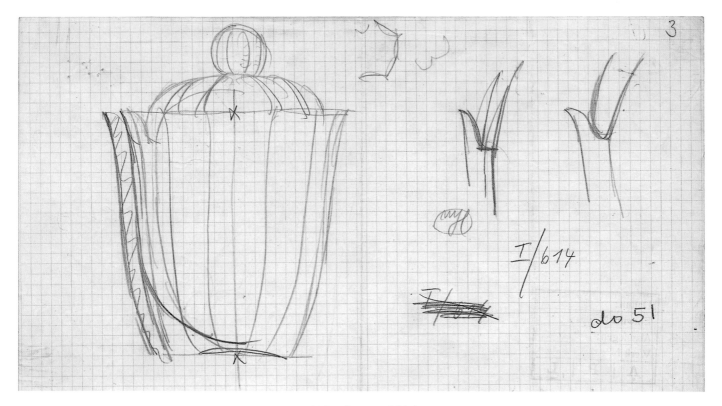

409   Jar, ca. 1914

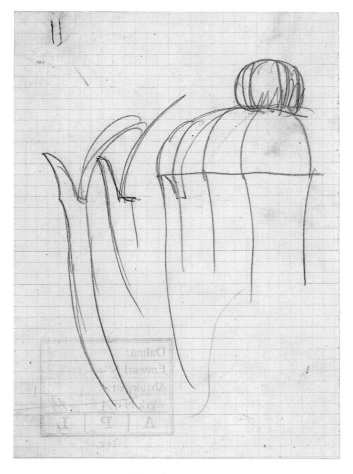

410   Jar, ca. 1914

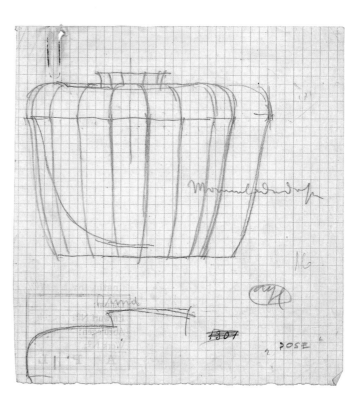

411   Jam jar, ca. 1915

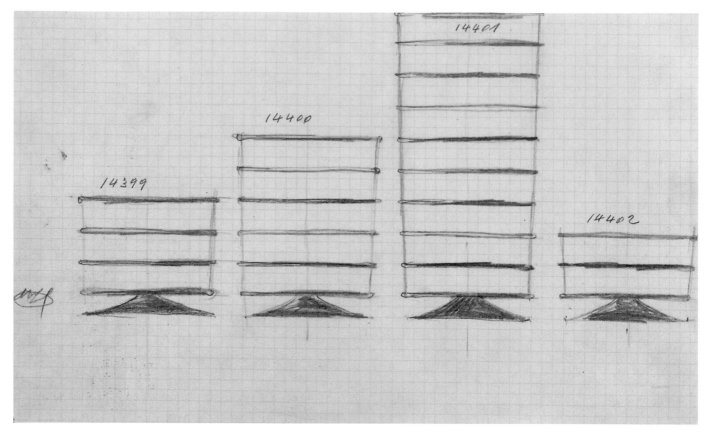

412   Four glasses, 1928

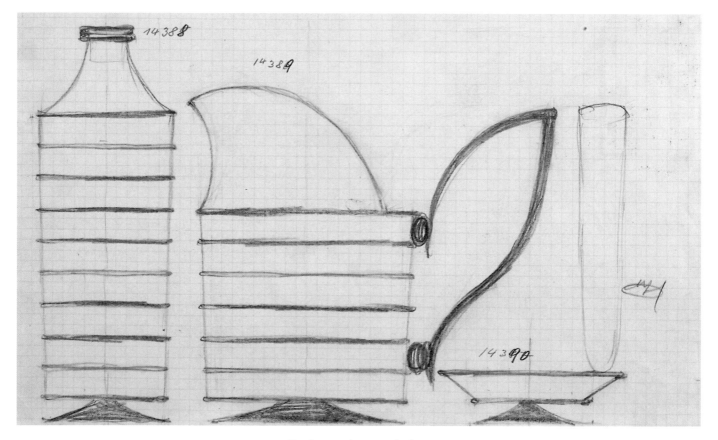

413   Bottle, pitcher, and glass, 1928

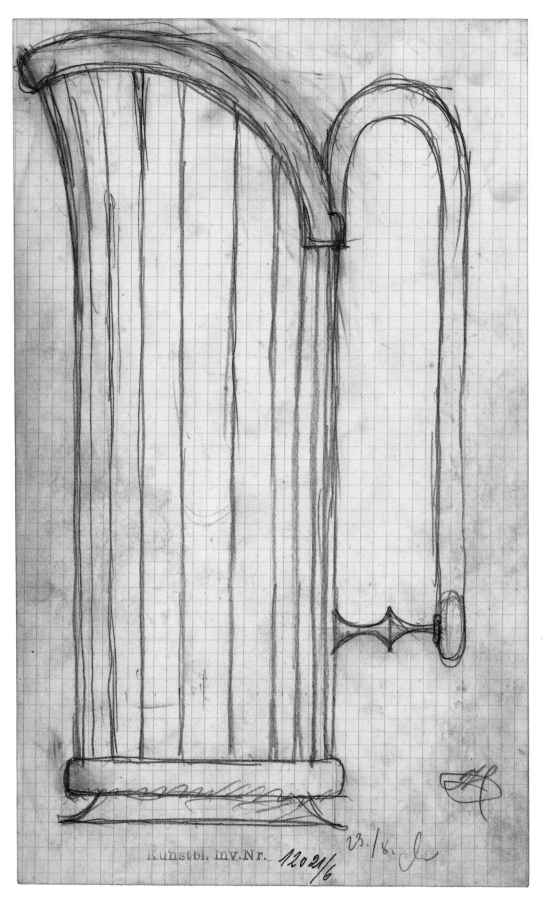

Kuhstbl. inv.Nr. *12021/6*

414   Water jug, ca. 1928

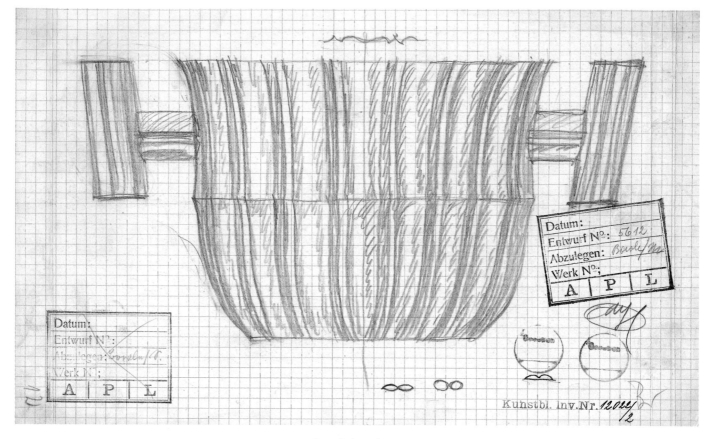

415   Punch bowl, ca. 1920

416   Coffeepot, 1925/28

417   Coffeepot and cup, 1928

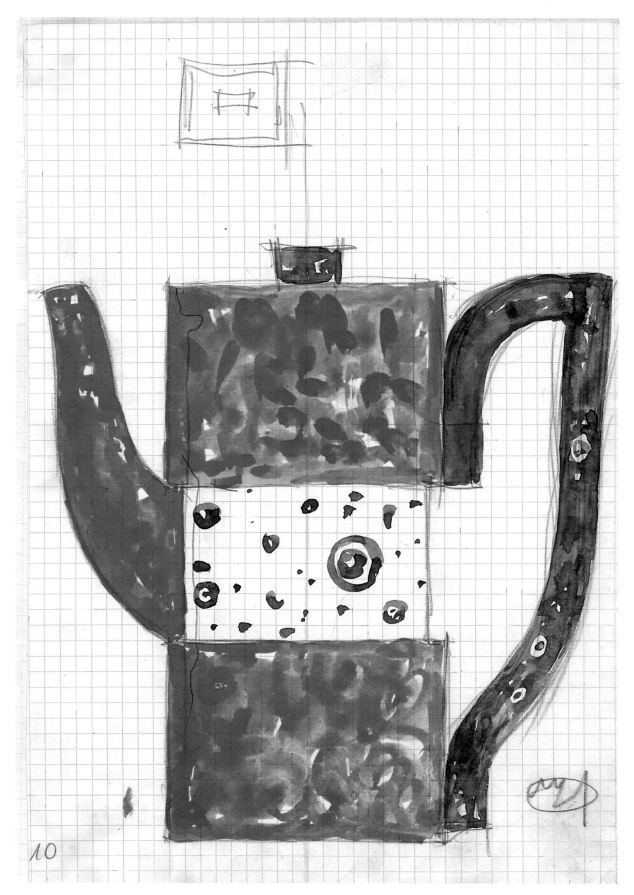

418   Coffeepot, 1928

419   Glass, before 1914 (designed 1910)   420   Glass, before 1914 (designed 1910)

421   Glass, before 1914 (designed 1910)   422   Glass, before 1914 (designed 1910)

423   Vase (designed before 1923)   424   Vase (designed before 1923)

425 Tumbler, ca. 1910

426 Tumbler, ca. 1910

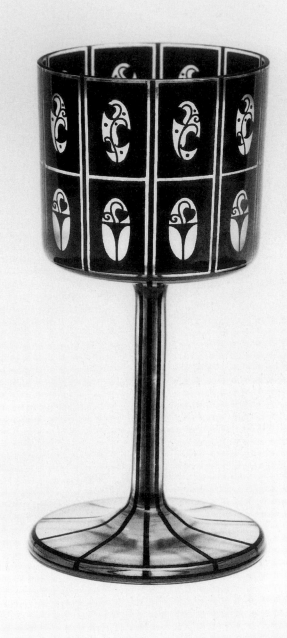

427   Wine glass (designed ca. 1911)   428   Wine glass (designed ca. 1911)

429   Liqueur glass, ca. 1911

430   Two liqueur glasses, ca. 1911

431   Champagne glass, ca. 1911

432   Two liqueur glasses, 1917/25

433   Jardinière, before 1914

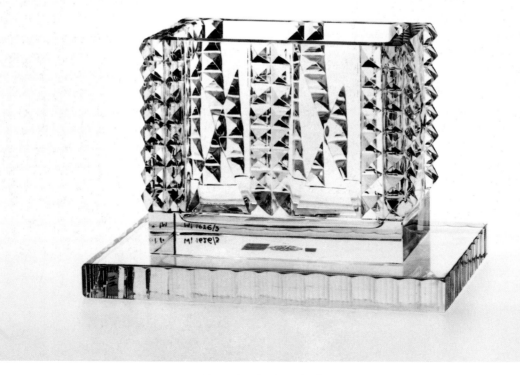

434   Jardinière, before 1914

435   Bowl, from 1915

436   Jar, after 1918 (designed 1915)

437   Bottle, after 1915

438　Bonbonnière, before 1914　　　　　439　Punch glass, before 1914

440   Punch bowl, before 1914

441   Vase, before 1914 (designed 1910)

442   Two glasses and a decanter from a set (designed ca. 1920)

443   Toiletry set, ca. 1913

444   Requisites for Holy Mass, before 1915

445　Vase, ca. 1913

446   Centerpiece, before 1914

447   Tumbler (designed before 1915)   448   Lidded vase, before 1914

449　Jug from a porcelain service, 1910/11

450   Mocca service (made before 1935)

451   Mocca service (made before 1938)

452   Sugar bowl from a porcelain service, 1910/11

453   Cup, ca. 1919 (designed ca. 1910)

454   Cup, ca. 1919 (designed ca. 1910)

455   Wooden models for parts of a porcelain mocca service, ca. 1910

Architecture and Monuments

Josef Hoffmann was a very productive architect. His first building dates from 1900, and his last from 1954. Although he built several dozen houses, most reference books on modern architecture mention, and usually illustrate, only two in any detail – the Purkersdorf Sanatorium near Vienna of 1904 and the Palais Stoclet in Brussels of 1905/11. This selectivity may seem an oversimplification, but these are certainly Hoffmann's major architectural works. They were almost contemporaneous and form a stylistic unity, which stands out from all the other buildings he designed, both before and after this peak. Hoffmann's earlier and later buildings display great architectural skill and confidence in design; above all, they are extraordinarily elaborate and costly. Hoffmann's biographer Eduard F. Sekler has aptly called this "richness as artistic possibility."[1] However, they are houses for which Biedermeier solidity is the only leitmotiv, and one must ask why the Purkersdorf Sanatorium and the Palais Stoclet are so unique. Most likely the explanation lies with Hoffmann's clients. The sanatorium was commissioned at the instigation of the art critic Berta Zuckerkandl, whose brother-in-law Viktor Zuckerkandl desired an outstanding example of the new style. The commission from the Stoclet family followed directly from the building of the sanatorium.

It may be assumed that had he found more such clients, Hoffmann would have produced other works of the same caliber at a later date. However, he was first and foremost a craftsman, in his architecture as in his other work, and he had no reformist or inventive ambitions.

Based on the many studies that he made for facades, historians of architecture have often felt that Hoffmann devoted too little attention to the real problems of architecture, such as blueprints and building techniques. Before he enrolled at the academy in Vienna, Hoffmann had graduated from the best school of architecture in Austria-Hungary, the Senior State Commercial and Technical School (Höheren Staatsgewerbeschule) in Brünn, and while still a student at the academy he was already a full-fledged architect. Many of the challenges of designing and building, such as blueprints, were so familiar to him that he did not need to concern himself with them in more detail, nor did he wish to do so. Hoffmann's skill as an architect is probably one of the reasons why he was not an inventive builder and remained a decorative architect, with an almost blind sureness of touch, right from 1900 (the forestry office for the Wittgenstein Forestry Administration) until 1954 (residential housing for the City of Vienna).

Note

1 Eduard F. Sekler, *Josef Hoffmann: The Architectural Work*, translated by the author; catalogue translated by John Maas (Princeton, N.J., 1985) [Salzburg and Vienna, 1982].

456   Design for a high-rise building, 1927

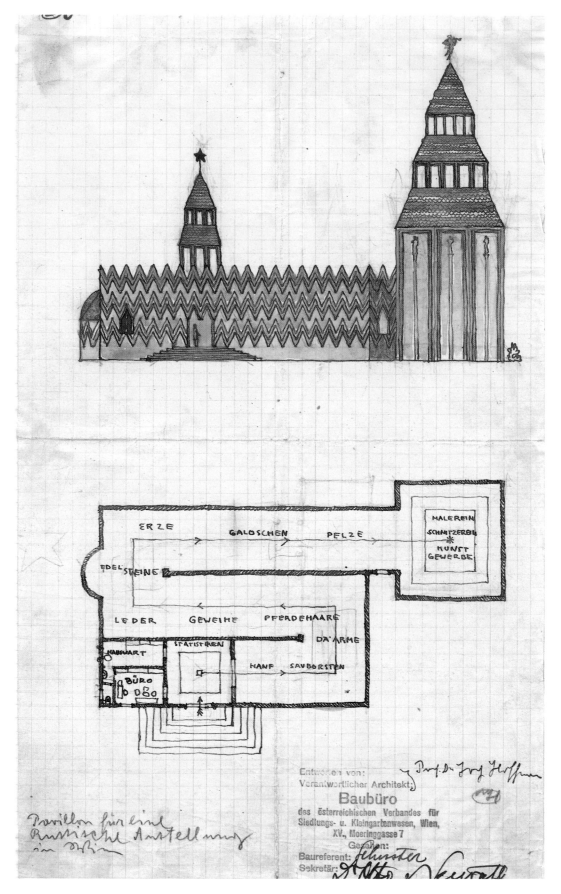

457   Plan and elevation of a pavilion for a Russian exhibition in Vienna, 1923/25(?)

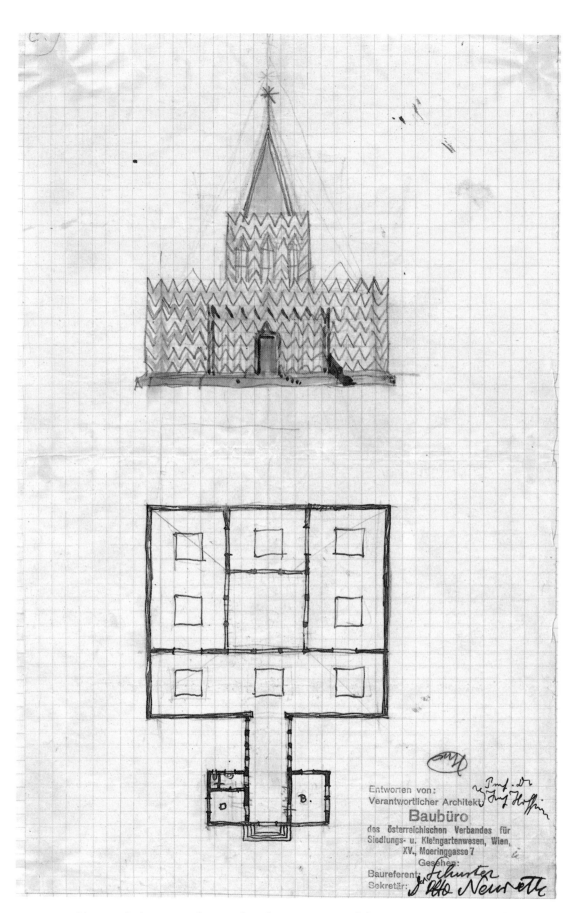

Entworfen von:
Verantwortlicher Architekt
Baubüro
des österreichischen Verbandes für
Siedlungs- u. Kleingartenwesen, Wien,
XV., Moeringgasse 7
Gesehen:
Baureferent:
Sekretär:

458   Plan and elevation of a pavilion for a Russian exhibition in Vienna, 1923/25(?)

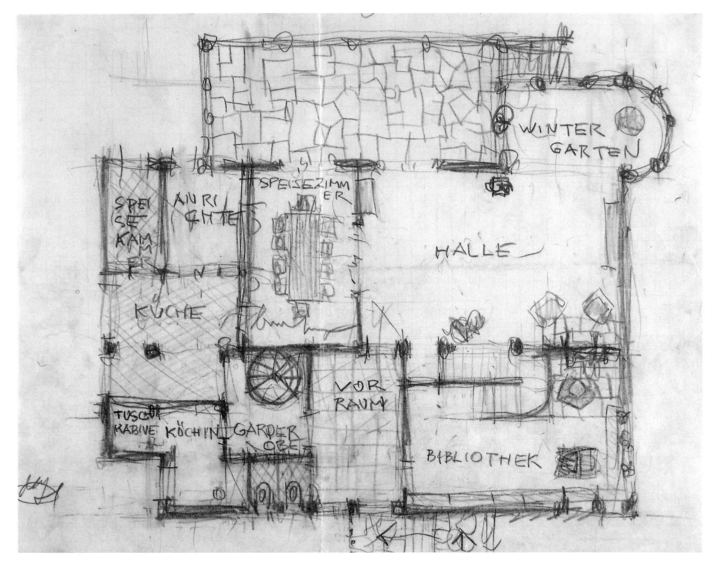

459 Plan of the Ast country house, 1923/24

460   Design for the facade of the Ast country house, 1923/24

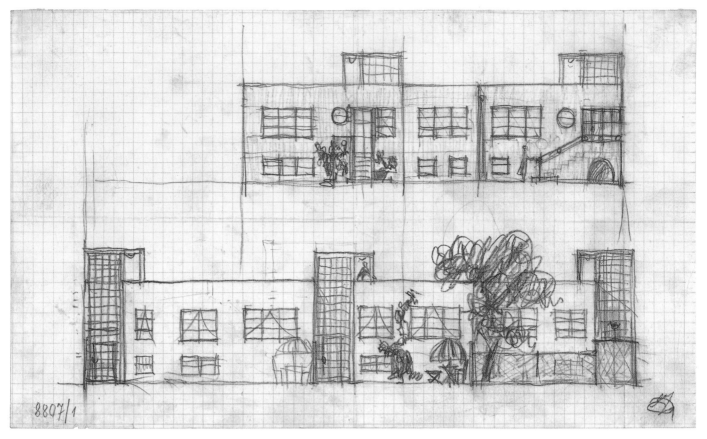

461   Design for the facade of a row house in the Werkbund housing estate, 1930/32

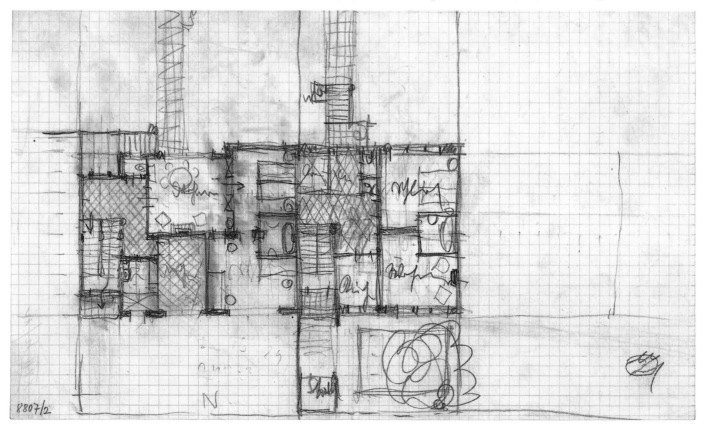

462   Plan of a row house in the Werkbund housing estate, 1930/32

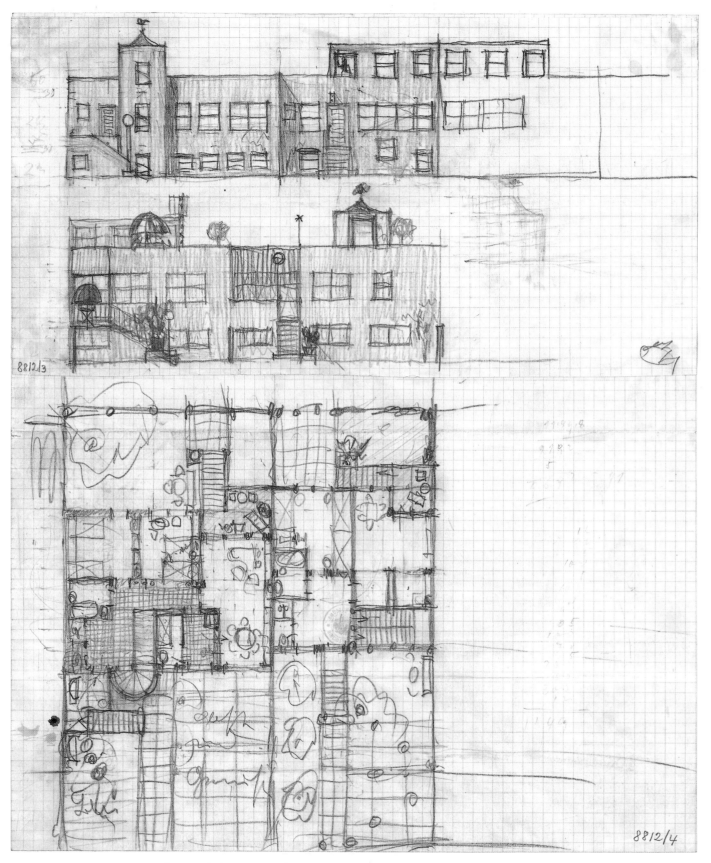

463   Plan and elevations of a row house in the Werkbund housing estate, 1930

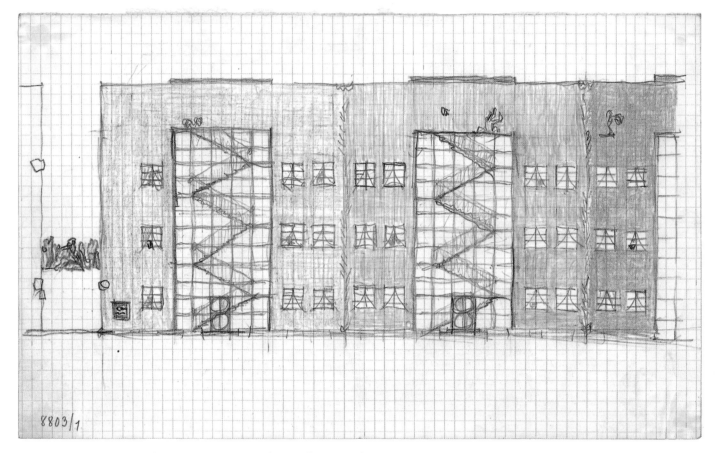

464   Design for the facade of an apartment building, 1930

465   Design for the facade of a three-story apartment building, 1929

466   Design for the facade of a public housing project in Vienna, 1929

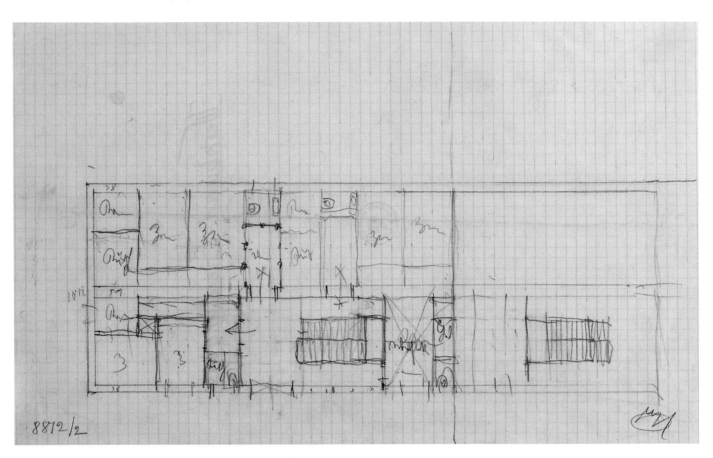

467   Plan of the Werkbund housing estate, 1930

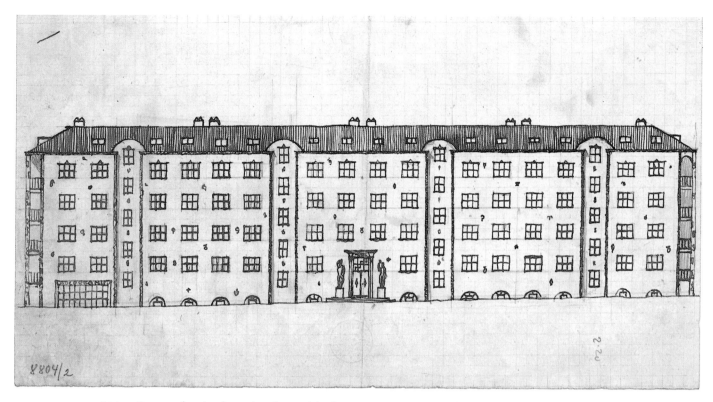

468   Design for the facade of a public housing project on Billrothstrasse in Vienna, 1923

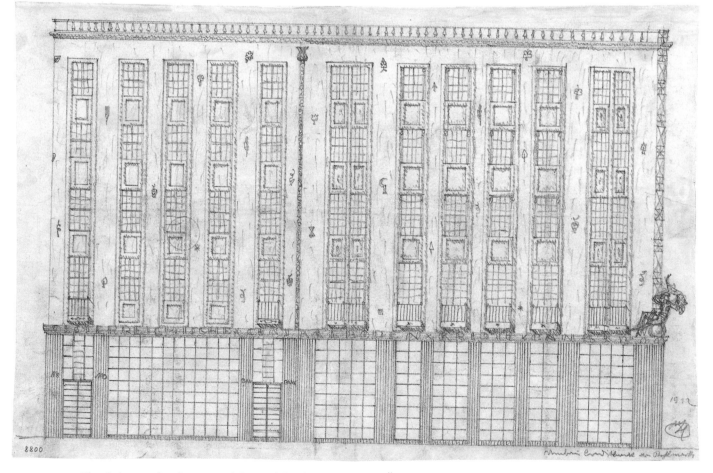

469   Third design for the remodeling of the facade of the Österreichische Central Boden Credit Bank, 1912

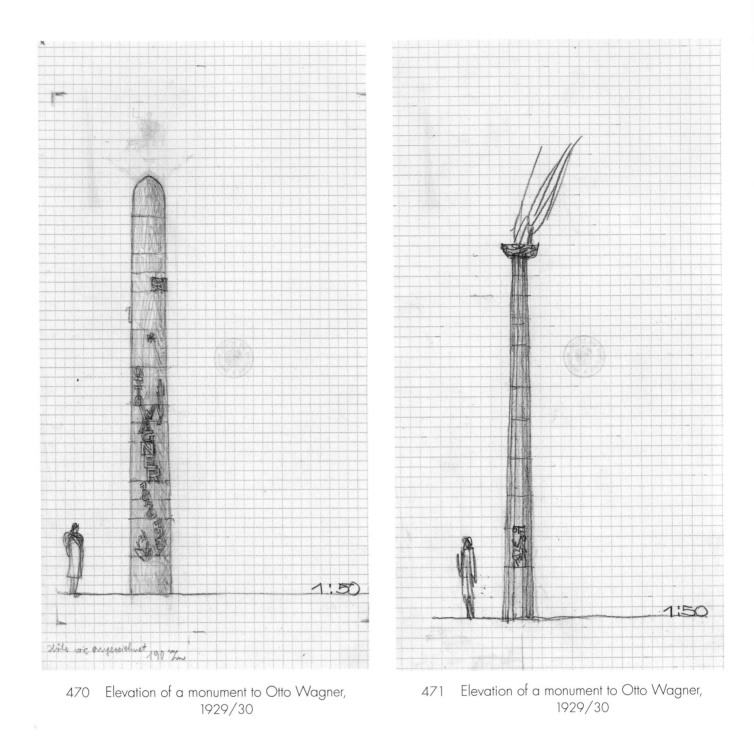

470   Elevation of a monument to Otto Wagner, 1929/30

471   Elevation of a monument to Otto Wagner, 1929/30

472   Plan and elevation of a monument to Otto Wagner, 1929/30

473   Elevation of a monument to Otto Wagner,
1929/30

474   Elevation of a monument to Otto Wagner,
1929/39

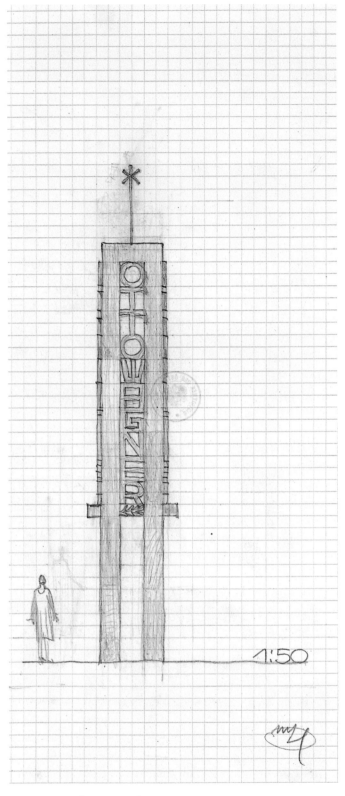

475　Elevation of a monument to Otto Wagner, 1929/30

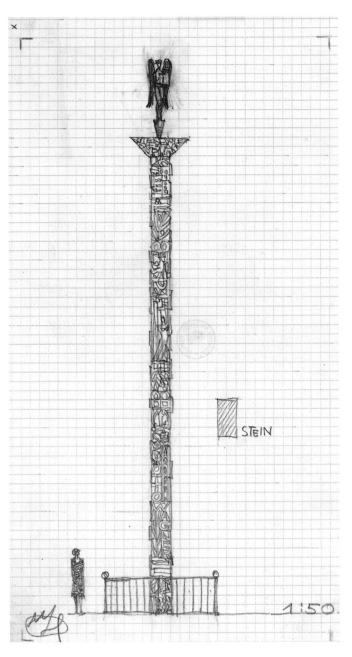

STEIN

476　Elevation of a monument to Otto Wagner, 1929/30

477   Model of the Purkersdorf Sanatorium, 1904/5

478   Model of the Beer-Hoffmann villa, 1905/6

479 Model of the Skywa/Primavesi villa, 1913/15

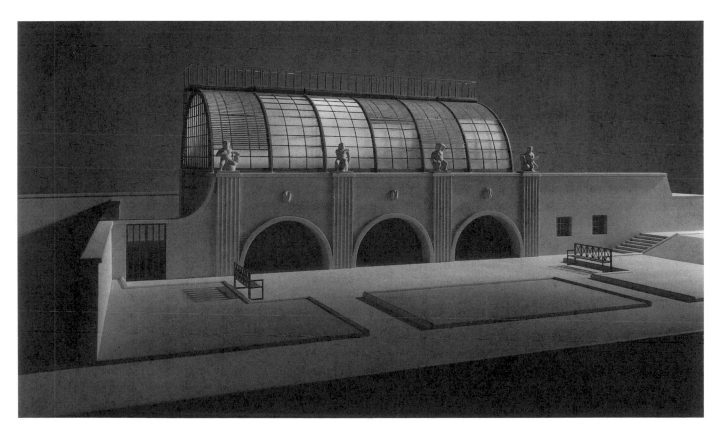

480 Model of the orangery for the Skywa/Primavesi villa, 1913/15

481   Model of the Palais Stoclet, 1905/11

The Strange Objectivity of a Mythical Artist's Hand: Notes on Josef Hoffmann's Design Drawings

Jan Tabor

Discovery in a Gallery Window

Josef Hoffmann's design drawings are peculiar. Although they are simple – occasionally even spare or banal – but consistent in their formal clarity, they can be irritating and sometimes raise serious problems even for experienced Hoffmann scholars.

In 1992 a well-established art gallery in Vienna displayed a drawing by Josef Hoffmann in its window. It was a notably typical Hoffmann drawing. Although it scarcely differs from hundreds of other familiar sketches by this celebrated Viennese Jugendstil artist – currently exploited by antique dealers, tourist promotion, and state offices that cultivate Austrian patriotism – and although it cannot be considered one of Hoffmann's artistically more interesting architectural drawings, it is nevertheless a rarity in the history of architecture, ideal for illustrating the problems posed by the drawings and by the legendary figure Josef Hoffmann has become.

The drawing is in pencil on an ordinary sheet of graph paper and shows the front elevation of an unspectacular architectural detail: the entrance to a building. The building is not immediately recognizable, nor is its type, as the sketch only shows in profile a cross-section of the facade up to the *bel etage*. The fluted columns supporting a lavishly decorated architrave set into the wall are architectural elements that Hoffmann used repeatedly in variations from 1911 on, after the completion of the Palais Stoclet. The balconied portico forms a kind of official platform, with a delicate, vertically structured metal railing. The corners have raised, ball-shaped handles. The lantern before the front columns of the portico has an urn-shaped shade, culminating in a ball-handled lid. A striking but indeterminate feature in an otherwise clear and economical drawing is the imposing emblem in stone, as is the richly decorated cordon cornice, apparently intended to start from the architrave and wrap around the building. The emblem is set in a prominent position directly above the high balcony door. As this is a side section, it is not entirely clear whether the emblem is a facade decoration in the historical style, the coat-of-arms on a nobleman's palace, or the German imperial eagle. But Hoffmann clearly indicates that the entrance was intended for a prestigious building, and not, for instance, an elementary school or even a family home, as might be assumed from the otherwise modest depiction. Apart from the scale 1:50 added in Hoffmann's own hand in ink, the sheet provides no other information on the building and its purpose or on the date of the drawing. Although it should have been relatively easy to identify the building and to date the drawing correctly, the gallery called it a "study of an entrance," from "about 1920." The shape of the railing and lantern clearly point to the Nazi period or the early postnationalistic phase in the fifties. Virtually no other architect or designer has ever remained so constant in his drawing style over the course of decades as did Josef Hoffmann. As he only rarely dated and identified his drawings, even experts on his work can err in reading and categorizing them. The Art-Deco decoration on the architrave and cornice, emphasized here by the bold lines, may possibly have induced the gallery to give the sketch such an early date. Moreover, the building no longer exists.

The Answer: A Building for the Wehrmacht

The drawing was made for the Wehrmacht building (Haus der Wehrmacht), in Vienna's 3rd district, Metternichgasse 3; thus it was made in 1939. Following Austria's Anschluss to the German Reich in March 1938, Josef Hoffmann was commissioned in the spring of 1939 to convert the building formerly used by the German Embassy in Vienna into an officers' club.[1] The Embassy was built about 1870 in the "Ringstrassen style," which Hoffmann considered "a weak imitation of Italian Renaissance." The remodeling was finished in 1940 for the architect's seventieth birthday. The Haus der Wehrmacht was one of the few examples of Nazi architecture in Vienna; it was damaged by bombs at the end of the war and later demolished to make room for the new German Embassy building (1963-65, by Rolf Gutbrod). The sketch that has now turned up on the art market is one of the few from Hoffmann's Nazi period that have survived, or have reached the public. Possibly to avoid the unpleasant issue of their own compliance, Viennese writers have long suppressed and neglected the Nazi involvement of major Austrian artists. Apart from the biographical gaps, there are other reasons why this sketch is particularly interesting for art historians working on Hoffmann's drawings. The conversion of the German Embassy to the Haus der Wehrmacht was one of the last designs that Hoffmann was able to realize – and with the honors lavished upon him on the occasion of his seventieth birthday by the National Socialists it may be assumed that the commission was a kind of a birthday present. In view of the political responsibility this commission entailed and the aesthetic expectations of the authorities, the building was the most monumental and, as such, politically the most questionable in Hoffmann's long career. Apart from the various exhibition pavilions that he designed, such as the Austrian pavilion for the Biennale in Venice in 1934, the Haus der Wehrmacht was his only public commission, his only "official" building. Comparing the preliminary

sketch to the completed building reveals the precision with which the design was executed. Everything in the sketch was in fact realized, down to the smallest detail, with all proportions and dimensions retained. Only the decorations on the architrave and the cornice seem to be substantially more emphatic in the drawing than in the more delicate three-dimensional construction; or so it appears from the photographs, which are perfectly in focus.

Exact congruence of design and execution was typical for Josef Hoffmann throughout his career, and it is unique in the history of design since Jugendstil. Unique because architects and designers endeavored (and still do today) to establish their projects as high art by the way they presented them, and every sketch was elevated to an autonomous work of art. Hoffmann's approach was fundamentally different: the sketch was intended to be a blueprint for a building, nothing more. If anything, less. The artist, who was an unparalleled mannerist in decoration and a congenial designer for the cultured bourgeoisie in Vienna, simply indicated how something was to be *made*, not, as is still the practice today, how it was to *look*. Hoffmann's drawings appear to be sketches of already existing structures or objects, as if they were notations on the form and other visible quali-

Haus der Wehrmacht, 1940

ties. They also look like the work of a not particularly talented or ambitious draftsman. Many in fact could be taken for exercises drawn by a novice. His sketches can all be described as the objective records of what does not yet exist.

Authenticity versus Antinomy

The concordance between the design sketch and the object – between idea and realization – is what the Hoffmann scholar Eduard F. Sekler calls "authenticity."[2] Hoffmann's drawings are also unique in that this authenticity is restricted to the formal and objective elements of the building – shape, dimensions, material, and decoration. In reality, however, there is always a clear, indeed, intentional discrepancy between the sketch and its execution, a discrepancy that might best be described as understatement. The simple, at times even casual nature of the sketch, its obvious lack of value judgment or emotion, avoidance of monumentality or symbolism, and its lack of pretension are in striking contrast to the reality of the objects and buildings when completed. The differences are almost reciprocal, antithetical: subjective reactions to Hoffmann's objects range from costly, exclusive, luxurious, noble, solemn, bombastic, monumental, golden, symbolic, sacred, refined, filigreed, fulminating, and so on to playful, pleasing, discursive, or kitsch. None of these adjectives could be applied to his drawings. This discrepancy can be called antinomy. The astonishing thing is that there is no contradiction between the authenticity and the antinomy in Hoffmann's drawings.

"In the Simple, Soldierly Way"

Of all Hoffmann's works, the Wehrmacht building may be the one exhibiting the greatest discrepancy between the modesty of the sketch and the unambiguous political symbolism of the actual building. In this case Hoffmann, the apolitical and sensitive designer for the cultured, slightly avant-gardistic, and sometimes decadent Viennese bourgeoisie, faced aesthetic criteria (Nazi Neoclassicism) diametrically opposed to that of his former clientele. Whereas before Hoffmann had been able to reflect in his work the aesthetic of "richness as artistic possibility," as Eduard F. Sekler aptly entitles a chapter in his Hoffmann monograph,[3] the commission from the Nazis in 1939 confronted him with the problem of "propaganda as an artistic mission." He himself said it was a question of "expressing the present use of the building in a simple, clear, soldierly way, through its form.... All components [the facade, flagpoles, insignia of the Wehrmacht, railings, layout of the garden, etc.] would have to establish the military character of the building without making it look like a barrack, for the building is to be a clubhouse and official building for the Wehrmacht, as shown by the monumental inscription over the main entrance."[4]

Hoffmann's reluctance to discuss art and architectural theory, and particularly his reluctance to comment on his own work, was proverbial. His 1940 article in *Die Pause*, a publication of the Vienna Cultural Department (Wiener Kulturamt), may well be the only instance of him expressing in detail his thoughts on a concrete project and providing explanations of his work. The decoration of the cornice, which is so striking in the sketch and which delineates the smooth façade at the level of the portico balcony, was, according to Hoffmann, taken from the "motif of the shoulder strap on our uniforms." Apart from this "shoulder strap" decoration (and it is probably only now, when the Wehrmacht uniforms are no longer familiar, that we fail to recognize it), the design for the monumental portico was so clearly drawn that the building could and may well have been erected from this simple sketch. There may have been other drawings for the decoration. The cornice decoration on this building is also the only sketch of an ornament by Hoffmann for which we have an authentic statement regarding his source of inspiration. This late design, which looks as if it had been made in the twenties, is impressive testimony to a unique feature of Hoffmann's art and his personality: his almost playful ability to adapt to a wide variety of tasks and clients. It was an adaptability rooted in a basic aesthetic and formal consistency. Naturally, the design of the facade for the Haus der Wehrmacht owed much to National Socialist Neoclassicism in the manner of Ludwig Troost (Hitler's first architect), but it is also a fine example of the Viennese decorative style, to which Hoffmann remained faithful throughout his life. Strangely, an architect from the *Altreich*, as Germany was called prior to the expansion under Hitler, was entrusted with the interior design of the Wehrmacht building in Vienna.

Originality beyond the Idiosyncrasy of Style

Josef Hoffmann's drawings are unique. Although they do not employ a clear "artistic handwriting," they can be distinguished from the designs and drawings of Hoffmann's teachers at the Vienna Academy, Karl von Hasenauer and Otto Wagner, or of his fellow contemporaries – such as Josef Olbrich, Adolf Loos, Josef Frank, Frank Lloyd Wright, or Le Corbusier – whether opponents or admirers. When one compares the sketches of these architects, all of whom had a distinctive drawing style, only Hoffmann's can be said to be free of the fashionable trends to which architectural drawing is subject no less than architecture. However, the objects and buildings that he designed were fashionable, extremely fashionable, with a basic repertoire of adaptable ideas. Hoffmann did not change his way of designing throughout his life. His sketches were always reduced to the bare essentials but detailed enough for authentic Hoffmann objects to be made from the drawings, provided one had craftsmen as experienced and capable as he had to do the work. The simplicity of the drawings can be compared with the brevity of mathematical formulas. Each formula is unique, but it appears in a kind of chain: an idea is repeated with slight deviations or variations in different stages. The schematic nature of the designs, despite their casual look, was obviously intentional.

The Cult of the Artistic Architectural Sketch

Like all students of architecture and graduates of the academy in Vienna, Hoffmann was an excellent draftsman. This is evident from his student projects, travel sketches, and architectural studies. Skill in drawing was an essential for acceptance at the academy. Even Otto Wagner, who was critical of an exaggeratedly artistic approach to architectural drawing, assessed applicants for his master class (many of whom were graduates or senior students already) primarily on the basis of their draftsmanship. Rudolf Weiss (1890-1980), one of Wagner's pupils, told Marco Pozzetto, when he was researching the Wagner school, that he had spent an entire summer in Sirmione, Salzburg, and Passau making the ten drawings required by Otto Wagner for his application portfolio.[5] At the time there was a veritable cult of artistic drawing, as we see from Wagner's comments in his obituary for Josef Olbrich (1867-1908). Here he states that one of his study projects "surpassed everything else in its skillful drawing.... As far as his method of depiction was concerned, I can only set one other beside him, but even he is hardly in the same class, and that is one of my teachers, Professor van der Nüll."[6] The cult of artistic draftsmanship, the cult of artistic self-representation, was inseparable from the cult of the Wagner school. "Gentlemen, we are Number

One in the world!" proclaimed Professor Wagner in 1905 to his students at the banquet given to mark the tenth anniversary of the establishment of his school.[7] Selected works by students were published almost every year between 1898 and 1907 in the periodicals *Aus der Wagnerschule* and *Wagnerschule*, glossy brochures edited by the students themselves and distributed worldwide. In the third issue (1900), the stage designer Alfred Roller stated:

The work of art is not only of interest in its finished state, but at every stage of its genesis. That explains the new appreciation of architectural sketches and their equation with the first notations by the painter or sculptor, which, happily, we are encountering again today.[8]

His comment is a reflection of two important new phenomena in the history of architectural drawing; firstly, the greater importance now accorded to the drawing as a means of distinguishing the architect from the nonartistic builder, and secondly, the drawing as a dynamic record of the design process. This was a radical break with the principles of historicism that had been obligatory until then.[9] The architectural revolution that came about just before the turn of the century was heralded and accompanied by a revolution in architectural drawing. The historical importance accorded to architectural drawing is evident in the work of the Italian Futurist Antonio Sant'Elia (1888-1916), who was influenced by the drawings of the Wagner school to such an extent that he was regarded as "un Wagnerschüler in absentia (a Wagner student in absence)."[10] This radical change in the attitude toward architecture can be seen as the end of canonized architecture, that is, architecture bound to historical styles. A free and inventive use of form, materials, and constructive and decorative elements became possible. The shift in the paradigm in architecture was preceded by the decanonization of architectural drawing and design; the revolution came first on the drawing boards and in the sketchbooks. The first rapid sketch of an idea, until then regarded as without artistic merit, had come to be valued as a work of art by about 1900, as the remark by Roller illustrates. At a time of ever fiercer competition, artistically impressive and easily comprehensible architectural drawings became an increasingly important medium for an architect's self-representation. In fact, even though the number of architects was rapidly growing, their quality still remained questionable.

"According to the records, we have 850 architects practicing in Vienna today, but anyone who knows the situation here would have the greatest difficulty in naming a hundred true artists among them," Otto Wagner complained as early as 1895.[11] Architectural drawing, until then hardly more than a matter of technical draftsmanship, had become a serious and fiercely debated issue for architecture and the architect's professional image during the second half of the nineteenth century. Architectural drawing moved away from its subject, architecture, threatening to determine or perhaps even replace it entirely. Wagner went on to make the following demands:

To begin with the essentials in architectural drawing, it must be stressed that a facile manner is entirely reprehensible; the architect must always endeavor to put his thoughts on paper as clearly, precisely, purely, deliberately and convincingly as possible. Every architectural drawing should document the taste of the artist, and it should never be forgotten that he is showing something that will exist in the *future*, not what already exists. The addiction to offering an illusory picture of the future must be considered wrong, because it involves a lie. All the enticing coincidences and moods that nature can offer, laid down in a good watercolor and transferred to a nonexistent object, are deliberate deceptions, and they should be rejected if only for that reason.[12]

He also rejected the use of catalytic or automatic methods in drawing: "A good, great thought should be conceived and carefully considered before the pencil is taken up."[13] Clearly his advice had little effect, possibly because Wagner himself supported the cult of modern artistic drawing in order to establish the worldwide reputation of his school. When Wagner's book *Moderne Architektur* was published in a Czech translation in 1910, Pavel Janák, a pupil of Wagner and co-founder of Czech Cubism, criticized in his article "From Modern Architecture to New Architecture" the attitudes of the Wagner school:

So far modern architecture has been a rare, happy entity between two forces – the creative force of the artist and the force of the accepted principles, with the main accent on coordination through the creative hand of the artist. Modern architecture is based mainly on the driving inventiveness of the creative hand of the artist; only for a minority has it been accompanied by intellectual speculation [i.e. theoretical deliberations], although the innovations were justified with theoretical proclamations and rationales. The movement had various characteristics, because, after fifteen years, as the force of the creative hand slackened, speculative forces gained the upper hand.... The spontaneously creative hand does not, as formerly, guide the artistic will; it follows it and is beginning to judge it. The creative hand is losing its former dominance and is being replaced by theory.[14]

In other words, "modern architecture," that is, Jugendstil, which depended on the draftsman's hand, had come to an end. The "new architecture," which was later to be called *Neues Bauen* (New Building) would derive from theory and not from intuition.

The Rejection of "Built Sketches"

Particularly fierce criticism of the "trashy cult of drawing" and the self-representational work of the Vienna academy came at the early date of 1908 from the Wagner pupil Marcel Kammerer, who wrote:

The decorative effect the drawing was intended to have naturally influenced the object shown; everything was designed to achieve a favorable impact, just as the painter treats the objects he depicts as best suited to the effect the picture is intended to have. Sheer love of drawing was undeniable in many [architects], and it exacted a heavy price. If some of the designs were ever realized, the result was "built sketches" but rarely works of architecture.... In short, our representations should be in keeping with their purpose and be clear, easily understandable and precise. In view of the economic factors the projects should be realizable with simple and easily available technical means and the construction not too time-consuming. In the teaching institutions particularly the students should be instructed to concentrate on the object.... Later, the school exhibitions, which are practically valueless, should be dropped; indeed, architects will have to realize that their art is not suitable for exhibitions, and they should seek their exhibition arena in the streets and alleys, in real life.[15]

Strangely, and this is also evidence of the contradictory nature of the Wagner school, Kammerer stopped working as an architect in 1920. He became a painter, a fanatical National Socialist and anti-Semite, and one of the most powerful Nazi politicians in Vienna. He was one of the Nazi artists whose kitschy pictures Hitler admired and bought. Kammerer was not the only Wagner pupil who ceased to work as an architect and turned to painting. Others were Oskar Laske (1874-1954), Mario Sandonà (1877-1957), and Frantisek Fiala (1878-1927).[16]

It was said of Adolf Loos (1870-1933) – obviously with justification – that he was a wretched and unwilling draftsman. He repeatedly attacked the artist-architect, and cursed his "authority over the master builder." He hated everything to do with the artistic image of the architect, praising the craftsman, the guarantor of true "building culture." In his 1909 essay "Architektur," he wrote:

The architect has displaced the craftsman. He learned to draw and learned nothing else, so draw he does. The craftsman cannot draw. His hand has grown heavy. The blueprints by the old masters are clumsy – any student of architecture today can do better. To say nothing of the so-called skillful draftsman who is sought out and highly paid by every architectural firm! Architecture has been degraded to graphic art by architects. It is not the architect who can build best who receives the most commissions, but the architect whose work looks best on paper. The two are quite irreconcilable.... The best draftsman can be a bad architect, the best architect a bad draftsman. Simply choosing the profession of architect requires a talent for graphic art. All our new architecture is invented on the drawing board and the drawings are then reproduced three-dimensionally, like paintings on waxworks.... Today the skillful draftsman predominates, and it is not the tool that creates the forms, but the pencil.[17]

This justified criticism of the prevailing mania for drawing and the consequent excesses it wrought – whether advanced, but not necessarily heeded, by Wagner, Kammerer, or Loos – could not be applied to Josef Hoffmann. On the contrary. He had long anticipated the demand for clearer and more economical drawing. His distinctive way of fusing the sketch and final blueprint into one drawing was radically ahead of his time, more so than that of anyone before or after him, including Adolf Loos, his most vociferous opponent.

Hoffmann drew clearly and precisely, as if he were writing instructions. He drew as if he wanted to put into practice Loos's demand that architecture should be such that a verbal description would suffice to order a house by telephone and build it. Loos, reformer and preacher of simplicity and naturalness, cultivated the expressive, monumental, measureless gestural drawing. Hoffmann's drawing style illustrated a simple thesis: drawing is nothing, execution is everything. The spareness of his sketches was admittedly motivated by an ideology. Like Adolf Loos, Josef Hoffmann glorified the eternal genius of the craftsman.

The Myth of the Creative Hand

The creative hand, the hand of the craftsman, not yet corrupted by mass industrial production, and craftsmanship itself – threatened with extinction – were highly regarded by the Vienna Jugendstil architects, most of whom themselves came from small-town artisan families living somewhere in the provinces of the Austro-Hungarian Empire. Hoffmann's father, for example, had been co-owner of a small cotton workshop in Brtnice; Loos's father was a cemetery stonemason in Brno; Olbrich's was a pastrycook in Opava. The father of perhaps the most gifted of Wagner's students, Josef Plecnik, was a carpenter in Ljubljana. The parents of Leopold Bauer, Otto Wagner's successor in the School of Architecture, were innkeepers in Krnov. The Jugendstil architects saw the hand as a kind of extension of the brain, and it was held to have almost magical properties. Hoffmann's glorification of the hand went so far that, as former staff members tell us, he would never take anyone with "bad hands" as a student or into his employ.[18]

In the lecture "Meine Arbeit" (My Work), which Hoffmann gave in February, 1911, he stated:

Modern education shall set us the task to bring to our elementary schools also the sense for reality and work instead of a world of purely abstract concepts. More important than hair-splitting instruction in grammar is manual dexterity, the awakening of the creative forces; these are almost paralyzed and atrophied by a purely literary education. It is high time that we awaken them again.... But we feel how for us the forces grow, through them, and how we must not lose respect for the sanctity of work. Our art-craftsmen are an elite of the first rank. They are not slaves of a machine but creators and shapers, makers of form and masters. Their labors are not loveless patchwork by various hands but the work of one man. Therefore they are all signed with the signet, that is, with the name of the craftsman. We know that we do not work for individual profit but for the cause, and that makes us free. We know no differences in rank; we recognize only an order of work and the higher quality of performance.... This work of the hands guided by healthy creative force shall not degrade but elevate and lead to highest perfection through the correct appreciation of its worth.[19]

The words are emotional, but the emotion was genuine, and this was indeed Hoffmann's attitude to his work. What he said on that occasion is the key to an understanding of his drawing and sketches. Their spareness in fact expressed his "respect for the sanctity of work," the work of his craftsmen and co-workers. They appreciated the trust he placed in them and Hoffmann knew he could rely on them.

About 1898 Josef Hoffmann began to use ordinary graph paper for almost all his drawings and sketches. He did not use transparent paper or the method used by most architects, even today, of tracing from one drawing the areas to be retained in the new. He simply tore sheets of varying size out of ordinary sketchbooks or school exercise books. The geometric structure of the squares forced him to discipline his imagination, to put down his ideas more objectively. It also enforced an economy of line, helped to maintain the inherent order of the buildings or objects, and facilitated accuracy in proportion and scale. Hoffmann almost always drew exactly to scale, and usually in the following proportions: 1:1, 1:10, 1:50, or 1:100. On rare occasions he indicated the scale on the sheet.

For him the square pattern on the paper was not a constructive system or grid, as it was for many architects, including Frank Lloyd Wright, but only an aid for his freehand drawing, which he retained even for long strokes or rectangular shapes. Freehand drawing corresponded to the cult of the creative hand; it also prevented an inclination to perfectionism on the part of the craftsman, which could result in the seemingly mechanical appearance of Hoffmann's objects and buildings. The freehand sketch was the basis for the craftsmanship: "manual labor," "handmade things," were values in themselves. Hoffmann used a ruler only in exceptional cases, for instance to design particularly graceful glasses with thin stems and sides, where irregularities in the drawing could distort the execution. Moreover, Hoffmann could not rely on these designs being executed by congenial craftsmen whom he knew personally, as was the case with the Wiener Werkstätte. Thus his glass designs are more like technical drawings than design sketches for artifacts. Otherwise there are few differences in type or scale in Hoffmann's drawings and designs, whether he was drawing buildings, architectural details, interiors, tableware, or items of jewelry. This may have been due to the fact that he frequently used his ideas for decorative objects and artifacts in his architecture and vice versa. Form follows object, object follows form.

Hoffmann's usual drawing procedure, as can be reconstructed from isolated statements and from thousands of drawings, was the following: He took a sheet of graph paper, rarely bigger than A4 (9 × 10″) and usually smaller, picked up a medium pencil with a rather dull point in his carefully manicured hand, drew the axis in the middle of the sheet, closed his eyes and waited – usually only for a moment – until the idea came. "There are two kinds of artists, the ones who construct an object rationally and develop it systematically, and the others who have a sudden inspiration – I am more for those with inspiration. One should not obstruct the intuition.... I for myself have always to close my eyes and imagine the object before I begin it," said Hoffmann in 1942 in an interview.[20] Sometimes he sang softly while he was working. Often he drew while at a concert. The object that he had imagined very exactly was then put down in outline with a few strokes and at one sitting. The strokes are firm and they give the impression that the designer knew exactly what he wanted. They are as finished and precise as if Hoffmann had sketched from already existing objects. He never pondered with his pencil; he did not need to wrest an idea out of his subconscious (or wherever the imagination may be located) with his drawing tool; he did not think with his hand or through its movements.

His drawing hand was not a catalyst for the imagination, or its driving force. He did not work out his themes in approximation, employing a strategy against the horror vacui of the empty sheet (often synonymous with the empty head) by putting down the initial mark, any arbitrary automatic stroke, and scratching a possible and usable shape, the right shape, out of it. For Hoffmann, who believed perhaps more than any other artist in the particular significance of the creative hand, his own hand was only a registering apparatus for the ideas that were already drawn in his head.

He drew as if he wanted to make an objective depiction of a finished object. He was deliberately anti-artistic and anti-emotional in his drawing as he wanted only to register and describe. Mostly, as it would appear, the first idea was the right one and so the only one that was drawn for the task at hand. It may also have been the only one he conceived. But it is not certain whether, when only one sketch is known of an object or design, it was really the only one ever made. It would seem that Hoffmann's creative work had become routine after years of intensive exercise; conceiving, testing, rejecting, and correcting many different variants had become an automatic process in his head. If so, it was comparable to the routine of an acrobat. This would seem to be confirmed by projects that were not by any means routine, such as the synagogue for Zilina (Slovakia), of which Josef Hoffmann drew at least fourteen different variants in 1928. Or, also in 1928, the design for a monument to Otto Wagner, of which nine preliminary sketches or variants are known, not including the one that was actually executed. In the latter case, it is striking that the executed sketch is by far the most successful. The concept of "preliminary design" or "variant" does not strictly apply to Hoffmann's sketches. "Examples" or "case studies" would be better terms, for there seem to be seven different monuments for seven different places and seven different occasions. The same is true of the synagogue designs, where it looks as if the building had been intended for twelve different sites. Sekler believes that the picturesque and exotic forms in these sketches were inspired by the architecture of Slovenian wooden churches, but some of the drawings recall Hoffmann's design for the pavilion of a Soviet exhibition in Vienna in 1924, seemingly a paraphrase of the Kremlin in Moscow. One small change – the star of David instead of the red star – and a new design was made. As is evident, Hoffmann was economical, not only with his drawing resources but with his imagination as well. Typical of his drawings is also the lack of any descriptive details – objective or atmospheric – of place or architectural site. The buildings he designed were always seen as individual cases unrelated to the situation for which they were created and in which they were to stand. Hoffmann's drawings are flat and two-dimensional. He primarily drew outlines, and they are free of three-dimensional modeling. Only in exceptional cases, when it was a matter of clarifying complicated shapes, did he indicate the form by shading a small part of the sketch. He used color not to achieve "pretty effects" but to lay down the coloring he wanted. Sometimes he used colored adhesive foil instead of watercolor or colored pencils. His sketches only provide information on shape, decoration, measurements, and materials. All other explanations – as to the purpose, the client, the time, etc. – are left out. Sometimes the purpose of an object can hardly be guessed at without the inscription on the drawings. Still, one learns nothing about the intended function, technical qualities, construction, or structural details from the drawing, since, as Hoffmann explained, the execution was a matter for the craftsmen entrusted with the task. It is clear that Hoffmann was only a designer, a decorator, not a constructor. In contrast, Otto Wagner or Frank Lloyd Wright would draw their very first sketches with a ruler – in other words, they would construct and only make freehand additions and corrections later.

Hoffmann largely avoided theoretical statements on his work and on the problems of craftmanship and architecture. Unlike Adolf Loos, his former classmate in Brno and later his bitter enemy for so many years, Hoffmann was not a cultural critic, life reformer, or Utopian. He did not want to change the world, improve, or beautify it. His lack of interest in theory, in larger cultural and social issues is related to the fact that, apart from student works, he made no designs for which he did not already have a commission or at least the probability of getting one. He never drew Utopian or fantasy architecture or architectural manifestoes. Architecture as an event in drawing, as literature, as a form of artistic expression was alien to him. He cannot be compared with any of his visionary contemporaries, such as Tony Garnier, whose experimental socialist project developed in the novel *Une Cité industrielle: Etude pour la construction des villes* and published in 1917, includes drawings of painstaking exactitude, from the urban ground plan down to the last details of window latches;[21] Bruno Taut with his Expressionist architectural poems; the picturesque ideas of Michel de Klerk in the early Expressionist "Amsterdamer Schreckenskammer" (Amsterdam Chamber of Horrors);[22] and the dynamic architectural sculptures of Erich Mendelsohn. Admirable as Hoffmann's imagination was, it was always the sober imagination of the businessman.

The Axonometric Revolution

Kasimir Malevich (1878-1935) painted a picture in 1914 that evinced a new method of depiction: axonometry. The first axonometric architectural drawings were shown in a De Stijl exhibition in Paris in 1923 and soon axonometry be-

came the predominant method of representation for the modern movement in architecture, particularly in Soviet revolutionary work.[23] Axonometry was more than an objective and economical method of drawing that enabled ground plans, sections, and views to be visualized on one sheet. It was a manifesto of the "new architecture" which, as Pavel Janák had correctly predicted in 1910, was now based on theory. Josef Hoffmann was always open to the new. In his essay "Die Schule des Architekten" (The School for Architects), he wrote in 1924:

The paintings of the new Russians remind us of beautiful old working drawings with their sections, dimension lines and hatching. It is a sign that the sense for the spatial is growing. Modern sculpture no longer has merely the figurative in its program; it begins to feel architecturally and to construct. We can almost speak of a unified style already, and this hope gives us support.[24]

By "painting" and "modern sculpture" he clearly meant the formal experiments of the Soviet Constructivists, most likely of El Lissitzky in particular.

Hoffmann, who must have been familiar with axonometry and its objectivity and economy, did not use it. One can hardly draw freehand in axonometry, and his craftsmen would never have understood it.

Notes

1 Josef Hoffmann, *Die Pause* 12 (Vienna, 1940): 50.
2 Eduard F. Sekler, "Gedanken zu den Zeichnungen Josef Hoffmanns," lecture given on July 19, 1987 in Vienna; from notes by Jan Tabor.
3 Eduard F. Sekler, *Josef Hoffmann: The Architectural Work*, translated by the author; catalogue translated by John Maas (Princeton, N. J., 1985) [Salzburg and Vienna, 1982]: 75–100.
4 Hoffmann, op. cit., note 1.
5 Marco Pozzetto, *Die Schule Otto Wagners 1894–1912* (Vienna, 1980): 14.
6 Otto Wagner, "Josef Olbrich," *Der Architekt* 14 (Vienna, 1908): 161, quoted in op. cit., note 5.
7 Pozzetto, op. cit., note 5: 26.
8 Alfred Roller, as quoted in Otto Antonia Graf, *Die vergessene Wagnerschule* (Vienna, 1969):10.
9 Ibid.
10 Iain Boyd White, "Antonio Sant'Elia un Wagnerschüler in absentia," in *Antonio Sant'Elia L'architettura disegnata*, exh. cat. (Venice, 1991).
11 Otto Wagner, *Moderne Architektur: Seinen Schülern ein Führer auf diesem Kunstgebiet* (Vienna, 1895); 4th ed. retitled *Die Baukunst unserer Zeit: Dem Baukunstjünger ein Führer auf diesem Gebiet* (Vienna, A. Schroll, 1914). Citation here is to reprint edition (Vienna: Löcker Verlag, 1979): 21.
12 Ibid: 73.
13 Ibid: 44.

14 Pavel Janák, "Od moderní Architektury k architekture," *Styl* 2 (Prague, 1910): 105–9. Quoted in Pozzetto, op. cit., note 5: 159.

15 Marcel Kammerer, "Über die Art der Darstellung unserer Entwürfe," *Der Architekt* 14 (Vienna, 1908): 41–42. Quoted in Pozzetto, op. cit., note 5: 194ff.

16 Pozzetto, op. cit., note 5: 14.

17 Adolf Loos, "Architektur," in Adolf Loos, *Trotzdem 1900–1930* (Vienna, 1982, reprint of the first ed., Innsbruck, 1932): 98.

18 Quoted in op. cit., note 3: 490–92.

19 Josef Hoffmann, lecture of February 22, 1911, "My Work," as quoted in op. cit., note 3: 490, 492.

20 Quoted in op. cit., note 3: 236–37.

21 Tony Garnier, *Une Cité industrielle: Etude pour la construction des villes* (New York, 1989) [France, 1917; 2nd ed. 1932].

22 Werner Hegemann, "Aus der Amsterdamer Schreckenskammer," *Wasmuths Monatsheft für Baukunst* 9, no. 1 (Berlin, 1925): 147–51. Quoted in Vittorio Magnago Lampugnani, *The Architecture of the Twentieth Century in Drawings: Utopia and Reality* (New York, 1982): 9.

23 Lampugnani, op. cit., note 22: 12.

24 Josef Hoffmann, "The School of the Architect," *Das Kunstblatt* (April 1924). Quoted in Sekler, op. cit., note 3: 495.

Excerpts from "My Work"

Lecture, given on 22 February 1911

Josef Hoffmann

We live in a time that tries to connect with a broken [continuity of] culture, that therefore begins its work without experience and without years of tradition.

It is unclear but determined in its intention to create a modern setting for our modern life.

This appears to us as important and as difficult as the solution of the social questions. I speak of these things to characterize the period of our development.

We studied at the Academy around 1890, and you may be interested how this was done.

In the first year we designed a villa and then a princely castle.

In the second year an apartment house, then some larger project like a school or a savings bank. In the third year a government building or a theater.

One had the project and was permitted to work. There was no question of guidance or an instruction in any relevant manner. One studied the projects of one's predecessors and made something similar.

The atmosphere was entirely uninteresting and inartistic. All we had [to go on] was the study in the library which we did on our own initiative. Consider, at that time we did not learn anything about Ruskin and Moris [*sic*], nothing of all that which across the Channel guided the direction [of developments] with enormous impetus. We knew nothing of Beardslei [*sic*], nothing of Oscar Wilde.

We had seen no *Studio* and had not heard anything about modern French painting, nor about the efforts of the modern Belgians. We lived on, uninformed and untutored. And yet that period also had something curious. We were seized with an endless longing to want and to attempt something other than what we saw every day.

I had just met Olbrich and Moser. Olbrich, a man full of sparkling ideas and perhaps a romanticism that was too great, was a colossal worker and indefatigable doer.

He was obsessed by Wagner's music and would have loved to build Walhalla. Fantasizing with him was too beautiful. No task was too great for him, and [there was] nothing he did not at least try to draw....

Beside him appeared the painter Moser, who, thanks to his activity as an illustrator, already knew more of the outside [art world] and henceforth gained the greatest influence over us. His talent for two-dimensional artistic design and for every kind of arts and crafts invention appeared fabulous to us. He knew how to promote and stimulate everywhere. He excelled not only by his great imagination but equally by his practical and organizational abilities....

Meanwhile Otto Wagner had been appointed at the Academy, and with him a new life entered. He understood how to strengthen us in our intentions and ideas, and to stimulate us with sparkling spirit to all sorts of things.

His ideas stressing purpose and material had meanwhile become known to us; and while we had to recognize them as something absolutely right, they could not eradicate a certain romanticism [that] unfortunately at that time was within us. Unfortunately, I was only briefly under his influence, then went to Italy, beginning my official Roman journey.

At first I was desperate. All official, art-scholarly architecture failed to interest me. I was looking for new impulses at any price. Library studies and the perpetual learning of certain styles and architectural forms had spoiled me, had robbed me of the entire delight of seeing for the first time, and had dulled me to the true beauties of this divine land.

Finally I fled into the Campagn [*sic*] and refreshed myself at the simple peasant buildings, that without pomp and without stylistic architecture nevertheless give the land its special character. There, for the first time, it became clear to me what matters in architecture; henceforth I studied all the little places on my way with fiery zeal. At last I came also to Pompeii and Paestum. I saw the Doric temple, and suddenly it fell from my eyes like scales why I did not like the stuff learned at school. There we learned only the proportions of the average of fifty temples and their columns and their entablatures. Here I saw columns with capitals almost as wide as the height of the column, and I was simply transfixed with admiration. Now I knew that what mattered above all was the proportion [?] and that even the most accurate application of the individual forms of architecture meant nothing at all. In Vienna, where I returned, much had changed greatly in the meantime. The Secession was founded, the whole modern progress suddenly became known to us, and we stood on the threshold of those events that gave Vienna for a time the character of a true city of art. We worked with great enthusiasm.

First [we were] confused by the pressure of so many new ideas, groping here and there, trying everything, throwing most of it away again. It is characteristic of this era that almost all artists from Wagner to Van de Velde saw the exact fulfillment of construction as the only right thing but that the expression, i.e., the formal fulfillment of this idea, was tried in incredibly varied ways. One would hardly believe that one is facing works of one and the same time.

From this can be seen how much this time strove for new forms.

Yet, certain things nevertheless became slowly clear, and were recognized, and determined as unshakable truths.

On the one hand, a strong opposition demanded blind imitation of old styles, those in the English taste at least, and found its home at the Austrian Museum under Skala; on the other hand it saw salvation in fighting every individual touch and even in the denial of all artistic intentions. This educated us in strict self-criticism and only after long inner struggles led again to a free and fearless unfolding of our efforts....

Back however, to the old styles. It might seem that initially we have conceded the justification of using them again. But this is not the case. ...

A connoisseur will reject with indignation any copy, his esthetic sense will guard him from the tastelessness of showing himself in the period room of some firm. Isn't it ridiculous in Vienna to own a room costumed as a Tyrolean peasant's chamber when its painted furniture betrays at first glance the citified master painter. It would really be interesting to see the behavior of the famous studios if they were asked for the style of Queen Semiramis, the Normans, or the Fiji Islanders. We are almost certain that they would be able to deliver even such things promptly due to their colossal knowledge and first-class employees; we know after all of the priceless case of a recently ordered and delivered Moorish billiard table. We hear from the antique dealers that they are always doing more business. This is a gain for our efforts; for, once the public has acquired a taste for only genuine things, they will logically also have to encounter us along the way.

The public should, however, be careful even so; for as soon as the demand for genuine things becomes great, industries capable of doing anything will begin to serve in this respect too....

It is, for example, absolutely necessary that our carpet manufacturers should create patterns similar to those of necktie fabrics; they should seek value in distinctive weave, originality of color, quality of material and its use, instead of weaving only bad patterns whose use becomes a torment for all and leads to complete dullness.

The modern possibilities are very great and known only to the technician. Industry could suddenly face fruitful and indisputable, therefore economically enormously important, tasks. Just as it does not occur to anyone to have Renaissance ornaments applied to his automobile, so it would not occur to anyone to use such designs in his home, given the elevated and conscious interest of the manufacturer. What, however, is then the state of the modern designs?

Naturally they would only be demanded rarely by quite specific people; they would then be ordered from an artist who in his very own field of handicraft would be in a position to meet this rare demand of a perhaps vanishing artistic sensibility. The false struggle between handicraft and industry would then have ended, and the limits of each would be determined and naturally protected. For this, however, we need a work of modern education on a large scale.

This will have to consist above all in recognizing the value of technology and creative work. It will have to emphasize the absolute fulfillment of the demand for genuine material and the limitation of the available means. There is still a long way to go.

In a textbook of vocational education I recently read the following: Staining woods serves to give inferior kinds of wood the appearance of costlier and better woods! Instead it should say that staining serves to achieve colors that do not occur in natural wood, and therefore do not copy any [natural wood]. Thus gray, blue, and green above all are proper. Of course, one can also use other tones, but one should try to show the material itself, perhaps through an emphasis on the veining, by rubbing a lighter color into the graining.

We have to present everything the way it really is.

Therefore we shall, for example, use opaque glass only when it is not commercially marbled; we shall use only tiles, not sheet metal formed and enameled like tiles.

In our architectural plasterwork we will not use wire netting for corbels and vaulting but will display the surface plane; if need be, we shall ornament it with free decoration but not stick on pressed plaster.

In our gas heaters we will not put seemingly glowing wooden logs of asbestos but we will show the flame and the reflector; we will design our electric lighting not as candle but as hanging lightbulb. Then only shall we recognize again the charm of candlelight and use it on festive occasions instead of spoiling our old chandeliers forever by ridiculous adaptation.

Our doors shall no longer have to be so high because it does not happen that guards carrying halberds march through them, but they will be all the wider because our social rooms are too small anyhow and will serve our needs better when they are linked by wide openings. All our doors, narrow or wide, should have the same height throughout because by this their relationships become properly apparent and a pleasant restfulness is achieved. We shall, for example, orient our rooms by the sun and not by the facade, and we shall establish the fulfillment of all reasonable needs, of comfort, as the supreme principle. We shall set great value by the design of our gardens, for gardens are magic, wonder, and delight for our life. They, however, are not plant collections of botanically well-grouped beings. Gardens must be rooms, festive halls, and cosy corners. Then they are … [?] and playgrounds. Gardens must always have closure. A gate of perforated decoration shall open them. Public gardens too are not passages and deserts or collections of herbs. They shall be invented not only by the competent gardener but by the artist. In them our youth dreams its first dreams. They are important like schools and churches. Their instruction is gentle and unconscious, considerate of every temper.

They teach us all that the soul needs to rise above the workaday. Modern education shall set us the task to bring to our elementary schools also the sense for reality and work instead of a world of purely abstract concepts. More important than hairsplitting instruction in grammar is manual dexterity, the awakening of the creative forces; these are almost paralyzed and atrophied by a purely literary education. It is high time that we awaken them again. These are our thoughts of six, seven years ago. Meanwhile we had been called to the School of Arts and Crafts as a teacher and had to try and lead the young people in our care on a productive path. Many of our intentions were hindered by the lack of workshops of our own. It is therefore clear that we were anxious to establish them. For this we required the necessary capital or a generous Maecenas. We had the good fortune to find one in the person of Fritz Waerndorfer.

After a long stay in London, Waerndorfer had returned to Vienna, and he was immediately interested in the then new movement.

I recall that we met him one fine day on the scaffolding of the Secession building.

He came to us out of pure interest with his young wife, and he has since helped and supported us with great understanding in every respect.

The idea of workshops was not alien to him. There already had been beginnings in England and Germany; he needed no explanation; he plunged head over heels into this work with ardent zeal. We wanted to start out gently but he had no desire to do a halfway job and dared to realize the ideas fully with all his means. If this enterprise had met with full understanding, we would today have a model institute, the envy of the world. But in Vienna it is not easy to prevail. It takes much, much patience.

To show what we wanted, we then wrote to our friends:

"We want to establish intimate contact between public, designer, and craftsman and to produce good simple household utensils. We start from purpose, utility is our first condition."
[Then follows citation of the well-known work program of the Wiener Werkstätte to the penultimate sentence which reads: "We shall try to fulfill what is in our powers. We can only take a step forward through the cooperation of all our friends."] Our program is approximately defined in this. We did not lack opponents; we were accused of presumption in imagining we could master so many crafts at once….

But we also owed the happiest hours to this enterprise. Each of you will have experienced often in life what a pleasure it is … talking to a good cabinetmaker or other craftsman, and to get to know a world that stands on its two feet, and knows and fulfills its function.

Now we have the good fortune to dwell every day in a circle of such people and to enjoy with sincere admiration their devoted, heartfelt perseverance, deep understanding, and manly strength. We see with pride that they stand at the worktable with pleasure and without distaste, and that they gladly help us to realize ideas they apparently sense as made for their dexterity. But we feel how for us the forces grow, through them, and how we must not lose respect for the sanctity of work. Our art-craftsmen are an elite of the first rank. They are not slaves of a machine but creators and shapers, makers of form and masters. Their labors are not loveless patchwork by various hands but the work of one man. Therefore they are all signed with the signet, that is, with the name of the craftsman. We know that we do not work for individual profit but for the cause, and that makes us free. We know no differences in rank; we recognize only an order of work and the higher quality of performance....

We hope for and dream again of garden-rich, beautiful, bright cities, without oppressive ugliness; we dream of handsome, healthy people in handsome rooms and of the open cheer of positive work.

This work of the hands guided by healthy creative force shall not degrade but elevate and lead to highest perfection through the correct appreciation of its worth.

Our time should at last recall that art alone preserves the value of its colossal epoch-making works as an inspiration for the future, and that we will vanish from the earth with all the things of our civilization if a vigorous art will not transmit them by its inner value.

Published in English in Eduard F. Sekler, *Josef Hoffmann – The Architectural Work*, pp. 486-492. © 1985 by Princeton University Press. Reprinted by permission of Princeton University Press.

Biography

Brigitte Huck

1870

Josef Franz Maria Hoffmann was born on December 15 in the small town of Pirnitz (Brtnice) in Moravia, an industrial center of the Austro-Hungarian Empire. He was the third of six children. His father, Josef Franz Karl, was the town mayor and co-owner of the cotton division of Prince Collalto's textile factory. The living tradition of Moravian folk art, the fertile landscape, and a family life close to that of Biedermeier days – these were the strongest aspects of a childhood that exercised a powerful influence on Hoffmann's later life.

1879

Hoffmann attended grammar school in Iglau (Jihlava), where Adolf Loos, who came from Brünn (Brno), was also a student. It was his father's wish that Hoffmann should study law and enter into public service. He was traumatized by the severe, authoritarian school system, but his interest in art and architecture was now awakened, and he visited building sites with the son of the local architect to help with the work. Finally, after numerous family battles, he was allowed to go to Brünn in 1887 to enter the Architecture Department of the Höhere Staatsgewerbeschule (Senior State Commercial and Technical School), where in 1888/89 he met up with Adolf Loos again. After passing his final examination, he enrolled in a practical course at the Militärbauamt (Military Building Office) in Würzburg, Germany in 1891 and one year later applied to the Akademie der bildenden Künste (Academy of Fine Arts) in Vienna.

1892

Hoffmann began studying at the Akademie der bildenden Künste (Academy of Fine Arts) in the School of Architecture, which was then directed by Karl Freiherr von Hasenauer. Von Hasenauer, co-architect of the new Ringstrasse, was at that time at the peak of his career. After his death in 1894 Otto Wagner took over the class. His was a dynamic program, with stimulating courses and projects. For his third-year diploma work, Hoffmann chose to design an "Island of Peace," an international convention center of immense scale. He won an award for the work and the Rome Prize of the École des Beaux Arts. Hoffmann repeatedly referred to the great influence his teacher Otto Wagner had on his work, and all his life he remained a devotee of Wagner.

1895-1896

The Club of Seven was established, a group of Hoffmann's friends that included such artists and architects as Josef Maria Olbrich, Koloman Moser, Max Kurzweil, Max Fabiani, and Friedrich Pilz. Meeting in the back rooms of Viennese cafés to discuss current problems, they were the avantgarde forum for the heated architectural discussions. Otto Wagner's manifesto of 1895, *Moderne Architektur*, was conceived of in the Club of Seven. With Olbrich, Hoffmann went to Italy; from his travel sketches that have survived their route can be traced from Venice through Rome to Naples and on to Capri. The vernacular architecture of the island and the visual qualities of the plain white houses are described by Hoffmann in his article "Ein Beitrag für malerische Architekturempfindungen" (A Contribution to Picturesque Architecture). They served as a source of inspiration, expressive of social contentment as well as characteristic of the qualities of a particular landscape and its people.

1897

Back in Vienna, Hoffmann began working in Otto Wagner's studio on the design and construction of the Viennese Stadtbahn (city train). He also made designs for the Municipal Pavilion at the Kaiser's Jubilee exhibition in 1898 as well as for the Gewerbebank in Prague, and created a drawing competition for the new Bohemian municipal theater in Pilsen. His article "Architektonisches von der Insel Capri" (Architecture on the Island of Capri) was published in *Der Architekt*. In the same year the Vienna Secession was founded. With all the avant-garde artists in Vienna as members, it was to have a decisive impact on the city's artistic scene. Josef Maria Olbrich's programmatic design of an exhibition building for the Secession gave Hoffmann scope to design the interior; he was responsible for the room belonging to the Secessionist publication *Ver Sacrum*.

1898

The British Arts and Crafts Movement influenced Hoffmann in his designs for the *Ver Sacrum* room in the Secession building, the Viribus Unitis room for the Secession at the Kaiser's Jubilee exhibition, and the studio designs for Koloman Moser and the painter Ernst Stöhr that were created at the same time. Stylized ornamentation, particularly the characteristic palmetto patterns, was typical of the furniture, as was the choice of materials according to moral principles. Secessionist artists would not, for instance, accept wood stained to look like another natural wood; staining should be honestly evident, using gray, blue, or green, but never brown tones. Hoffmann's designs for the third Secessionist exhibition, which was dedicated to Max Klinger, established him as an impressive creator of installations. In this year he married Anna Hladik.

1899

Hoffmann continued to play a major role in designing the Secessionist exhibitions, which had become an important part of Viennese cultural life. He was also making his first contacts with potential customers. First commissions included the furnishings and portico for the local branch of the Apollo Soap and Candle Factory and the revamping of the industrialist Paul Wittgenstein's country house, Bergerhöhe. This client would continue to be a loyal patron and friend of Hoffmann for the rest of his life. At the age of only twenty-nine, Hoffmann was appointed professor at the Vienna Kunstgewerbeschule (School of Applied Arts), along with Koloman Moser. Hoffmann taught in the departments of architecture, metalwork, enameling, and applied art at the school until his retirement in 1936. The appointment of the Secessionists Hoffmann and Moser at the renowned school was greeted with enthusiasm as a victory of the "modern artists" over the "old school."[1] The school also

Dining room, executed by Anton Pospischil for the winter 1899 exhibition at the Österreichisches Museum für Kunst und Industrie

recruited its new director from among the Secessionists, Felician Freiherr von Myrbach.

1900

Hoffmann designed the rooms for the Vienna Kunstgewerbeschule and the Secession at the Paris Exposition Universelle; these designs reveal his sense of proportions. He also designed and exhibited a dining room. He undertook study tours to England to see the workshop practices of the Guild of Handicrafts in London. Hoffmann became interested in the furniture by C. B. Ashbee, and through his future business partner Fritz Waerndorfer invited Charles Rennie and Margaret Mackintosh to exhibit a tearoom at the eighth Secessionist exhibition. Its austerity and simplicity fired the Viennese artists with enthusiasm and confirmed the ideals of the Secession. While working on the preparations for the eighth Secessionist exhibition, Hoffmann was also developing his idea for a colony of villas, or artists' colony in the Hohe Warte suburb on the outskirts of Vienna and was commissioned to design the houses for his friends the painters Karl Moll and Koloman Moser, the photographer Hugo Henneberg, and the art collector Victor Spitzer. His son Wolfgang was born.

1901

Design of the forestry office for the Wittgenstein Forestry Administration in Hohenberg, Lower Austria (for Karl Wittgenstein), and of the house for the foresters.

The two semi-detached houses for Moll and Moser in Hohe Warte and the Henneberg house were finished and provided the first evidence of Josef Hoffmann's concern with achieving unity of the house and its furnishings as an ideal integration of building and living. He received numerous commissions for interiors of private homes, among others for Helene Hochstätter, Magda Mautner Markhof, Hugo Koller, Gustav Koller, and Hans Salzer. These were created with his student Franz Messner and members of the studio at the Kunstgewerbeschule.

1902

Fourteenth Secessionist exhibition. Hoffmann was in charge of the artistic direction and the design of the rooms. The centerpiece of the exhibition was the polychrome statue of Beethoven by Max Klinger, around which Gustav Klimt realized the ideal of a *Gesamtkunstwerk* (total work of art) devoted to an artist, the famous Beethoven frieze. Josef Hoffmann's ornamental reliefs, above the doorways, were of eminent importance in the development of an abstract, constructive direction in Austrian art, marking the move away

Koloman Moser and Fritz Waerndorfer, 1903

from the organic to clear-cut, cubic forms. In the same year his dining room for Fritz Waerndorfer was created, as were the furnishings for the apartment of Hans Salzer, a doctor in Wittgenstein's family.

1903

The Wiener Werkstätte (Vienna Workshop) was founded. Josef Hoffmann and Koloman Moser were responsible for its artistic direction, while the industrialist Fritz Waerndorfer acted as financier and managed its commercial activities. In a factory building in Neustiftgasse, studios were set up for work in metal and in leather, for carpentry and for lacquering; other spaces were allocated to a bookbinding workshop and to offices and sales rooms. All were designed by Josef Hoffmann. Initially an architectural office was also attached to the workshops. The main concern of the Wiener Werkstätte was, in addition to producing individual objects of superior quality, to develop a formal language of the time and to produce complete interiors that expressed the creative vision of its founders. The Wiener Werkstätte continued in operation until 1932.

In the same year Hoffmann built a summerhouse and boathouse for the Knips family in Seeboden, Kärnten. Another major building project was the Gewerkschaftshotel der Poldihütte (Poldihütte Trade Union Hotel) in Kladno, Czechoslovakia.

1904

The Purkersdorf Sanatorium near Vienna was built, one of the highlights of Hoffmann's architecture. Commissioned by Viktor Zuckerkandl, brother-in-law of art critic and Secession promoter Berta Zuckerkandl, the luxurious spa

Exhibition rooms of the Wiener Werkstätte, Neustiftgasse, 1903

building was a milestone in architectural history with the clarity of its formal arrangement, the radical simplicity of its cubic design, and its concept of space. Hoffmann, together with Koloman Moser, designed the entire interior and all the technical and decorative elements that the Wiener Werkstätte would produce. With Koloman Moser he also designed the interior for the Flöge fashion salon, managed by Gustav Klimt's companion and her sisters.

1905

House and interior for Alexander Brauner at Hohe Warte and a villa for the poet Beer-Hofmann. Hoffmann went to Belgium and signed the contract with Adolphe Stoclet for the Palais Stoclet in Brussels. He met the sculptors Constantin Meunier and Georg Minne. A group of artists around Gustav Klimt, including Hoffmann, left the Secession.

1905-1911

Palais Stoclet built in Brussels. Hoffmann designed the building, the complete interior, the garden, and all subsidiary buildings. The two-story structure with its distinctive tower is edged with façade profiles that give the building its typically atectonic appearance. The interiors are conceived as a graduated series of impressions, culminating in the central two-story hall. Artists such as Gustav Klimt (mosaic frieze in dining room), Georg Minne (marble fountain), Karl Otto Czeschka (glass windows), Michael Powolny (ceramics), Leopold Forstner (mosaics), and Franz Metzner (sculptures) contributed to the subtle atmosphere of the villa, a *Gesamtkunstwerk* that has survived almost entirely intact.

1906-1907

Parallel to the Palais Stoclet, Hoffmann worked on two other villas in Vienna, one for the engineer Alexander Brauner and the other for Richard Beer-Hofmann. Stylistically they owe a debt to the British Arts and Crafts movement and to Neoclassicism. They certainly deviate from the severe Secessionist style. He also made numerous designs for monuments and tombs.

1907

Koloman Moser left the Wiener Werkstätte to devote himself to painting, and Eduard Wimmer, a student of Hoffmann, took over his position and directed the fashion department for many years. The Cabaret Fledermaus was founded, a nightclub to provide "cultural entertainment." The bar, stage, and auditorium were created by Hoffmann, who also collaborated on the interior with artists such as Gustav Klimt, Oskar Kokoschka, Berthold Löffler, and Emil Orlik. Writers such as Peter Altenberg, Egon Friedell, and Alfred Polgar read from their works, the Wiesenthals danced, and the bartender was especially brought from America. The town sales outlet of the Wiener Werkstätte am Graben was designed by Hoffmann. In Vienna he met Charles Edouard Jeanneret (Le Corbusier), who was skeptical of the decorative Viennese architecture.

1908

The 1908 *Kunstschau* was held on the site of what is now the Concert Hall, and Hoffmann was responsible for designing the temporary exhibition building, the interior, and the overall design of the exhibition, which included an Oskar Kokoschka room. He met the Paris fashion designer Paul Poiret in Vienna. Josef Olbrich, creator of the artists' colony "Mathildenhöhe" in Darmstadt, died. Adolf Loos gave his legendary lecture "Ornament und Verbrechen" (Ornament and Crime), not published until 1913.

1909-1910

The "transportable hunting lodge" for Alexander Pazzani was built near Vienna. It was a wooden house, and Hoffmann used prefabricated construction for the first time. The last of the houses on the Hohe Warte, the Villa Ast, was also built. His first contacts were made with Otto Primavesi, a major industrialist and banker in Olmütz, for whom Hoffmann was to build a country house in Czechoslovakia (Winkelsdorf) and a villa for his cousin in Vienna. Like many of Hoffmann's clients, Primavesi had close contacts with Viennese artists, and his wife's and daughter's portraits were painted by Klimt. The Austrian Werkbund was founded.

1911-1912

Hoffmann worked on interior designs for Hugo Marx in Hinterbrühl near Vienna and for Mimi Marlow, star of the Cabaret Fledermaus. He designed the exhibition rooms for the sculptor Anton Hanak at the *Kunstausstellung* in Dresden, the façade and interior for the Grabencafé and the reception room for the exhibition *Österreichisches Kunstgewerbe* (Austrian Arts and Crafts) at the Österreichisches

Anteroom, executed by L. Schmidt for the winter 1913/14 exhibition at the Österreichisches Museum für Kunst und Industrie, Vienna

Museum für Kunst und Industrie (now the MAK). He also designed the Austrian pavilion for the international art exhibition in Rome.

1912-1914

First plans for the Austrian Biennale pavilion in Venice, built in 1934. Interiors for the industrialist Moritz Gallia in Vienna and the painter Ferdinand Hodler in Geneva, both in the monumental, Neoclassical, decorative style characteristic of 1910-14. Starts work on the Kaasgraben colony of eight single-family homes arranged in pairs and fitted unobtrusively into their surroundings, a modest version of the Hohe Warte houses in a Neoclassical tradition. Two other architectural projects of this period were also stylistically very similar: the villa for Josefine Skywa and Robert Primavesi in Gloriettegasse in Vienna, with a porter's lodge, conservatory, and garden pavilion, and the Austrian pavilion for the German Werkbund exhibition in Cologne (with Anton Hanak and Oskar Strnad). The buildings both have gabled side sections and a colonnaded front.

The financier of the Wiener Werkstätte, Fritz Waerndorfer, went bankrupt. His place was taken by Otto and Mäda Primavesi, who appointed a commercial director and, in 1915, Dagobert Peche as artistic director. He was to bring an entirely new style to the Wiener Werkstätte.

1915-1918

The years 1915/16 brought mainly interiors, such as those for Anton and Sonja Knips in Vienna, Heinrich Böhler in

Munich and St. Moritz, Berta Zuckerkandl, and Paul Wittgenstein. In addition Hoffmann provided the interior decoration for some Wiener Werkstätte sales rooms: the branch in Marienbad, the fashion department in Kärntner Strasse (together with Wimmer-Wisgrill), and the department for fabrics, lace, and lighting in Kärntner Strasse/Führichgasse. In Burghausen am Inn an electrochemical factory was built for Dr. Alexander Wacker. The influence of Dagobert Peche on the style of the Wiener Werkstätte and upon Hoffmann's formal language became increasingly evident, with the painterly-graphic element almost replacing the severe structures of the early designs. Peche opposed the idea of industrial production and thus resisted demands of the Werkbund. In 1918 Otto Wagner, Gustav Klimt, Egon Schiele, and Koloman Moser all died.

1919-1925

The first plans were made for the last of the Vienna villas, the house for Sonja Knips, which was only to be built five years later. The clients of the postwar period came mainly from Austria's economically more powerful successor state, Czechoslovakia. Hoffmann built a house for the textile industrialist Fritz Grohmann in Würbenthal and for Sigmund Berl in Freudenthal, continuing the type developed in the prewar period – a blockish shape with sectional divisioning and a hip roof. For the Ast house, a country seat on Wörther

Sales rooms of the Wiener Werkstätte in Zurich, 1915

Lake and his first major postwar commission in Austria, Hoffmann used a flat roof and designed the famous arched pergola in concrete. At the 1925 Exposition Internationale des Arts Décoratifs in Paris he showed his "Lady's Salon," a new type of room between the boudoir and the bedroom. Its erotic iconography caught the mood of the twenties. Hoffmann's design for the Austrian pavilion, in collaboration with Peter Behrens, Oskar Strnad, and Josef Frank, created speculation about a possible Neobaroque revival. Adolf Loos turned down an invitation to join the project. The art and architecture critics applauded the pavilion as one of the most original creations in the exhibition. This was the peak of Hoffmann's international career, and it brought him the Order of the French Légion d'Honneur and an invitation to write the article on modern interior design for the fourteenth edition of the Encyclopedia Britannica. The profile of the Paris pavilion was mimicked in an apartment building on Seventy-second Street in New York, and many of the stylistic features of American Art-Deco architecture derive from Hoffmann. Josef Urban, an Austrian architect who had emigrated to the United States, opened the Wiener Werkstätte of America in the twenties, with exhibition space on Fifth Avenue.

The City of Vienna commissioned Hoffmann to design low-income housing at Klosehof (Vienna 19, 140 apartments) and Winarskyhof (Vienna 20, 76 apartments), together with Peter Behrens. Second marriage, to Karla Schmatz, a model at the Wiener Werkstätte.

1927

In the *Kunstschau* arranged by Oswald Haerdtl at the Österreichisches Museum für Kunst und Industrie, Hoff-

Josef Hoffmann and Franz v. Zülow, August 1931

mann showed two rooms. He also designed an interior for Ernst Bauer in Vienna. The Wiener Werkstätte found itself in financial difficulties and had to cease payments. Hoffmann was deeply depressed by the embittered opposition of Adolf Loos, who was unleashing a flood of polemic lectures and articles against the "eclectic trash" produced by the Wiener Werkstätte.

1928-1930

Hoffmann began to concern himself with major projects – housing and the "New Building." He developed an interest in Le Corbusier and the Bauhaus and undertook a number of urban planning projects, including an art and exhibition hall on Karlsplatz in Vienna. He provided the plans for the renovation of the old city in Vienna and designed a Palast für Kunst und Kultur (Center for Art and Culture in steel and glass in the manner of Mies van der Rohe), as well as a monument for Otto Wagner for the Heldenplatz in Vienna.

Installations for the 1934/35 exhibition *Das befreite Handwerk* (Crafts Liberated) at the Österreichisches Museum für Kunst und Industrie, Vienna

He designed the interior and portal of the Confiserie Altmann & Kühne together with Oswald Haerdtl, with whom he also converted the Grabencafé. He built a house for Isidor Diamant in Klausenburg, Romania, and designed the music room for the exhibition *Wiener Raumkünstler* (Viennese Interior Designers) at the Österreichisches Museum für Kunst und Industrie. He was a member of the jury for the League of Nations building competition in Geneva and held general responsibility for the exhibition by the Austrian Werkbund at the Museum für Kunst und Industrie. He was appointed vice-president of the Austrian section of the Werkbund, and designed four terraced houses for the pilot housing project built by the Werkbund in Vienna.

1932-1940

The cost of the duplexes for the Werkbund estate exceeded all expectations. Hoffmann left the Artist's Association in the face of heated criticism. The Wiener Werkstätte was dissolved and the complete inventory was sold at auction. In 1934 the Austrian pavilion for the Biennale in Venice was built. Hoffmann also designed the rooms for the exhibition celebrating fifty years of the Wiener Kunstgewerbeverein (Vienna Applied Arts Association) at the Österreichisches Museum für Kunst und Industrie (1934). Henceforth Hoffmann concentrated mainly on projects and studies, including a competition project for the Great National Assembly Palace in Ankara, Turkey, a Viennese park project for a Hall of Fame and a mausoleum for Austrian musicians, and designs for the Austrian pavilion for the Exposition Universelle in Paris in 1937. In 1936 Hoffmann retired from his teaching post at the Kunstgewerbeschule. Despite ideological reservations about the new National Socialist system, Hoffmann welcomed the economic upswing he hoped it would bring for his architectural practice and accepted the commission to convert the former German Embassy in Vienna to the House der Wehrmacht, a club for officers of the German Wehrmacht.

Josef Hoffmann at his desk, 1951

1941-1956

Hoffmann's attention focused primarily on residential housing for the City of Vienna in Blechturmgasse, Silbergasse, and Heiligenstädter Strasse, but this work is not among his outstanding achievements. He became a member of the Kunstsenat (Art Senate) and the General Commissioner of the Austrian Department of the Biennale in Venice. He celebrated his eighty-fifth birthday in the Palais Stoclet in Brussels and died shortly afterward, in 1956, of a stroke in Vienna.

Note

1 Ludwig Hevesi, *Ver Sacrum* (Vienna, April 1899).

List of Illustrated Works

The designations WWE, WWKA, and WWMB at the end of some entries refer to the Wiener Werkstätte records: WWE = Wiener Werkstätte Entwurf (sketch); WWKA = Wiener Werkstätte Kartei (card index); WWMB = Wiener Werkstätte Modellbuch (design book). Unless otherwise stated, Hoffmann's monogram has the initials intertwined.

Furniture and Wooden Objects

1 Chair, 1904 (detail)
See cat. no. 9

2 Interior, 1899
Pencil, India ink, and red and yellow crayon on graph paper, 6 × 4″ (15.3 × 10.2 cm)
Monogrammed (lower left): JH, dated (verso): 1899
K.I. 10439/2

3 Cupboard, 1899
Pencil, India ink, and blue and red crayon on graph paper, 4¹⁵⁄₁₆ × 4³⁄₁₆″ (12.6 × 10.7 cm)
Monogrammed (lower left): JH
K.I. 10439/5

4 Hall, 1899
Pencil, India ink, and red crayon on graph paper, 3¹¹⁄₁₆ × 3¹⁄₈″ (9.3 × 8 cm)
Monogrammed (lower left): JH, dated (verso): 1899
Illustration for Alfred Lichtwark's essay "Palastfenster und Flügelthuer" (Palace Window and Folding Door)
K.I. 10439/6, 7

5 High window seat, 1899
Pencil, India ink, and red crayon on graph paper, 4⁷⁄₁₆ × 3¹⁄₈″ (11.3 × 8 cm)
Monogrammed (lower right): JH, dated (verso): 1899
Illustration for Alfred Lichtwark's essay "Palastfenster und Flügelthuer" (Palace Window and Folding Door)
K.I. 10439/6, 7

6 Bed arrangement, 1901
India ink on graph paper, 7⁵⁄₁₆ × 7″ (18.6 × 17.8 cm)
Monogrammed (lower left): JH
K.I. 8972

7 Bookcase, 1900
Pencil and India ink on graph paper, 6⁵⁄₁₆ × 4¹⁄₈″ (16.1 × 10.4 cm)
Monogrammed (lower left): JH
K.I. 10439/3

8 Metal vitrine, 1903/4
Pencil and India ink on graph paper, 12¹⁄₈ × 7″ (30.8 × 17.7 cm)
Monogrammed (center right): JH, stamped (upper right): JH
K.I. 12132/12
WWMB 3, p. 305 (model nos. H 128, 305)

9 Three chairs, 1904
Pencil, India ink, and green, blue, and red crayon on graph paper, 8¹⁄₈ × 13³⁄₈″ (20.6 × 33.9 cm)
Monogrammed and dated (center right): 19JH04, stamped (upper left): JH
Probably for the furnishings of the Flöge fashion house
K.I. 8819/1

10 Dressing table, stool, and armchair, ca. 1930
Pencil on graph paper, 8¹⁄₈ × 13¹⁄₄″ (20.6 × 33.6 cm)
Signed (lower right): Josef Hoffmann
Dated (inventory stamp): 1.6.31
K.I. 12129/24

11 Nursery, 1927
Pencil and crayon on graph paper, 8¹⁄₄ × 13³⁄₈″ (20.9 × 34 cm)
Monogrammed (lower right): JH
For the nursery of Dipl.-Ing. Ernest Bauer's apartment
K.I. 8819/12

12 Cupboard and a dressing table, 1927
Pencil on graph paper, 8¹⁄₄ × 13³⁄₈″ (21 × 34 cm)
Monogrammed (lower left): JH
Hoffmann studio stamp

Executed by Anton Pospischil for the *Kunstschau*, Vienna, 1927
K.I. 8819/14

13 Buffet and stove, ca. 1925
Pencil on graph paper, 7¹⁵⁄₁₆ × 12¹³⁄₁₆″ (20.2 × 32.6 cm)
Monogrammed (lower right): JH
K.I. 8819/9

14 Wooden table and stand, ca. 1930
Pencil, India ink, and orange crayon on graph paper, 8¹⁄₈ × 13³⁄₈″ (20.7 × 33.9 cm)
Monogrammed (lower right): JH
K.I. 12133/11

15 Tailor's wooden dummy, ca. 1930
Pencil, India ink, and red crayon on graph paper, 13³⁄₈ × 8¹⁄₄″ (33.9 × 20.9 cm)
Monogrammed (lower right): JH
Pencil sketches on verso
K.I. 12133/12

16 Chair, 1928
Pencil on graph paper, 7¹¹⁄₁₆ × 13¹⁄₈″ (19.6 × 33.4 cm)
Monogrammed (lower left): JH, dated (lower right): 1928
K.I. 8819/15

17 Chair and stool, ca. 1930
Pencil on graph paper, 8¹⁄₁₆ × 13¹⁄₈″ (20.5 × 33.3 cm)
Monogrammed (lower right): JH
Dated (inventory stamp): 1.6.1931
K.I. 12129/21

18 Sofa, table, chair, and glass cabinet, 1920/30
Pencil and ocher, blue, orange, red, and green crayon on graph paper, 8¹⁄₈ × 13¹⁄₄″ (20.6 × 33.7 cm)
Monogrammed and (incorrectly) dated (lower right): JH 1912
K.I. 8819/3

19 Cabinet, ca. 1930
Pencil and yellow, red, green, and ocher
crayon on graph paper, $8\frac{1}{4} \times 13\frac{5}{16}''$
(21×33.8 cm)
Monogrammed (lower right): JH
K. I. 8819/13

20 Two chairs and an armchair, 1927
Pencil and red crayon on graph paper,
$8\frac{3}{16} \times 13\frac{3}{8}''$ (20.8×34 cm)
Monogrammed (lower right): JH
Hoffmann studio stamp
Executed by Anton Hergesell & Co., Vien-
na, for the *Kunstschau*, Vienna, 1927
K. I. 8819/17

21 Two chairs, 1928
Pencil and yellow, green, and orange cray-
on on graph paper, $8\frac{1}{4} \times 13\frac{3}{8}''$
(20.9×34 cm)
Monogrammed and dated (lower right):
JH 1928
K. I. 8819/16

22 Chair, ca. 1898
Pine and beech; $34\frac{1}{4} \times 17\frac{1}{4} \times 16\frac{3}{4}''$
($87 \times 44 \times 42.5$ cm), height of seat $17\frac{3}{4}''$
(45 cm)
From the furnishings of Ernst Stöhr's
house and studio at St. Johann on Wocheiner Lake, Slovenia
H 2721/1983

23 Chair, 1934
Made by Johann Soulek & Co., Vienna
Walnut, solid and carved, and leather;
$34\frac{3}{4} \times 20\frac{1}{2} \times 19''$ ($88 \times 52 \times 48$ cm), height
of seat $19''$ (48 cm)
Made for the exhibition *Das befreite
Handwerk*, Vienna, 1934
H 1701/1934 (acquired at exhibition)

24 Chair, 1910
Made by Jacob & Josef Kohn, Vienna
Beech, solid, turned and bent, and
plywood, stained black and shellacked;
$37 \times 19 \times 17$ ($94 \times 48 \times 43$ cm), height of
seat $18\frac{3}{4}''$ (47.5 cm)
Label: JACOB & JOSEF KOHN, WIEN
Mark: 21 X J. & J. KOHN WIEN. AUSTRIA
Shown at the winter 1910/11 exhibition of
the Österreichisches Museum für Kunst
und Industrie, Vienna
W. I. 880/1911

25 Chair (model no. 728), ca. 1907
Made by Jacob & Josef Kohn, Vienna

Beech, solid, bent, and stained brown, and
patterned plush fabric; $29\frac{1}{4} \times 20\frac{3}{4} \times 17''$
($74.5 \times 53 \times 43$ cm), height of seat $18\frac{1}{2}''$
(47 cm)
The same chair design was used for the
cabaret "Die Fledermaus"
H 2870/1987

26 Chair, ca. 1904
Made by Jacob & Josef Kohn, Wsetin
Beech, stained light brown and shellacked,
plywood, and red oilcloth; $39 \times 18 \times 17''$
($99 \times 46 \times 43$ cm), height of seat $17\frac{3}{4}''$
(45 cm)
Mark: JaJ. KOHN/WSETIN-AUSTRIA
(burned into the wood)
For the dining hall of Purkersdorf
Sanatorium
H 2189/1969

27 Armchair, 1903
Pine, stained black; $41\frac{1}{4} \times 26 \times 19\frac{3}{4}''$
($105 \times 66 \times 50$ cm), height of seat $17\frac{3}{4}''$
(45 cm)
From the bedroom furnishings of the
Knips' country house at Seeboden on
Millstätter Lake, Austria
H 2702/1983

28 Chair, 1906
Made for the Wiener Werkstätte
Beech, painted white; $35\frac{1}{2} \times 18 \times 18''$
($90 \times 46 \times 46$ cm), height of seat $18\frac{1}{2}''$
(47 cm)
From the furnishings of Dr. Hermann
Wittgenstein's apartment
H 2089/1966

29 Chair, 1907/8
Made for the Wiener Werkstätte
Beech, painted white and linen (not origi-
nal); $35\frac{1}{2} \times 26 \times 18''$ ($90 \times 66 \times 46$ cm),
height of seat $18''$ (45.5 cm)
From the nursery furnishings of Dr. Her-
mann Wittgenstein's apartment
H 2090c/1966

30 Chair, 1902
Pine and beech, painted white, and yellow
oilcloth (fragments); $51\frac{1}{4} \times 18\frac{1}{2} \times 18''$
($130 \times 47 \times 46$ cm), height of seat $17\frac{3}{4}$
(45 cm)
For the anteroom of Dr. Hans Salzer's
apartment
H 2545/1977

31 Chair, 1930
Beech, solid, zebrawood veneer, and

epinglé; $33\frac{1}{4} \times 18 \times 17\frac{1}{4}''$
($84.5 \times 46 \times 44$ cm), height of seat $17\frac{3}{4}''$
(45 cm)
Upholstery designed by Lucia Stadlmayer
and made by Philip Haas & Sons, Vienna
For the coffeehouse at the Vienna Werkbund exhibition, 1930
H 2722/1983

32 Chair, ca. 1913
Made by Jacob & Josef Kohn, Vienna
Beech, solid and bent, and plywood, ebo-
nized; $36\frac{1}{4} \times 18 \times 16\frac{1}{4}''$ ($92 \times 46 \times 41$ cm),
height of seat $18\frac{1}{2}''$ (47 cm)
Label: JACOB & JOSEF KOHN, WIEN
Mark: J. & J. KOHN Teschen Austria
H 2301

33 Chair, ca. 1907
Made for the Wiener Werkstätte
Beech; $36\frac{1}{4} \times 18\frac{1}{4} \times 18''$ ($93 \times 46.5 \times 46$
cm), height of seat $18''$ (45.5 cm)
Upholstery (not original): pattern no. 6324
of the Backhausen company, after a 1907
design by Hoffmann
Formerly owned by Karl Bräuer
H 2599/1980
WWF 103, p. 179

34 Chair, 1930
Made by Thonet Brothers, Vienna
Beech, solid, bent, and stained brown, and
cane; $30 \times 18 \times 16\frac{1}{4}''$ ($76 \times 45.5 \times 41$ cm),
height of seat $16\frac{1}{4}''$ (41.5 cm)
Label: THONET
The same model was used on the terrace of
the coffeehouse at the Viennese Werkbund
exhibition, 1930
H 3041/1989

35 Chair, 1929
Made by Jacob & Josef Kohn, Vienna
Beech, solid, and stained black;
$35\frac{1}{2} \times 16\frac{1}{8} \times 16\frac{1}{8}''$ ($90 \times 41 \times 41$ cm),
height of seat $18\frac{1}{2}''$ (47 cm)
Upholstery (worsted fabric): pattern no.
6643 of the Backhausen company, after a
1907 design by Hoffmann
Originally designed for the dining room of
Dr. Lengyel's villa in Pressburg (Brati-
slava), Slovakia, 1929. The chair from the
MAK's collection is a slightly altered recon-
struction of 1961, which architect Hermann Czech had carried out for the Ball-
haus restaurant on Schauflergasse, Vienna 1.
H 2597/1980

36/37 Piano chair, 1910
Made for the Wiener Werkstätte
Oak, solid, stained black, with white rubbed into the grain, and metal mechanism to adjust the height of the seat;
$37^{1}/_{8} \times 16^{1}/_{2} \times 16''$ (94.3 × 42 × 40.5 cm), height of seat $18^{1}/_{2}''$ (47 cm)
H 2597/1980

38 Armchair, 1900
Oak, solid and veneered, brass, and yellow pigskin (originally yellow Swedish leather);
$31 \times 22^{3}/_{4} \times 20^{1}/_{2}''$ (79 × 57.5 × 52 cm), height of seat $17^{3}/_{4}''$ (45 cm)
For the dining room of a Viennese apartment
H 2735/1983

39 Armchair, 1910
Made by Jacob & Josef Kohn, Vienna
Beech, solid, turned, and bent, and plywood, stained black and shellacked;
$32 \times 28 \times 20^{1}/_{2}''$ (81 × 71 × 52 cm), height of seat $18^{1}/_{4}''$ (46.5 cm)
Label: JACOB & JOSEF KOHN, WIEN
Mark: 21 X J. & J. KOHN WIEN, AUSTRIA
Shown at the winter 1910/11 exhibition of the Österreichisches Museum für Kunst und Industrie
W. I. 881/1911

40 Tea cart, ca. 1908
Made for the Wiener Werkstätte
Oak, carved, ebonized, and with white rubbed into the grain, brass, glass, and woolen braid, $28^{3}/_{4} \times 24^{1}/_{2} \times 14^{1}/_{2}''$
(73 × 62 × 37 cm)
From the furnishings of Dr. Hermann Wittgenstein's apartment
H 2081/1966
WWF 105, p. 254

41 Armchair, 1905
Made for the Wiener Werkstätte
Oak, solid, veneered, stained black, and with white rubbed into the grain, and upholstery (not original); $39 \times 33 \times 29^{1}/_{4}''$
(99 × 84 × 74.5 cm), height of seat $17''$
(43 cm)
From the inglenook of Dr. Hermann Wittgenstein's apartment
H 2086/1966
WWF 101, p. 456

42 Armchair, 1914
Made by Jacob & Josef Kohn, Vienna
Beech and plywood, stained black and bent, and blue leather; $32^{5}/_{8} \times 22^{7}/_{8} \times 20^{1}/_{2}''$

(83 × 58 × 52 cm), height of seat $17^{3}/_{4}''$
(45 cm)
Mark: J. & J. KOHN/WSETIN/-AUSTRIA/ 7 IV 14
H 2990/1989

43 Armchair, 1907/8
Made for the Wiener Werkstätte
Beech, painted white, and linen (not original); $35^{1}/_{2} \times 26 \times 18''$ (90 × 66 × 46 cm), height of seat $19''$ (48 cm)
From the nursery furnishings of Dr. Hermann Wittgenstein's apartment
H 2090b/1966

44 Armchair, ca. 1912
Probably made by Ludwig Schmitt
Oak, solid, veneered, stained black, and with white rubbed into the grain, and beige cotton (not original); $48^{1}/_{2} \times 26 \times 20^{3}/_{4}''$
(123 × 66 × 53 cm), height of seat $19^{1}/_{4}''$
(49 cm)
From the furnishings of a dining room
Lhg 1472

45 Stool, 1898
Pine, painted black (later treatment);
height $18^{1}/_{2}''$ (47 cm), diameter $16^{1}/_{2}''$
(42 cm)
From the furnishings of Koloman Moser's studio
H 2063a/1964

46 Stool, 1937
Made by Max Welz & Co., Vienna
Linden, carved and silvered, and pink velvet, $15^{1}/_{4} \times 19^{1}/_{4} \times 19^{1}/_{4}''$ (39 × 49 × 49 cm)
From the furnishings of "Lady's Salon"
Shown at the Exposition Universelle, Paris, 1937
H 2061/1964

47 Upholstered chair, 1937
Made by Max Welz Co., Vienna (frame and decoration) and Hedwig Pöchlmüller (upholstery)
Linden, carved and silvered, and wool, embroidered; $32 \times 25^{1}/_{2} \times 27^{1}/_{2}''$
(81 × 65 × 70 cm), height of seat $17^{1}/_{4}''$
(44 cm)
From the furnishings of "Lady's Salon"
Shown at the Exposition Universelle, Paris, 1937
H 2060/1964

48 Table, 1905
Made for the Wiener Werkstätte

Oak, solid, veneered, stained black, and with traces of white rubbed into the grain, and white-veined black marble,
$26 \times 43^{1}/_{4} \times 26''$ (66 × 110 × 66 cm)
From a furniture grouping in Dr. Hermann Wittgenstein's apartment
H 2082/1966
WWF 101, p. 46

49 Piano stool, ca. 1908
Made for the Wiener Werkstätte
Oak, solid, veneered, stained black, and with white rubbed into the grain, and blue woolen fabric; height $19^{1}/_{4}''$ (49 cm), diameter $17''$ (43 cm)
From the furnishings of Dr. Hermann Wittgenstein's apartment
H 2083 a, b/1966
WWF 105, p. 252

50 Coffee table, 1902
Maple, solid, stained dark brown, and purple-veined white marble; $24 \times 37^{3}/_{4}''$
(61 × 96 cm)
From a furniture grouping in Dr. Hans Salzer's apartment
H 2079/1966

51 Table, 1899
Pine, painted white; $30^{3}/_{4} \times 39^{1}/_{4} \times 25^{1}/_{2}''$
(78 × 99.7 × 65 cm)
From the kitchen furnishings of Paul Wittgenstein's country house, "Bergerhöhe"
H 2801/1985

52 Kitchen table, 1905
Spruce, painted white, maple, solid, and nickeled brass; $30^{1}/_{2} \times 54^{1}/_{4} \times 31''$
(77.5 × 137.5 × 78.5 cm)
From the kitchen furnishings for Dr. Hugo Koller
H 2849/1983

53 Table, 1907/8
Made for the Wiener Werkstätte
Beech and pine, painted white (apron panels originally framed in blue);
$29^{1}/_{2} \times 51^{1}/_{4} \times 25^{1}/_{2}''$ (75 × 130 × 65 cm)
From the nursery furnishings of Dr. Hermann Wittgenstein's apartment
H 2090o/1966

54 Table, ca. 1898
Pine, originally stained green;
$30^{3}/_{4} \times 38^{1}/_{2} \times 26^{1}/_{4}''$ (78 × 98 × 66.5 cm)
From the furnishings of Ernst Stöhr's house and studio in St. Johann

on Wocheiner Lake, Slovenia
H 2716/1983

55 Washstand, ca. 1898
Pine, originally stained green, and brass;
28³/₄ × 42³/₄ × 21″ (73 × 108.5 × 53.5 cm)
From the furnishings of Ernst Stöhr's
house and studio in St. Johann
on Wocheiner Lake, Slovenia
H 2717/1983

56 Cabinet, ca. 1898
Pine, originally stained green, and brass;
56 × 32 (45 open) × 14″ (142.5 × 81.5 (114)
× 35.5 cm)
From the furnishings of Ernst Stöhr's
house and studio in St. Johann on Wocheiner Lake, Slovenia
H 2714/1983

57 Dressing table, ca. 1898
Pine, originally stained green, and brass;
65 × 46³/₄ × 16″ (165 × 119 × 40.5 cm)
From the furnishings of Ernst Stöhr's
house and studio in St. Johann
on Wocheiner Lake, Slovenia
H 2715/1983

58 Lady's desk, 1905
Made for the Wiener Werkstätte
Oak, solid and veneered, stained black, and
with white rubbed into the grain, tombac,
and leaded glass; 42¹/₄ × 35¹/₂ × 26¹/₂″ (107
× 90 × 67 cm)
Marks (on drawer locks): rose mark
(embossed)
From the furnishings of Dr. Hermann
Wittgenstein's apartment
H 2084/1966
WWF 101, p. 44

59 Desk, 1909
Made for the Wiener Werkstätte
Oak, massive, veneered, stained black, and
with white rubbed into the grain, and
brass; 46 × 60⁷/₈ × 31¹/₈″
(117 × 154.5 × 79 cm)
From the furnishings of the Österreichi-
sche Staatsgalerie, Lower Belvedere,
Vienna, 1909
H 3134

60 Desk, ca. 1910
Made for the Wiener Werkstätte
Oak, solid and veneered, ebonized, and
with white rubbed into the grain, and tombac; 49¹/₂ × 61³/₄ × 33¹/₂″

(126 × 157 × 85 cm)
Marks (on drawer locks): rose mark
(embossed)
Josef Hoffmann's personal desk
H 2043/1960

61 Cabinet, 1898
Alder, solid, stained black and polished
(originally stained green), and copper;
83³/₄ × 51¹/₄ × 26″ (213 × 130 × 66 cm)
From the furnishings of Koloman Moser's
studio
H 2062/1964

62 Buffet, 1899
Pine, painted white, pear wood, solid, and
copper; 78¹/₄ × 51¹/₂ × 25¹/₂″
(199 × 130.5 × 64.7 cm)
From the kitchen furnishings of Paul Wittgenstein's country house, "Bergerhöhe"
H 2800/1985

63 Cabinet, ca. 1898
Pine, originally stained green, maple inlay,
palisander, and brass; 55¹/₄ × 31 × 37″
(140.5 × 79 × 94 cm)
From the furnishings of Ernst Stöhr's
house and studio in St. Johann
on Wocheiner Lake, Slovenia
H 2713/1983

64 Cupboard, ca. 1898
Pine, originally stained green, walnut,
maple, and brass;
80³/₄ × 46 × 19³/₄″ (205 × 117 × 50 cm)
From the furnishings of Ernst Stöhr's
house and studio in St. Johann
on Wocheiner Lake, Slovenia
H 2710/1983

65 Cupboard, ca. 1898
Pine, originally stained green, walnut,
maple, and brass; 80³/₄ × 46 × 19³/₄″
(205 × 117 × 50 cm)
From the furnishings of Ernst Stöhr's
house and studio in St. Johann
on Wocheiner Lake, Slovenia
H 2711/1983

66 Cupboard with mirrored door,
ca. 1898
Pine, originally stained green, walnut, and
brass; 80³/₄ × 46 × 19¹/₄″
(205 × 117 × 49 cm)
From the furnishings of Ernst Stöhr's
house and studio in St. Johann
on Wocheiner Lake, Slovenia
H 2712/1983

67 Cupboard, 1903
Pine, stained black, and nickeled brass;
73¹/₂ × 43¹/₄ × 21³/₄″ (187 × 110 × 55 cm)
From the bedroom furnishings of the
Knips' country home in Seeboden on
Millstätter Lake
H 2699/1983

68 China cabinet, 1908
Made for the Wiener Werkstätte
Oak, solid and veneered, carved, stained
black, and with white rubbed into the
grain, leaded glass, and burnished metal;
78³/₄ × 47¹/₄ × 17³/₄″ (200 × 120 × 45 cm)
From the dining room furnishings for Frau
Dr. Rappaport
H 2221 a/1970

69 Buffet, 1908/9
Made for the Wiener Werkstätte
Oak, solid and veneered, carved, stained
black, and with white rubbed into the
grain, leaded glass, burnished metal, and
white- and brown-veined black marble;
78³/₄ × 78³/₄ × 17³/₄″ (200 × 200 × 45 cm)
Marks (on door locks): rose mark (em-
bossed)
From the dining room furnishings for
Frau Dr. Rappaport
H 2222/1970

70 Broom cupboard, 1906
Pine, painted white and gray, and brass;
70³/₄ × 35¹/₂ × 13³/₄″ (180 × 90 × 35 cm)
From the furnishings of Dr. Hermann
Wittgenstein's apartment
H 2091/1966

71 Desk and shelf arrangement,
ca. 1914
Pine and pear wood, painted white and
black, white-wood veneer, and mirror;
84³/₄ × 70 × 19³/₄″ (215 × 178 × 50 cm)
"Rax" lining designed by Dagobert Peche
for the Wiener Werkstätte, ca. 1910/15
From Dr. Adolf Vetter's villa
H 2212/1969

72 Cupboard, 1906
Pine, repainted white and gray, and brass;
78³/₄ × 42¹/₂ × 12¹/₂″ (200 × 107 × 31 cm)
From the anteroom furnishings of
Dr. Hermann Wittgenstein's apartment
H 2088 a/1966

73 Cupboards, 1906
Pine, repainted white and gray, and brass;

a) upper part (2 pieces)
35¹⁄₂ × 23¹⁄₂ × 19¹⁄₄″ (90 × 60 × 49 cm),
b) lower part (2 pieces)
43¹⁄₄ × 23¹⁄₂ × 12¹⁄₄″ (110 × 60 × 31)
From the anteroom furnishings of
Dr. Hermann Wittgenstein's apartment
H 2088 b-e/1966

74 Wardrobe, 1906
Pine, repainted white and gray, and brass;
a) wardrobe sections 78³⁄₄ × 37″
(200 × 94 cm), b) mirrored section
78³⁄₄ × 23¹⁄₄″ (200 × 59.3 cm)
From the anteroom furnishings of
Dr. Hermann Wittgenstein's apartment
H 2087/1966

75 Etagère, ca. 1898
Pine, originally stained green;
88¹⁄₂ × 14¹⁄₂ × 11¹⁄₂″ (220 × 37 × 29 cm)
From the furnishings for Ernst Stöhr's
house and studio in St. Johann
on Wocheiner Lake, Slovenia
H 2720 a,b/1983

76 Longcase clock, 1908/9
Made for the Wiener Werkstätte
Oak, solid and veneered, carved, stained
black, and with white rubbed into the
grain, leaded glass, and white metal;
78³⁄₄ × 17³⁄₄ × 9³⁄₄″ (200 × 45 × 25 cm)
From the dining room furnishings for Frau
Dr. Rappaport
H 2224/1970
WWF 104, pp. 225f.
WWMB 31, pp. 1036, 1040

77 Shelves, ca. 1914
(Attributed to Josef Hoffmann)
Pine and pear wood, painted white and
black, white-wood veneer, mirror, and
printed linen; 87 × 24¹⁄₂ × 17¹⁄₄″
(221 × 62.3 × 44 cm)
From the furnishings of Dr. Adolf Vetter's
villa
H 2212/1969

78 Bed, chest, and two night tables,
ca. 1898
Pine, originally stained green, and English
cotton velvet (bedspread); a) bed 54¹⁄₄
(headboard) × 32 (footboard) × 84¹⁄₄ ×
63¹⁄₄″ (138 × 81 × 214 × 160.5 cm), b) chest
15¹⁄₂ × 49 (72 open) × 19″ (39.5 × 124.5
[183 open] × 48.5 cm), c) night tables
17¹⁄₈ × 16¹⁄₈ × 15¹⁄₈″ (43.5 × 41 × 38.5 cm)
From the furnishings of Ernst Stöhr's
house and studio in St. Johann

on Wocheiner Lake, Slovenia
H 2708/1983 (bed), H 2709/1983 (chest),
H 2719 a, b/1983 (night tables)

79 Bed, 1903
Pine, stained black; 43¹⁄₂ × 78 × 37¹⁄₂″
(110.5 × 198 × 95 cm)
From the bedroom furnishings of the
Knips' country house in Seeboden on
Millstätter Lake
H 2700/1983 (bed), H 2709/1983 (chest),
H2719 A, B/1983 (night tables)

80 Bed, ca. 1905
Spruce, painted white;
39¹⁄₄ (headboard) × 31¹⁄₂ (footboard) × 79¹⁄₂
× 41¹⁄₄″ (100 × 80 × 202 × 104.5 cm)
From the bedroom furnishings for
Dr. Hugo Koller
H 2871/1983

81 Bed, ca. 1905
Cherry wood and beech, solid, painted
white; 41¹⁄₂ (headboard) × 33¹⁄₄ (footboard)
× 80³⁄₄ × 39¹⁄₄″
(105.5 × 84.5 × 205 × 100 cm)
From the bedroom furnishings for
Dr. Hugo Koller
H 2872/1983

82 Stool, 1899
Pine, painted white; 19¹⁄₂ × 18 × 17¹⁄₄″
(49.5 × 45.5 × 44 cm)
From the kitchen furnishings of Paul Witt-
genstein's country house, "Bergerhöhe"
H 2802/1985

83 Stool, 1907/8
Made for the Wiener Werkstätte
Beech, painted white, and linen (not origi-
nal); 18 × 16¹⁄₄ × 16¹⁄₄″ (46 × 41 × 41 cm)
From the nursery of Dr. Hermann Witt-
genstein's apartment
H 2090 d/1966

84 Night table, ca. 1905
Alder, solid, painted white, brass, and gray-
ish white marble; 27¹⁄₂ × 15¹⁄₂ × 14¹⁄₂″
(70 × 39.5 × 37 cm)
From the bedroom furnishings for
Dr. Hugo Koller
H 2873 a,b/1983

85 Night table, 1903
Pine, stained black, grayish white marble,
and nickeled brass; 27¹⁄₂ × 21³⁄₄ × 15³⁄₄″
(70 × 55 × 40 cm)

From the bedroom furnishings for the
Knips' country house in Seeboden on Mill-
stätter Lake
H 2701/1983

86 Sewing table, 1905
Made for the Wiener Werkstätte
Oak, solid and veneered, stained black, and
with white rubbed into the grain, tombac,
and blue silk; 27³⁄₄ × 16¹⁄₂ × 16¹⁄₂″
(70.5 × 42 × 42 cm)
From the furnishings of Dr. Hermann
Wittgenstein's apartment
H 2080/1966
WWF 101, p. 27

87 Liquor cabinet, 1908/9
Made for the Wiener Werkstätte
Oak, solid and veneered, stained black, and
with white rubbed into the grain, tombac,
faceted glass, and linoleum,
24¹⁄₂ × 31¹⁄₂ × 21³⁄₄″ (62 × 80 × 55 cm)
From the dining room furnishings for
Frau Dr. Rappaport
H 2225/1970

88 Vitrine, 1934
Made by Max Welz & Co., Vienna
Wood, polychromed and gilded;
32¹⁄₄ × 28¹⁄₄ × 13³⁄₄″ (85 × 72 × 35 cm)
Made for the exhibition *Das Befreite
Handwerk*, Vienna, 1934
H 1703/1934 (acquired at exhibition)

89 Vitrine, 1934
Made by Franz Konecny
Walnut, solid and veneered, carved, and
glass; 50 × 37 × 18¹⁄₂″ (127 × 94 × 47 cm)
Made for the exhibition *Das Befreite
Handwerk*, Vienna, 1934
H 2156/1969 (acquired from the
manufacturer)

90 Music stand, ca. 1908
Made for the Wiener Werkstätte
Oak, solid and veneered, plywood, stained
black, and with white rubbed into the
grain, and brass; 50 × 17³⁄₄ × 17″
(127 × 45 × 43 cm)
From the furnishings of Dr. Hugo Koller's
apartment
H 2848/1983
WWF 101, p. 53

91 Box, 1950
Made by Österreichische Künstlerwerkstätten, Vienna I.

Walnut, solid, turned and carved; 4 × 4¹/₄″
(10 × 11 cm)
Mark (underside): KK
H 2012/1952

92 Box, 1940 (?)
Walnut, solid, turned; 2³/₄ × 4³/₄″
(7 × 12 cm)
H 2816

93 Cigarette box, ca. 1910
Made by Wiener Werkstätte
Mother of pearl, ebony veneer, and ebonized pear wood (inside); 5 × 7³/₄ × 4¹/₄″
(12.5 × 19.5 × 10.5 cm)
Mark (underside): WIENER/WERK/STÄTTE (in silver)
W.I. 1064/1912 (acquired from the Wiener Werkstätte)

94 Cigarette case, 1923
Made by Wiener Werkstätte
Ivory, carved; ³/₄ × 3¹/₂ × 2³/₄″ (2 × 9 × 7 cm)
Pl 565/1932 (acquired at the Wiener Werkstätte's liquidation auction)
WWK Schtzel 1

95 Bonbonnière, 1942
Made by Hugo Kirsch, Entwurf- und Versuchswerkstätte für das Kunsthandwerk, Vienna
Walnut, solid and carved; 3¹/₂ × 4¹/₂″
(8.8 × 11.3 cm)
H 1880/1942

96 Easter egg, ca. 1906
Made by Wiener Werkstätte (Therese Trethan)
White beech, solid, painted brown and white; 4 × 2¹/₂″ (10 × 6.6 cm)
Marks (inside): rose mark, WW, JH, TT (Therese Trethan)
H 2657/1969

97 Box, 1943
Made by Versuchswerkstätte des Kulturamtes der Gemeinde Wien, Vienna
Macassar ebony, walnut and cherry tree wood on veneered mahogany;
2³/₈ × 6¹/₄ × 3³/₈″ (6 × 16 × 8.5 cm)
H 1890/1943

98 Jewel box, before 1904
Made by the Wiener Werkstätte
Marquetry in Swedish birch, ebony, mahogany, and solid ebony; 8¹/₄ × 18 × 12¹/₂″

(21 × 46 × 32 cm)
Marks (underside): rose mark,
WIENER/WERK/STÄTTE, JH (embossed in white)
Shown at a Wiener Werkstätte exhibition, Berlin, 1904 and at the *Kunstschau*, Vienna, 1908
H 1182/1908 (acquired at the *Kunstschau*)
WWF 101, pp. 16, 18

99 Box, 1950
Made by Österreichische Künstlerwerkstätten, Vienna
Linden wood, solid, painted pink;
3¹/₄ × 6¹/₄ × 4¹/₄″ (8 × 16 × 11 cm)
Marks (inside lid): JH, ÆB
H 2817

100 Box, 1950
Rosewood and palisander, solid;
2³/₄ × 6 × 3¹/₂″ (7 × 15 × 9 cm)
Marks (inside lid): JH, ÆB
H 2011/1952

101 Box, 1950
Made by Österreichische Künstlerwerkstätten, Vienna
Walnut, solid; 2¹/₂ × 6 × 4″
(6.5 × 15.3 × 10 cm)
Marks (inside lid): JH, ÆB
H 2010/1952

102 Cigarette case, 1950
Made by Österreichische Künstlerwerkstätten, Vienna
Burl, solid; ¹/₂ × 3¹/₄ × 2³/₄″ (1 × 8.5 × 7 cm)
Marks (inside lid): JH, ÆB
II 2013/1952

103 Box, 1943
Made by Versuchswerkstätte des Kulturamtes der Gemeinde Wien, Vienna
Macassar ebony, solid; 2³/₄ × 7¹/₂ × 3¹/₂″
(7 × 20 × 9 cm)
Mark (inside lid): JH
H 1889/1943

Metal Objects

104 Spoon, 1905
Pencil, India ink, and blue crayon on graph paper mounted on graph paper;
8¹¹/₁₆ × 4¹/₈″ (20.5 × 10.5 cm) (design sheet),
13¹/₁₆ × 8¹/₁₆″ (33.2 × 20.5 cm) (whole)
Monogrammed (lower right): JH,

stamped (upper right): JH
Executed 1905/8
Buyers: Stoclet and Dr. H. Salzer
K.I. 12090/13

105 Compote spoon, 1905
Pencil on graph paper;
8³/₁₆ × 7⁹/₁₆″ (20.8 × 19.2 cm)
Stamped (upper left): JH
Executed 1905
Buyers: Artin and Jenny Mautner
K.I. 12086/20
WWMB 5, p. 1000 (model no. S 453)

106 Spoon, 1907
Pencil on graph paper; 13 × 8″
(33.1 × 20.3 cm)
Stamped (upper center): JH
Executed 1906/12
K.I. 12086/27
WWMB 9, p. 798 (model no. S 798)

107 Coffee spoon, 1906
Pencil on graph paper; 13¹/₁₆ × 8″
(33.2 × 20.3 cm)
Stamped (upper center): JH
Executed 1906/14
K.I. 12086/28
WWMB 9, p. 799

108 Demitasse spoon, 1907
Pencil on graph paper; 13 × 8¹/₁₆″
(33.1 × 20.5 cm)
Stamped (upper center): JH
Executed 1907/12
K.I. 12086/29
WWMB 9, p. 859 (model no. S 859)

109 Spoon, ca. 1905
Pencil, India ink, and yellow, blue, green, and brown crayon on graph paper mounted on graph paper; 7³/₁₆ × 3¹/₈″ (18.3 × 7.9 cm) (design sheet), 13¹/₈ × 8¹/₁₆″ (33.3 × 20.5 cm) (whole)
Monogrammed (center right): JH, stamped (upper right): JH
Pencil sketch on verso
Executed ca. 1905
K.I. 12090/2

110 Spoon, 1905
Pencil, India ink, and green crayon on graph paper mounted on graph paper;
10⁵/₈ × 1³/₄″ (26.9 × 4.5 cm) (design sheet), 13³/₁₆ × 8″ (33.5 × 20.4 cm) (whole)
Stamped (upper right): JH

Executed 1905
K.I. 12090/14
WWMB 8, p. 526 (model no. S 526)

111 Two spoons, 1905
Pencil and red crayon on graph paper;
$13 \times 7^{15}/_{16}''$ (33×20.2 cm)
Monogrammed (center): JH, stamped
(upper center): JH
Executed 1905 and 1912
K.I. 12090/8
WWMB 8, pp. 558, 559 (model nos. S 558,
559)

112 Cutlery, date unknown
Pencil on graph paper; $13^{1}/_{8} \times 8''$
(33.3×20.4 cm)
Stamped (upper left): JH
K.I. 12086/42

113 Ladle, 1904
Pencil on graph paper; $11^{15}/_{16} \times 7^{1}/_{2}''$
(30.4×19.1 cm)
Designs on recto and verso
Stamped (upper center): JH
Executed 1904/6
Buyers: Hirschwald and F. Waerndorfer
K.I. 12086/19
WWMB 5, p. 721 (model no. S 311)

114 Dessert cutlery, date unknown
Pencil on graph paper; $11^{7}/_{16} \times 5^{5}/_{8}''$
(29×14.2 cm)
Writing on verso
K.I. 12087/8

115 Ice cream servers, 1904
Pencil on graph paper; $11^{1}/_{8} \times 8''$
(28.3×20.3 cm)
Monogrammed (lower right): JH
Executed 1904/6
Buyers: Hirschwald, F. Waerndorfer, and
Fanto
K.I. 12086/12
WWMB 7, pp. 441-43 (model nos. S 210-
12)

116 Carving, sardine, and escargot
forks, 1904
Pencil on graph paper; $12^{7}/_{8} \times 7^{1}/_{2}''$
(32.7×19.1 cm)
Monogrammed (lower right): JH
Pencil sketches on verso
Executed 1904/8
Buyers: Fanto, Hirschwald, F.
Waerndorfer, and others
K.I. 12086/17

WWMB 7, pp. 463-65 (model nos. S 464,
S 230-32)

117 Soda water stirrer, cake server,
and skewer, 1904
Pencil on graph paper; $12^{3}/_{4} \times 7^{15}/_{16}''$
(32.4×20.2 cm)
Monogrammed and dated (lower right):
19JH04
Executed 1904/6
Buyers: Fanto, Hirschwald, F.
Waerndorfer, and Seewald
K.I. 12086/11
WWMB 7, pp. 438-39 (model nos. S 207-9)
Cf. nos. 250, 253

118 Cheese and butter knives, 1904
Pencil on graph paper; $7^{15}/_{16} \times 5^{3}/_{4}''$
(20.1×14.6 cm)
Monogrammed (lower right): JH
Executed 1904/10
Buyers: Hirschwald and Dr. H.
Wittgenstein
K.I. 12086/13
WWMB 7, pp. 445-46 (model nos.
S 213-14)

119 Spoon and eggcup, 1904
Pencil on graph paper; $8 \times 6^{1}/_{4}''$
(20.3×15.8 cm)
Monogrammed and dated (lower right):
19JH04
Executed 1904/6
Buyers: August Waerndorfer, Fanto,
Hirschwald, and F. Waerndorfer
K.I. 12086/14
WWMB 7, pp. 447-48 (model no. S 215)

120 Three spoons, 1905
Pencil and India ink on graph paper;
$8^{1}/_{8} \times 13^{1}/_{4}''$ (20.7×33.7 cm)
Monogrammed (center): JH,
stamped (upper right): JH
Executed 1905
WWE 3
WWMB 8, pp. 573-75 (model nos.
S 573-75)

121 Oyster fork, cutlery for fish and
for crab, date unknown
Pencil and India ink on graph paper;
$7^{7}/_{8} \times 13^{1}/_{8}''$ (20×33.4 cm)
Monogrammed (lower center): JH,
stamped (lower center): JH
K.I. 12086/10

122 Sandwich server, 1912
Pencil, India ink, and blue crayon on graph

paper; $7^{1}/_{4} \times 3^{7}/_{8}''$ (18.4×9.8 cm)
Wiener Werkstätte stamp (lower center)
Executed 1912 and 1914
K.I. 12087/47
WWMB 16, p. 2953

123 Fish knife and fish fork, 1904
Pencil and India ink on graph paper;
$10^{11}/_{16} \times 7^{3}/_{8}''$ (27.1×18.7 cm)
Stamped (upper center): JH
Executed 1904/6
Buyers: Fanto, Hirschwald, F. Waern-
dorfer
K.I. 12086/9
WWMB 7, p. 438-39 (model nos. S 207-9)
Cf. nos. 245-46

124 Children's cutlery, 1925
Pencil in graph paper; $13^{9}/_{16} \times 8^{1}/_{16}''$
(34.5×20.5 cm)
K.I. 12087/76
WWKA S be 6/1-3

125 Cutlery for fish and for fruit, 1927
Pencil on graph paper; $13^{9}/_{16} \times 8^{1}/_{16}''$
(34.5×20.5 cm)
Executed 1927
K.I. 12086/30
WWKA S be 5/9-12

126 Skewer, 1913
Pencil on graph paper; $13^{1}/_{4} \times 7^{15}/_{16}''$
(33.7×20.1 cm)
Monogrammed (center): JH
Executed 1913
K.I. 12091/4
WWMB 16, p. 3051

127 Skewer, ca. 1911
Pencil and green crayon on graph paper;
$13^{1}/_{4} \times 8''$ (33.6×20.3 cm)
Monogrammed (center): JH
Executed (date unknown)
K.I. 12091/3
WWMB 16, p. 2858

128 Sandwich server, after 1918 (?)
Pencil on graph paper; $13^{3}/_{16} \times 7^{11}/_{16}''$
(33.5×19.5 cm)
Monogrammed (lower left). JH
K.I. 12089/9

129 Milk pitcher, sugar bowl, and
sugar tongs, ca. 1927
Pencil on graph paper; $7^{13}/_{16} \times 13''$
(19.9×33 cm)
Plan drawing on verso

Executed 1927/30
K.I. 12057/26
WWKA Sse 27/2-4 (model no. 27/2-4)
Cf. 263

130 Tea service, 1912
Pencil on graph paper; $7^5/_8 \times 13^3/_{16}''$
(19.4 × 33.5 cm)
Pencil sketches on verso
Executed 1912 and 1919
K.I. 12054/20
WWMB 15, p. 2765-68 (model nos.
S 2765-68)
Cf. no. 257

131 Coffeepot and milk
pitcher,1925/30
Pencil on graph paper; $7^{11}/_{16} \times 13^1/_8''$
(19.6 × 33.4 cm)
Monogrammed (lower right): JH
K.I. 12015/3

132 Sugar bowl, cup and saucer,
1925/30
Pencil on graph paper; $13^1/_8 \times 17^{11}/_{16}''$
(33.4 × 19.6 cm)
Monogrammed (lower right): JH
K.I. 12040/14

133 Teapot, 1918
Pencil on paper; $18^1/_8 \times 13''$
(20.7 × 33.1 cm)
Monogrammed (lower right): JH
Pencil sketches on verso
Executed 1918/20
K.I. 12016/9
WWMB 19, p. 3909 (model no. S 4027)
Cf. nos. 140, 142, 261

134 Sugar bowl and creamer, 1918
Pencil on paper; $18^1/_8 \times 13''$
(20.7 × 33.1 cm)
Pencil sketches on verso
Executed 1918/20
K.I. 12016/8
WWMB 19, pp. 3999-4000 (model nos.
S 4209, 4211)
Cf. nos. 140, 142, 261

135 Tea- or coffeepot, ca. 1927
Pencil on graph paper; $13^1/_4 \times 7^{13}/_{16}''$
(33.6 × 19.8 cm)
Monogrammed (lower right): JH
Executed 1927/30
K.I. 12057/25
WWKA Sse 27/1 (model no. 27/1)
Cf. no. 263

136 Coffee service, ca. 1907
Pencil on holed paper mounted on thin
cardboard; $13 \times 8^1/_8''$ (33 × 20.7 cm)
Monogrammed (lower right): JH,
stamped (upper left): JH
Executed 1908/12 and 1915/16
K.I. 12052/35
WWMB 10, pp. 1073-77, 1107 (model nos.
S 1073-77, 1107)

137 Teapot, ca. 1928
Pencil on graph paper; $7^{13}/_{16} \times 13^1/_8''$
(19.8 × 33.3 cm)
Monogrammed (lower right): JH
Dated (inventory stamp): 3.VIII.28
Executed 1929
K.I. 12057/43
WWKA Sse 32/1 (model no. Sse 32/1)

138 Coffeepot and creamer, ca. 1928
Pencil and red crayon on graph paper;
$16^7/_{16} \times 13^5/_{16}''$ (41.8 × 33.8 cm)
Monogrammed (lower right): JH
Executed 1928/9
K.I. 12059/15
WWKA Sse 29/1, 2 (model nos. Sse 29/1, 2)

139 Milk pitcher, 1923
Pencil and blue crayon on paper;
$7^7/_8 \times 11^{11}/_{16}''$ (20 × 29.7 cm)
Pencil sketches on verso
Executed 1923 and 1925
K.I. 12016/12
WWKA SSe 3/7 (model no. S 4820)
Cf. no. 261

140 Coffeepot, 1923
Pencil and red and black ink on graph
paper; $8^7/_{16} \times 12^1/_4''$ (21.5 × 31.1 cm)
Pencil sketches on verso
Executed 1923/4
K.I. 12016/10
WWKA Sse 3/8 (model no. S 4672)

141 Teapot, 1904
Pencil on graph paper; $8^1/_{16} \times 12^{13}/_{16}''$
(20.5 × 32.5 cm)
Monogrammed (lower right): JH
Executed 1904/6
Buyers: Wittgenstein, F. Waerndorfer,
Hirschwald, and Mautner
K.I. 12052/21
WWMB 7, p. 488 (model no. M 201)

142 Coffeepot, 1923
Pencil and red and black ink on paper;
$8^9/_{16} \times 11^1/_8''$ (21.8 × 28.2 cm)

Executed 1923/25
K.I. 12016/11
WWKA Sse 3/ 6 (model nos. Sse 3/ 6 and
S 4672/1)
Cf. nos. 133, 134, 261

143 Teakettle, 1909
Pencil and yellow crayon on graph paper;
$13^5/_{16} \times 16^9/_{16}''$ (33.8 × 42 cm)
Monogrammed and dated (lower right):
19JH09, stamped (upper left): JH
Wiener Werkstätte stamp (lower right)
Pencil sketches on verso
Executed 1911
K.I. 12018/1
WWMB 12, p. 1909 (model no. S 1909)

144 Tea service, 1903
Blue and red crayon on graph paper;
$8^1/_4 \times 13^3/_8''$ (21 × 34 cm)
Monogrammed and dated (lower left):
19JH03, stamped (upper left): JH
Pencil sketches on verso
Executed 1903
Buyer: K.R. Flesch
K.I. 12051/14
WWMB 3, pp. 182-84 (model nos. S 82-84)
Cf. nos. 136, 256

145 Tea service, 1903
Pencil and blue crayon on graph paper;
$8 \times 12^{13}/_{16}''$ (20.4 × 32.6 cm)
Monogrammed and dated (lower center):
19JH03, stamped (center left): JH
Executed 1904/5
Buyers: Artin, Fanto and Karl Wittgenstein
K.I. 12053/1
WWMB 4, pp. 137-40 (model nos. S 58-61)

146 Samovar, 1903
Pencil and blue and red crayon on graph
paper; $12^{15}/_{16} \times 7^{15}/_{16}''$ (32.8 × 20.1 cm)
Monogrammed and dated (lower right):
19JH03
Executed 1903
Buyer: K.R. Flesch
K.I. 12018/21
WWMB 3, p. 181 (model no. S 81)
Cf. nos. 144, 256

147 Tea service, 1904
Pencil on graph paper; $15^{11}/_{16} \times 13^1/_4''$
(39.9 × 33.7 cm)
Monogrammed and dated (upper left):
19JH04, stamped (lower left and upper
center): JH
Executed 1904
Buyer: F. Waerndorfer

K.I. 12058/26
WWMB 7, pp. 525-29 (model nos.
S 246-50)

148 Milk pitcher and creamer,
1928/29
Pencil on graph paper; $7^3/_4 \times 13^1/_4''$
(19.7 × 33.6 cm)
Monogrammed (lower right): JH
Dated (inventory stamp): 27.9.1928,
22.3.1929
Executed 1929
K.I. 12058/7
WWKA Sse 31/2, 6
Cf. no. 149

149 Sugar bowl, sugar tongs, and cup,
1928/29
Pencil on graph paper; $7^7/_8 \times 13^3/_{16}''$
(20 × 33.5 cm)
Monogrammed (lower right): JH
Dated (inventory stamp): 16.VII.31
Pencil sketch of details on verso
Executed 1929
K.I. 12058/14
WWKA Sse 31/3-5 (model nos. Sse 3-5)
Cf. no. 148

150 Sugar tongs, sugar bowl,
and creamer, 1909
Pencil on holed graph paper; $7^7/_8 \times 12^{15}/_{16}''$
(20 × 32.9 cm)
Monogrammed (lower right): JH, stamped
(three times, upper left and upper right): JH
Executed 1909 and 1914
K.I. 12052/36
WWMB 12, pp. 1779-81 (model nos.
S 1779-81)

151 Sugar bowl and spoon, ca. 1910
Pencil and green crayon on graph paper;
$7^{15}/_{16} \times 13^1/_4''$ (20.1 × 33.6 cm)
Executed 1911 and 1915
Buyer: Stoclet
K.I. 12026/15
WWMB 14, pp. 2371-72 (model nos.
S 2371-72)

152 Bonbonnière, sugar caster, and
napkin ring, ca. 1924
Pencil and red crayon on graph paper;
$8^3/_4 \times 13^1/_8''$ (22.2 × 33.3 cm)
Monogrammed (lower right): JH
Possibly amended by Philipp Häusler
Initialed and dated (lower right, by
Häusler): ‚PH 15.XI.24
Executed 1924/27
K.I. 11998/5

WWKA Sdi 35, 36 and Ssh 29 (model nos.
Sdi 35, 36 and Ssh 29)
Cf. no. 260

153 Centerpiece (bonbonnière), 1912
Pencil on graph paper; $7^1/_4 \times 12^{13}/_{16}''$
(18.5 × 32.6 cm)
Monogrammed (lower center): JH
Plan drawing on verso
Executed 1912
K.I. 12005/23
WWMB 15, p. 2647
Cf. no. 266

154 Silver centerpiece (bonbonnière),
1912
Sketch
Pencil on graph paper; $7^3/_4 \times 12^{13}/_{16}''$
(19.7 × 32.6 cm)
Monogrammed (upper right): JH
Wiener Werkstätte stamp (lower right)
Executed 1912
K.I. 12033/11
WWMB 15, p. 2615
Cf. nos. 151, 266

155 Silver centerpiece (bonbonnière),
1912
Production drawing
Pencil and blue crayon on graph paper;
$7^{13}/_{16} \times 22^{15}/_{16}''$ (19.9 × 32.8 cm)
Executed 1912
K.I. 12033/12
WWMB 15, p. 2615
Cf. nos. 150, 266

156 Centerpiece for fruit, and vinegar
and oil cruets from a tableware set, 1908
Pencil, India ink, and yellow, green,
brown and red crayon on graph paper;
$7^{15}/_{16} \times 11^9/_{16}''$ (18.5 × 29.4 cm)
Monogrammed (lower right): JH
Stamped (upper left): JH
Executed 1908
Buyer: Adolphe Stoclet
K.I. 12026/17
WWMB 10, p. 1133

157 Centerpiece, 1924/25
Pencil on graph paper; $16^1/_8 \times 13^1/_4''$
(41 × 33.6 cm)
Executed 1925/31
K.I. 12059/9
WWKA M sh 17
Cf. no. 268

158 Centerpiece, 1907
Pencil on graph paper, holed for filing;

$13^1/_4 \times 8^1/_8''$ (33.7 × 20.7 cm)
Monogrammed (lower right): JH,
stamped (upper center): JH
Executed 1907
K.I. 12003/9
WWMB 9, p. 921

159 Sauceboat, 1908
Pencil, India ink, and green crayon on
graph paper; $8 \times 4^7/_{16}''$ (20.4 × 11.3 cm)
Wiener Werkstätte stamp (upper center)
K.I. 12024/2A

160 Basket, 1906
Pencil on graph paper; $12^{15}/_{16} \times 7^{15}/_{16}''$
(32.8 × 20.2 cm)
K.I. 12032/31
WWMB 30, p. 643 (model no. M 643)

161 Jardinière for laurel, ca. 1907
Pencil, India ink, and ocher, green, and
brown crayon on graph paper; $7^{15}/_{16} \times 13''$
(20.2 × 33 cm)
Wiener Werkstätte stamp (lower center)
K.I. 12134/31

162 Basket, 1906/10
Pencil, India ink, and silver body color on
graph paper; $8^1/_{16} \times 13^3/_8''$ (20.5 × 33.9 cm)
Wiener Werkstätte stamp (twice, lower
right)
K.I. 12032/2

163 Jardinière, 1905
Pencil, India ink, and green, brown, and
red body color on imitation parchment
mounted on graph paper; $6^1/_4 \times 2^5/_8''$
(15.9 × 6.7 cm) (parchment), $13^1/_4 \times 8^1/_{16}''$
(33.7 × 20.5 cm) (whole)
Monogrammed (on mounting): JH
Wiener Werkstätte stamp (twice, lower
center and lower left)
Executed 1905
Buyers: Stoclet and others
WWE 31/3
WWMB 7, p. 426 (as Koloman Moser)
(model no. M 183)

164 Jardinière, 1905
Pencil, India ink, and green, blue,
and red body color on imitation parchment
mounted on graph paper; $6^1/_8 \times 4^3/_8''$
(15.5 × 11.1 cm) (parchment), $13^1/_4 \times 8^1/_{16}''$
(33.7 × 20.5 cm) (whole)
Monogrammed (lower center): JH
Wiener Werkstätte stamp (lower center)
Executed 1905/7

Buyers: E. Löw-Beer and E. Pirringer
WWMB 2, p. 1312 (model no. M 417)

165 Jardinière, 1905
Pencil, India ink, blue crayon, and yellow
and green body color on imitation
parchment mounted on graph paper;
$6^{3}/_{16} \times 4^{3}/_{8}''$ (15.7 × 11.1 cm) (parchment),
$13^{1}/_{4} \times 8^{1}/_{16}''$ (33.7 × 20.5 cm) (whole)
Monogrammed (lower right): JH
Wiener Werkstätte stamp (lower right)
Executed 1905, 1906, 1908, and 1910
Buyers: Gzerwinka and Fellner
WWE 31/5
WWMB 2, p. 1313 (model no. M 418)

166 Jardinière, 1904/5
Pencil, India ink, and green and red body
color on graph paper; $13^{3}/_{8} \times 8^{1}/_{4}''$
(33.9 × 20.9 cm)
Monogrammed (lower right): JH
Wiener Werkstätte stamp
WWE 31/1

167 Jardinière, ca. 1908
Pencil, India ink, and green, red, and ocher
body color on graph paper; $13 \times 7^{15}/_{16}''$
(33.1 × 20.1 cm)
Monogrammed (lower center): JH
Wiener Werkstätte stamp (twice, lower
center and lower right)
WWE 31/2

168 Jardinière, 1912
Pencil on graph paper; $12^{7}/_{16} \times 7^{15}/_{16}''$
(31.6 × 20.1 cm)
Monogrammed (lower right): JH
Wiener Werkstätte stamp (lower right)
Executed 1912
K.I. 12037/2
WWMB 35, p. 2044 (model no. M 2044)
Cf. 279

169 Basket, ca. 1909
Pencil on paper; $13 \times 7^{15}/_{16}''$
(33.1 × 20.2 cm)
Monogrammed (lower left): JH,
stamped (upper center): JH
Pencil sketches on verso
Executed (date unknown)
K.I. 12031/7
WWMB 32, p. 1058 (model no. M 1058)

170 Wastepaper basket, 1906
Pencil on graph paper; $13^{1}/_{8} \times 8''$
(33.3 × 20.4 cm)
Stamped: JH

Executed 1906
Buyer: E. Waerndorfer (?)
K.I. 12031/37
WWMB 30, p. 677 (model no. M 677)

171 Basket, 1907
Pencil on graph paper; $13^{1}/_{8} \times 7^{13}/_{16}''$
(33.3 × 19.9 cm)
Design on recto and verso
Stamped (twice, upper left and upper
middle): JH
Executed 1907, 1909, and 1913
K.I. 12032/46
WWMB 31, p. 773 (model no. M 773)

172 Flowerpot holder, 1907/8
Pencil on graph paper; $13 \times 8''$
(33 × 20.3 cm)
Stamped (upper right): JH
Executed 1908 and 1910
Buyer: Czerwinka and Fellner
K.I. 12135/8
WWMB 31, p. 925 (model no. 925)

173 Flower basket, 1906
Pencil and blue crayon on graph paper;
$7^{3}/_{4} \times 12^{15}/_{16}''$ (19.7 × 32.8 cm)
Monogrammed (lower right): JH,
stamped (upper left): JH
Executed 1906
K.I. 12135/ 6
WWMB 30, p. 588 (model no. M 588)

174 Jardinière, 1905
Pencil on graph paper; $6^{3}/_{8} \times 10^{9}/_{16}''$
(16.2 × 26.8 cm)
Monogrammed (lower right): JH,
stamped (upper left): JH
Executed 1905/7
Buyers: E. Löw-Beer, Neumann, and
E. Pirringer
K.I. 12134/26
WWMB 2, p. 1312 (model no. M 417)

175 Candlestick, 1905
Pencil on graph paper; $13^{1}/_{4} \times 8^{1}/_{4}''$
(33.7 × 20.9 cm)
Monogrammed (right center); JH
Executed 1905
K.I. 12124/22
WWMB 8, p. 576 (model no. S 576)

176 Candlestick, 1904
Pencil on graph paper; $12^{7}/_{8} \times 7^{15}/_{17}''$
(32.7 × 20.1 cm)
Pencil sketches on verso
Executed 1904/7

Buyers; Hirschwald, Wittgenstein,
Professor Ceska, Therese Vogoin, and
others
K.I. 12123/10
WWMB 5, p. 977 (model no. M 247)

177 Candelabrum, ca. 1905
Pencil, India ink, and black watercolor on
graph paper; $11^{5}/_{16} \times 7^{1}/_{8}''$ (28.7 × 18.1 cm)
Stamped (upper left): JH
Executed (date unknown)
K.I. 12107/14
Model no. M 94, not confirmed by Wiener
Werkstätte records;
Cf. WWMB 3, p. 159 (model no. S 67)

178 Candelabrum, 1928
Pencil on graph paper; $13^{1}/_{16} \times 7^{13}/_{16}''$
(33.2 × 19.8 cm)
Monogrammed (lower right): JH
Pencil sketches on verso
Executed 1928
K.I. 12124/18
WWKA Sdi 72
Cf. no. 289

179 Candlestick, 1904
Pencil, black, blue, green, and yellow
crayon on graph paper; $16^{3}/_{8} \times 13^{3}/_{8}''$
(41.6 × 34 cm)
Monogrammed (lower right): JH,
stamped (upper left): JH
Executed 1904/ 6
Buyer: Baron Oppenheimer
K.I. 12123/36
WWMB, p. 932 (model nos. M 313, 314)

180 Lamp, 1903
Pencil, India ink, and blue and green
crayon on graph paper; $16^{5}/_{16} \times 12^{1}/_{16}''$ (41.4
× 30.6 cm)
Monogrammed and dated (lower right):
19JH03, stamped (upper left): JH
Executed 1904/ 6
Buyers: Hirschwald and Purkersdorf
Sanatorium
K.I. 12116/30
WWMB 3, p. 217 (model no. M 109)

181 Wall lamp, 1914
Pencil on graph paper; $10^{7}/_{16} \times 6^{7}/_{16}''$
(26.5 × 16.3 cm)
Monogrammed (verso): JH
Executed 1914
Buyer: Primavesi
K.I. 12113/4
WWMB 36, p. 2532 (model no. M 2532)

219 Brooch, 1912
Pencil and silver and blue body color on
graph paper; $7^7/_8 \times 11^3/_8''$ (20 × 28.8 cm)
Wiener Werkstätte stamp: 8.Feb.1912
Executed 1912
K.I. 12144/49
WWMB 68, p. 1477 (model no. G 1477)

220 Jewelry set, 1909
Pencil and red crayon on paper, mounted
on cardboard; $13 \times 7^{15}/_{16}''$ (33 × 20.2 cm)
Monogrammed (lower left): JH,
stamped (9 times): JH
Wiener Werkstätte stamp (lower right)
Executed 1909/16
K.I. 12159/22
WWMB 66, p. 955-63
(model nos. G 955-63)

221 Tiepin, 1911
Pencil on graph paper; $13^1/_4 \times 8^1/_8''$
(33.7×20.6 cm)
Monogrammed (lower right): JH
Executed 1911
K.I. 12151/2
WWMB 67, p. 1288 (model no. G 1288)

222 Pendant, 1915
Pencil and black, yellow, and blue body
color on graph paper; $11^3/_4 \times 5^1/_2''$
(29.8×13.9 cm)
Monogrammed (center right): JH
Executed 1915
K.I. 12140/19
WWMB 69, p. 1871 (model no. G 1871)

223 Gold ring, 1930
Pencil and yellow, blue, and black body
color on graph paper; $13^1/_8 \times 7^{11}/_{16}''$
(33.4×19.6 cm)
Monogrammed and dated (lower right):
JH 30
WWE 16/1

224, 227 Two medals, ca. 1904
India ink and black and gold body color on
cardboard, pasted on black uncoated
paper, mounted on graph paper;
$3^7/_8 \times 3^{15}/_{16}''$ (9.9 × 10 cm) (design sheet),
$13^5/_{16} \times 8^5/_{16}''$ (33.8 × 21.1 cm) (whole)
Monogrammed (on mounts): JH
Inscribed (no. 224); F J I
K.I. 8832/9, 10

225, 228 Two medals, ca. 1904
India ink and black and gold body color on
cardboard, pasted on black uncoated

paper, mounted on graph paper;
$3^{15}/_{16} \times 4''$ (10 × 10.1 cm) and
$3^7/_8 \times 3^7/_8''$ (9.8 × 9.9 CM)
(design sheets), $13^1/_{16} \times 8^5/_{16}''$
(33.2×21.1 cm) (whole, each)
Monogrammed (on mounts): JH
Inscribed (no. 225): F J I./MCMIV,
(no. 228): PRO/F J I/PATRIA
K.I. 8832/17, 18

226 Monogram, date unknown
Pencil and yellow body color on graph
paper; $12^{15}/_{16} \times 7^3/_4''$ (32.8 × 19.7 cm)
Monogrammed (bottom center): JH
Wiener Werkstätte stamp
K.I. 12096/5

227, 228 (See **224** and **225**)

229 Monogram, 1912
Pencil and yellow watercolor on graph
paper; $7^{15}/_{16} \times 13^3/_{16}''$ (20.2 × 33.5 cm)
Monogrammed: JH
Executed 1912
K.I. 12176/7
WWMB 15, p. 2590 (model no. S 2590)

230 Monogram, 1922 (?)
Pencil and black and brown body color on
imitation parchment; $12^5/_8 \times 9^1/_2''$
(32.1×24.1 cm)
Dated: 20./4.22 (?)
Signed (verso): Hoffmann
Executed (date unknown): Photo album of
Dr. Arthur Schneider, Zagreb
K.I. 12176/3
WWMB 51, p. 2902 (model no. L2952)

231 Paper knife, 1904
Pencil, India ink, and brown crayon on
graph paper; $12^3/_4 \times 8^3/_8''$ (32.4 × 20.8 cm)
Monogrammed and dated (lower right):
19JH04, stamped (upper left and upper
right): JH
Executed (date unknown)
K.I. 12072/13 (model no. BL 4)

232 Paper knife, ca. 1904
Pencil, India ink, and brown crayon on
graph paper; $12^1/_2 \times 7^{11}/_{16}''$ (31.8 × 19.5 cm)
Monogrammed (lower center): JH,
stamped (upper left and upper right): JH
Executed (date unknown)
K.I. 12072/14 (model nos. BL 14, 22)

233 Candlestick, 1912
Pencil, India ink, and blue crayon on graph

paper; $7^1/_2 \times 9^3/_{16}''$ (19.9 × 23.4 cm)
Monogrammed (center right): JH
Wiener Werkstätte stamp (lower right)
K.I. 12124/8

234 Candlestick, 1912
Pencil, India ink, and blue crayon on graph
paper; $13^7/_{16} \times 8^1/_{16}''$ (34.1 × 20.5 cm)
Dated (inventory stamp): 28. Nov. 1912
Wiener Werkstätte stamp (lower center)
Executed 1912
K.I. 12124/ 6
WWMB 16, p. 2951 (model no. S 2951)

235 Ink blotter, 1908/9
Pencil and India ink on holed graph paper;
$6^1/_2 \times 6^3/_4''$ (16.6 × 17.2 cm)
Stamped (upper center): JH
Wiener Werkstätte stamp (upper left)
Executed 1909
K.I. 12069/19
WWMB 10, p. 1312 (model no. S 1312)

236 Feather duster container, 1908/9
Pencil and India ink on holed graph paper;
$5^{13}/_{16} \times 6^1/_2''$ (14.8 × 16.6 cm)
Stamped (upper center): JH
Wiener Werkstätte stamp (upper left)
K.I. 12069/17
S 1310

237 Inkwell, 1903
Pencil and red crayon on graph paper;
$13^1/_{16} \times 8^1/_8''$ (33.1 × 20.6 cm)
Monogrammed and dated: JH 1903
Stamped (upper right): JH
Executed 1904/5
Buyers: Hirschwald, A. Ginzkey,
Dr. Hellmann, Klein brothers, and Zeileis
K.I. 12067/2
WWMB 3, p. 144 (model no. M 68)

238 Trophy, 1930
Pencil on graph paper; $13^7/_{16} \times 16^7/_{16}''$
(34.2×41.8 cm)
Monogrammed (lower right): JH
Dated (inventory stamp): 20.3.1930
Executed 1930
WWE 29/13
Cf. no. 302

239 Trophy, 1925/30
Pencil on graph paper; $7^1/_2 \times 12^1/_2''$
(19×31.7 cm)
Monogrammed (lower right): JH
K.I. 12049/12

240 Hammer (detail), 1913
Pencil on graph paper; $7^{13}/_{16} \times 13^{1}/_{8}''$
(19.8 × 33.4 cm)
Monogrammed (center): JH
WWE 25/4
Cf. no. 241

241 Freemason's hammer, 1913
Pencil on graph paper; $13^{1}/_{16} \times 7^{13}/_{16}''$
(33.2 × 19.8 cm)
Monogrammed (lower center): JH, dated
(upper center): 14/VII 13
Inscribed (on head): Zur Erinnerung an
das 25-Jahrjubiläum 1913 Wien
Executed 1913 in silver, 1914 in nickel
silver
Buyer: F.W. (silver)
WWE 25/3
WWMB 16, p. 3116; 36, p. 2402
(model nos. M 2402, S 3116)
Cf. no. 240

242 Bottle stoppers, ca. 1924
Pencil on graph paper; $10^{1}/_{8} \times 16''$
(25.7 × 40.7 cm)
Monogrammed (center left,
center right): JH
Executed 1924/28
K.I. 12094/30
WWKA Skk. 2, 7, 10, 13, 14, 16, 19
(model nos. M 3424-3432)

243 Bottle stoppers, 1917
Pencil and blue ink on graph paper;
$7^{15}/_{16} \times 13^{5}/_{16}''$ (20.1 × 33.8 cm)
Monogrammed (center right): JH
Executed 1917
K.I. 12094/3
WWMB 19, pp. 3842-43
(model nos. S 3893-94)

244 Hand mirror, 1914
Pencil on graph paper; $12^{3}/_{16} \times 7^{3}/_{8}''$
(31 × 18.7 cm)
Executed 1914
Buyer: Meda Primavesi
WWE 41/2
WWMB 17, p. 3404 (model no. S 3404)

245 Pieces from a 106-part cutlery set
for 12 people, 1904/8
Made by Wiener Werkstätte, partly by
Master FK
Steel, silver, and niello; lengths, a) knife
$8^{1}/_{2}''$ (21.5 cm), b) fork $8^{1}/_{2}''$ (21.5 cm),
c) spoon $9^{3}/_{4}''$ (21.8 cm), d) dessert fork
$7^{1}/_{8}''$ (18.2 cm), e) dessert knife $7^{1}/_{8}''$

(18.3 cm), f) coffee spoon $5^{1}/_{2}''$ (14.1 cm),
g) demitasse spoon 4″ (10.2 cm)
Marks: hallmarks, A, WW, rose mark, JH,
FK, LFW [Lilly and Fritz Waerndorfer]
Go 2009/1967
K.I. 12086/7, 9, 10-14 (designs)
WWF 93, p. 5
WWMB 3, p. 268ff.
Cf. no. 123
Known as the "flat" cutlery, with smooth
forms and four silver balls at the handle
ends.

246 Fish knife and fish fork from a 106-
part cutlery set for 12 people, silver,
1904/8
Made by Wiener Werkstätte, partly by
Master FK
Steel, silver, and niello; lengths, a) fork
$7^{1}/_{2}''$ (19.2 cm), b) knife $7^{5}/_{8}''$ (19.3 cm)
Marks: hallmarks, A, WW, rose mark, JH,
FK, LFW [Lilly and Fritz Waerndorfer]
Go 2009/1967
K.I. 12086/7, 9, 10-14 (designs)
WWF 93, p. 5
WWMB 3, p. 286ff.
Cf. no. 123
Known as the "flat" cutlery, see no. 245

247 Butter knife and cheese knife from
a 106-part cutlery set for 12 people,
1904/8
Made by Wiener Werkstätte, partly by
Master FK
Steel, silver, and niello; lengths, a) butter
knife $6^{5}/_{8}''$ (16.7 cm), b) cheese knife $6^{1}/_{2}''$
(16.6 cm)
Marks: hallmarks, A, WW, rose mark, JH,
FK, LFW [Lilly and Fritz Waerndorfer]
Go 2009/1967
K.I. 12086/7, 9, 10-14 (designs)
WWF 93, p. 5
WWMB p. 3, p. 268ff.
Cf. no. 118
Known as the "flat" cutlery, see no. 245

248 Pieces from a 106-part cutlery set
for 12 people, 1904/8
Made by Wiener Werkstätte, partly by
Master FK
Steel, silver, and niello; lengths, a) knife
$8^{1}/_{2}''$ (21.5 cm), b) fork $8^{1}/_{2}''$ (21.5 cm),
c) spoon $8^{1}/_{2}''$ (21.8 cm), d) coffee spoon
$5^{1}/_{2}''$ (14.1 cm), e) egg spoon $4^{1}/_{8}''$ (10.5
cm), f) eggcup, height $2^{1}/_{2}''$ (6.5 cm),
greatest diameter $4^{1}/_{2}''$ (11.5 cm)
Marks: hallmarks, A, WW, rose mark, JH,
FK, LFW [Lilly and Fritz Waerndorfer]
Go 2009/1967

K.I. 12086/7, 9, 10-14 (designs)
Known as the "flat" cutlery, see no. 245

249 Sugar tongs from a 106-part cut-
lery set for 12 people, 1904/8
Made by Wiener Werkstätte, partly by
Master FK
Steel, silver, and niello; length 4″ (10.2 cm)
Marks: hallmarks, A, WW, rose mark, JH,
FK, LFW [Lilly and Fritz Waerndorfer]
Go 2009/1967
K.I. 12086/7, 9, 10-14 (designs)
WWF 93, p. 5
WWMB 3, p. 268ff.
Known as the "flat" cutlery, see no. 245

250 Serving forks and cake server from
a 106-part cutlery set for 12 persons,
1904/8
Made by Wiener Werkstätte, partly by
Master FK
Steel, silver, and niello; lengths a) serving
fork $10^{1}/_{4}''$ (26 cm), b) cake server $8^{5}/_{8}''$
(21.9 cm), c) serving fork 10″ (25.4 cm)
Marks: hallmarks, A, WW, rose mark, JH,
FK, LFW [Lilly and Fritz Waerndorfer]
Go 2009/1967
K.I. 12086/7, 9, 10-14 (designs)
WWF 93, p. 5
WWMB 3, p. 268ff.
Known as the "flat" cutlery, see no. 245
Cf. no. 116, 117

251 Eggcup with spoon, 1904
Made by Wiener Werkstätte
Silver; a) cup, height $2^{11}/_{16}''$ (6.6 cm),
greatest diameter $4^{5}/_{8}''$ (11.7 cm),
b) spoon, length $3^{3}/_{8}''$ (8.6 cm)
Marks: hallmark, WW, rose mark, JH
Go 2057/1983
WWMB 2, p. 1084
WWF 93, p. 6
Cf. no. 119

252 Pieces from a 14-part cutlery set,
1907/12
Made by Wiener Werkstätte, partly by
Master FK
Nickel silver, silvered, and silver; lengths,
a) fork $8^{1}/_{2}''$ (21.5 cm), b) knife $8^{1}/_{4}''$ (20.9
cm), c) fish fork $7^{1}/_{2}''$ (19.1 cm), d) fish
knife $7^{1}/_{2}''$ (19.2 cm), e) demitasse spoon 4″
(10.3 cm)
Marks: Rose mark, WW, JH, c) and d) also
hallmark, A, FK
Go 1988/1964
K.I. 12086/22-56 (designs)
WWF 94, p. 67

WWMB 31, p. 849ff., and 9, p. 796ff.
Known as the "round model," this type of
cutlery, with smooth forms and rounded
handle ends, was used at the Fledermaus
Cabaret.

253 Pieces from a 14-part cutlery set,
1907/12
Made by Wiener Werkstätte, partly by
Master FK
Nickel silver, silvered; lengths, a) lemonade
spoon 8¹⁄₈″ (20.7 cm), b) snail fork 5″ (12.9
cm), c) demitasse spoon 4″ (10.3 cm),
d) sardine server 5¹⁄₈″ (13 cm),
e) corn holder 2³⁄₈″ (6.1 cm)
Marks: rose mark, WW, JH, d) also hall-
mark, A, FK
Go 1988/1964
K.I. 12086/22-56 (designs)
WWF 94, p. 67
WWMB 31, p. 849ff., and 9, p. 796ff.
Known as the "round model," see no. 252

254 Ice cream server, salad spoon, and
salad fork from a 14-part cutlery set,
1907/12
Made by Wiener Werkstätte, partly by
Master FK
Nickel silver, silvered; lengths, a) ice cream
server 7¹⁄₈″ (18.2 cm), b) salad spoon 11¹⁄₄″
(28.6 cm), c) salad fork 11¹⁄₈″ (28.3 cm)
Marks: rose mark, WW, JH
Go 1988/1964
K.I. 12087/22-56 (designs)
WWF 94, p. 67
WWMB 31, p. 849ff., and 9, p. 796ff.
Known as the "round model," see no. 252
Cf. no. 115

255 Fish knife and fish fork, 1916
Made by Wiener Werkstätte
Silver and ebony; lengths, a) knife 7⁹⁄₁₆″
(19.2 cm), b) fork 7⁹⁄₁₆″ (19.2 cm)
Marks: hallmark, rose mark, WW, JH
Go 2070/1985
K.I. 12087/52 (designs for further pieces)
WWMB 18, p. 3568, 3569
Made for the Primavesi family, this cutlery
has ebony handles bearing flower and leaf
motifs.

256 Tea service, 1903
Made by Wiener Werkstätte (Konrad Koch)
Silver, coral, and ebony: heights, a) milk
pitcher 2″ (5 cm), b) teapot 4¹⁄₄″ (11 cm),
c) burner 3¹⁄₂″ (8.5 cm), d) stand 4³⁄₄″ (12
cm), e) teapot 5¹⁄₄″ (13.5 cm), f) sugar bowl
3¹⁄₂″ (8.5 cm)

Marks: WW, rose mark, JH hallmark, A, KK
Go 2005/1965
WWMB pp. 181-84
WWF 93, p. 34
Cf. nos. 144, 146

257 Tea service, 1912
Made by Wiener Werkstätte
Silver and ivory; heights, a) teapot 3³⁄₄″
(9.5 cm), b) cookie jar 3″ (7.5 cm), c) milk
pitcher 3″ (7.5 cm), d) sugar bowl 3″
(7.5 cm), e) tray 1¹⁄₂″ (4 cm)
W.I. 1300/1914 (acquired from the Wiener
Werkstätte)
WWMB 15, p. 1764ff.
WWF 95, p. 194
Cf. no. 130

258 Samovar, 1909
Made by Wiener Werkstätte
Silver and ivory; 11¹⁄₂ × 11¹⁄₂ × 10¹⁄₄″
(29 × 29 × 26 cm)
Marks: WW, rose mark, WIENER WERK-
STÄTTE, JH, hallmark
Go 2010/1967
WWMB 11, p. 1483
WWF 94, p. 99

259 Tea service, 1923
Made by Wiener Werkstätte
Brass and ebony; a) sugar bowl, height 5¹⁄₂″
(14 cm), b) sugar tongs, length 3¹⁄₂″ (9 cm),
c) teapot, height 8″ (20 cm), d) milk pit-
cher, 3¹⁄₄″ (8 cm), e) tray 16¹⁄₂ × 14¹⁄₂″
(42 × 37 cm)
Marks: WIENER/WERK/STÄTTE; JH;
MADE/IN/AUSTRIA
Me 846/1930 (acquired from the Wiener
Werkstätte)
WWKA Mse 5/1
WWF 114, p. 3

260 Sugar caster, 1924
Made by Wiener Werkstätte
Silver; 3³⁄₄ × 2¹⁄₄″ (9.5 × 5.5 cm)
Marks: WIENER/WERK/STÄTTE, 900
Go 2066 (inventoried in 1986)
Cf. no. 152

261 Coffee and tea service with samovar, 1918/25
Made by Wiener Werkstätte
Silver and ivory; a) milk pitcher, height 7″
(17.5 cm), b) samovar, height 11³⁄₄″ (30
cm), c) tea sieve, length 5″ (12.5 cm),
d) sugar bowl, height 4″ (10 cm), diameter
5¹⁄₄″ (13.5 cm), e) sugar tongs, length 4³⁄₄″
(12 cm), f) coffeepot, height 7″ (18 cm),

g) teapot 6″ (15 cm), h) creamer, height
4″ (10 cm)
Marks: WIENER/WERK/STÄTTE, JH 900,
hallmark
Go 2035/1976
WWMB 19, nos. 4027, 4209, 4211
WWF 96, p. 202
Cf. nos. 133, 134, 139, 140, 142

262 Tea service, 1928
Made by Wiener Werkstätte
Silver and ebony; a) milk pitcher, height
4³⁄₄″ (12 cm), b) teapot, height 6³⁄₄″ (17
cm), c) sugar tongs, length 4″ (10 cm),
d) sugar bowl, height 5³⁄₄″ (14.5 cm),
e) tray, diameter 14″ (35.5 cm)
Marks: WIENER/WERK/STÄTTE, JH,
MADE/IN/AUSTRIA, hallmark
Go 2008/1967
WWF 115
Cf. no. 138

263 Coffee service, ca. 1927
Made by Wiener Werkstätte
Silver and ebony; a) sugar tongs, length
3¹⁄₄″ (8 cm); b) coffeepot, height 6¹⁄₂″
(16.5 cm), c) creamer, height 4¹⁄₄″
(11 cm), d) sugar bowl, height 3¹⁄₄″ (8 cm);
e) tray 15³⁄₄ × 8″ (40 × 20.5 cm)
Marks: WIENER/WERK/STÄTTE, 900,
MADE/IN/AUSTRIA
Go 1797/1930 (acquired from the Wiener
Werkstätte)
WWF 116
Cf. nos. 129, 135

264 Centerpiece, 1908/9
Made by Wiener Werkstätte
Silver; height 5¹⁄₂″ (14 cm), diameter 6¹⁄₄″
(16 cm)
Marks: WW, rose mark, JH, hallmark
W.I. 782/1910 (acquired from the Wiener
Werkstätte)
WWMB 10, p. 1264
WWF 94, p. 94

265 Centerpiece, 1910
Made by Wiener Werkstätte (Adolf Wert-
nik)
Silver; height 7³⁄₄″ (19.5 cm), diameter 8″
(20.5 cm)
Marks: WW, rose mark, JH,
WIENER/WERK/STÄTTE, hallmark, AW
Go 2012/1967
K.I. 12038/8 (design)
WWMB 12, p. 1859
WWF 94, p. 116

266 Bonbonnière, 1912
Made by Wiener Werkstätte
Silver and carnelian; height 4³/₄″ (12 cm),
diameter 5¹/₄″ (13.5 cm)
Marks: WW, rose mark, JH, hallmark
W.I. 1125/1912 (acquired from the Wiener
Werkstätte)
WWMB 15, p. 2647
WWF 95, p. 147
Cf. nos. 153-55

267 Centerpiece, 1905
Made by Wiener Werkstätte (Josef Wagner)
Silver and agate; height 17″ (43 cm),
diameter 11³/₄″ (30 cm)
Marks: WW, rose mark, JH, hallmark, JW
Go 2011/1967
WWMB 8, p. 490
WWF 93, p. 17

268 Centerpiece, 1924/25
Made by Wiener Werkstätte
Brass; height 7¹/₄″ (18.5 cm)
Marks: WIENER/WERK/STÄTTE, JH,
MADE/IN/AUSTRIA
Go 1987/1964
WWKA Msh 17
WWF 114, p. 6
Cf. no. 157

269 Centerpiece, 1907
Made by Wiener Werkstätte (Josef Hossfeld)
Silver; height 4³/₄″ (12 cm), diameter 7″
(18 cm)
Marks: WW, rose mark, JH (twice),
hallmark
Go 1394/1908 (acquired at the *Kunstschau*,
Vienna, 1908)
WWMB 9, p. 921

270 Centerpiece, 1940/42
Made by Ludwig Kyral, Entwurfs- und
Versuchswerkstätte für das Kunsthand-
werk, Vienna
Brass; height 10³/₄″ (27 cm), diameter
10¹/₂″ (26.5 cm)
Me 892/1942 (acquired from the Ent-
wurfs- und Versuchswerkstätte)

271 Goblet, 1940/42
Made by Ludwig Kyral, Entwurfs- und
Versuchswerkstätte für das Kunsthand-
werk, Vienna
Brass; height 5″ (12.5 cm), greatest diame-
ter 4³/₄″ (12 cm)
Me 893/1942

272 Vase, 1940/42
Made by Ludwig Kyral, Entwurfs- und
Versuchswerkstätte für das Kunsthand-
werk, Vienna
Tombac; height 5¹/₂″ (14 cm), greatest
diameter 7¹/₄″ (18.5 cm)
Me 890/1942

273 Bottle cooler, 1919
Made by Wiener Werkstätte
Brass; heights 9³/₄″ (24.6 cm), greatest
diameter 13¹/₈″ (33.4 cm)
Marks: WIENER/WERKSTÄTTE, JH
Me 910 (inventoried in 1958)
WWMB 38, p. 3076

274 Tumbler, 1940/42
Made by Ludwig Kyral, Entwurfs- und
Versuchswerkstätte für das Kunsthand-
werk, Vienna
Brass; height 4¹/₂″ (11.5 cm), greatest
diameter 3³/₄″ (9.5 cm)
Me 891/1942, (acquired from the Ent-
wurfs- und Versuchswerkstätte)

275 Goblet, 1940/42
Made by Ludwig Kyral, Entwurfs- und
Versuchswerkstätte für das Kunsthand-
werk, Vienna
Brass; height 6″ (15.5 cm), greatest diame-
ter 4³/₄″ (10.2 cm)
Me 888/1942, (acquired from the Ent-
wurfs- und Versuchswerkstätte)

276 Vase, 1911
Made by Wiener Werkstätte (Alfred Mayer)
Silver and tin; height 6″ (15.5 cm), greatest
diameter 4³/₄″ (12 cm)
Marks: WW, rose mark, JH, hallmark, AM
W.I. 1114/1912 (acquired from the Wiener
Werkstätte)
WWMB 14, p. 2502

277 Vase, 1909
Made by Wiener Werkstätte
Silver; height 9¹/₂″ (24 cm)
Marks: rose mark, JH,
WIENER/WERK/STÄTTE, hallmark
WWMB 970/1911 (acquired from the
Wiener Werkstätte), p. 1542
WWF 94, p. 97
K.I. 11983/26 (drawing)

278 Vase, 1940/42
Made by Ludwig Kyral, Entwurfs- und
Versuchswerkstätte für das Kunsthand-
werk, Vienna

Tombac; height 12¹/₄″, greatest diameter
4¹/₄″ (31.3 × 11 cm)
Me 889/1942 (aquired from the Wiener
Werkstätte)

279 Jardinière, 1912
Made by Wiener Werkstätte
Brass; height 7¹/₄″ (18.5 cm)
Marks: rose mark, JH,
WIENER/WERK/STÄTTE
W.I. 1123/1912 (acquired from the Wiener
Werkstätte)
WWMB 35, p. 2044
Cf. no. 168

280 Candlestick, 1912
Made by Wiener Werkstätte
Brass; height 23¹/₄″ (58.9 cm)
Marks: WIENER WERKSTÄTTE, JH
W.I 1122/1912 (acquired from the Wiener
Werkstätte)
WWMB 35, p. 2067

281 Candlestick, 1912
Made by Wiener Werkstätte
Brass; height 12¹/₄″ (31 cm)
Marks: rose mark, JH,
WIENER/WERK/STÄTTE
W.I. 1124/1912 (acquired from the Wiener
Werkstätte)
WWMB 35, p. 2055

282 Vase, 1912
Made by Wiener Werkstätte (Josef Husnik)
Brass; height 5¹/₂″ (14 cm), greatest diame-
ter 7³/₄″ (20 cm)
Stamped: rose mark, JH (twice),
WIENER/WERK/STÄTTE
W.I. 1120/1912 (acquired from the Wiener
Werkstätte)
WWMB 35, p. 2108

283 Box, 1919
Made by Wiener Werkstätte
Silver; 7 × 10¹/₂ × 9³/₄″ (18 × 26.6 × 24.5 cm)
Marks: WW, rose mark, JH, 900,
WIENER/WERK/STÄTTE
Go 2079 (inventoried in 1987)
WWMB 20, p. 4492
WWF 96, p. 213

284 Bowl, date unknown
Made by Wiener Werkstätte
Brass; 4 × 15¹/₄″ (10 × 38.5 cm)
Stamped: WIENER/WERK/STÄTTE, JH
Me 866/1932 (acquired at the Wiener
Werkstätte liquidation auction)

285 Jardinière, 1907
Made by Wiener Werkstätte

(Josef Hossfeld)
Silver; height 5¼″ (13.5 cm), greatest
diameter 9″ (23 cm)
Marks: WW, rose mark, JH (twice), hall-
mark
Go 1395/1908 (acquired at the *Kunstschau*,
Vienna, 1908)
WWMB 9, p. 996

286 Bowl, 1918
Made by Wiener Werkstätte
Silver; height 2½″ (6.6 cm), greatest
diameter 9½″ (24 cm)
Marks: rose mark, WIENER WERKSTÄTTE,
JH, hallmark, A
Go 2042/1978
WWMB 19, p. 4026
WWF 96, p. 210

287 Vase with handle, 1905/6
Made by Wiener Werkstätte
Sheet iron, painted, and glass;
4¾ × 1½ × 1½″ (11.8 × 3.7 × 3.7 cm)
Ei 961/1983
WWMB 30, p. 508
WWF 132

288 Basket, 1906
Made by Wiener Werkstätte
Silver; 9¾ × 5″ (24.8 × 13 cm)
Marks: WW, hallmark, 900
Go 2056/1983
WWMB 8, p. 698
WWF 113, p. 33

289 Candelabrum, 1928
Made by Wiener Werkstätte
Silver; height 12½″ (31.5 cm)
Marks: WW, JH, WIENER/WERK/STÄTTE,
900, MADE/IN/AUSTRIA
Go 1796/1930 (acquired from the Wiener
Werkstätte)
WWKA S di 72
WWF 115
Cf. no. 178

290 Table lamp, 1925
Made by Wiener Werkstätte
Brass and silk; height 36¼″ (92 cm)
Marks: WIENER/WERK/STÄTTE, JH
Me 867/1932 (acquired at the Wiener
Werkstätte liquidation auction)
WWKA MLA 39
WWF 119, p. 16

291 Table lamp, 1904
Made by Wiener Werkstätte (Konrad

Schindel)
Brass, silvered, and silk; height 16½″
(42 cm), greatest diameter 10¼″ (26 cm)
Marks: WW, rose mark, JH, KS
Go 2003/1965
WWF 97, p. 22

292 Candelabrum, 1930
Made by Wiener Werkstätte
Nickel silver; height 4½″ (11.2 cm), grea-
test diameter 9¾″ (25 cm)
Marks: WIENER/WERK/STÄTTE, JH,
MADE IN AUSTRIA
Go 2018/1972
WWKA 61

293 Paper knife, 1908
Made by Wiener Werkstätte
Silver and rock crystal; length 10″
(25.7 cm)
Marks: WW, rose mark, JH, hallmark
Bi 1301/1908 (acquired at the *Kunstschau*,
Vienna, 1908)
WWMB 15, p. 2588

294 Box, 1930
Made by Wiener Werkstätte
Silver, partly gilded; 3½ × 3½″ (9 × 9 cm)
Marks: WIENER/WERK/STÄTTE, JH, hall-
mark, 900, MADE/IN/AUSTRIA
Go 1810/1932 (acquired at the Wiener
Werkstätte liquidation auction)
Cf. no. 205

295 Box, 1908
Made by Wiener Werkstätte (Alfred Mayer)
Silver; 3 × 4¾ × 4¾″ (7.5 × 12 × 12 cm)
Marks: WW, rose mark, JH, hallmark, AM
Go 1396/1908 (acquired at the *Kunstschau*,
Vienna, 1908)
WWMB 10, p. 1167

296 Casket, 1910
Made by Wiener Werkstätte (Adolf Erbrich)
Silver; 3 × 9¾ × 9¾″ (7.5 × 24.5 × 24.5
cm)
Marks: WW, rose mark, JH, hallmark, AE
W. I. 781/1910 (acquired from the Wiener
Werkstätte)
WWMB 10, p. 1208

297 Casket, 1928/29
Made by Wiener Werkstätte
Decoration designed by Felicie Rix
Brass, ebony, and enamel; 2 × 16½ × 16¼″
(4.8 × 16.4 × 16 cm)
Marks: WIENER/WERK/STÄTTE, JH,

MADE/IN/AUSTRIA
Em 492/1967
WWMB 74, No. 1672

298 Wall lamp, 1912
Made by Wiener Werkstätte
Bronze; height 18½″ (47 cm)
Marks: WIENER/WERK/STÄTTE
Br 1643/1968
For the Grabenkaffee, Vienna
WWMB 35, p. 2165
WWF 98, p. 72

299 Toiletry set, 1908
Made by Wiener Werkstätte
Silver, partly gilded; a) stopper, height 1½″
(3.5 cm), diameter 2½″ (6.4 cm), b) cap,
diameter 2½″ (6.4 cm), c) lid, 7 × 2½″ (18
× 6.5 cm), d) brush, 9¼″ (23.5 cm), e) box,
2½ × 8¾ × 2½″ (5.4 × 22 × 6.6 cm), f) mirror, length 9¾″ (24.8 cm), g) candlestick,
height 6½″ (16.4 cm)
Go 2004/1965
WWMB 10, p. 1175ff.
WWF 94, p. 85

300 Carnet de ball, 1909
Made by Wiener Werkstätte
Brass, gilded; 5½ × 4½″ (14 × 11.5 cm)
Marks: WIENER/WERK/STÄTTE
Presented to the ladies at the
Concordia Ball
Me 980/1989
WWMB 32, p. 1110

301 Bottle stoppers, ca. 1910
Made by Wiener Werkstätte
Nickel silver, silvered; height 1½″ (3.8 cm),
diameter 2″ (5 cm)
Marks: WW, rose mark, JH
Go 2071/1985

302 Trophy, 1930
Made by Wiener Werkstätte (Augustin
Grötzbach)
Silver, partly gilded; height 12½″ (32 cm),
diameter 3½″ (9 cm)
Marks: WW, JH, hallmark, 900, HK, GA,
K.R.
Go 1798/1930 (acquired from the Wiener
Werkstätte)
Cf. no. 238

303 Lidded cup, 1911
Made by Wiener Werkstätte (Adolf
Erbrich)
Silver and lapis lazuli; height 7″ (17.5 cm)

Marks: WW, rose mark, JH, hallmark, AE
W.I. 1126/1912 (acquired from the Wiener
Werkstätte)
WWMB 14, p. 2399
WWF 95, p. 149

304 Goblet, 1940/42
Made by Ludwig Kyral, Entwurfs- und
Versuchswerkstätte für das Kunsthand-
werk, Vienna
Brass; height 5″ (13 cm), diameter 4¹⁄₂″
(11.5 cm)
Me 899/1942 (acquired from the Ent-
wurfs- und Versuchswerkstätte)

305, 306, and **307** Necklace, 1916
Made by Wiener Werkstätte
Gold and ivory; length 50³⁄₄″ (129 cm),
width 1″ (2.5 cm)
Marks: WW, hallmark
Go 1833/1941
WWMB 69, p. 1887
WWF 92, p. 94

308 Ring, 1912
Made by Wiener Werkstätte
Gold and pearls; diameter ³⁄₄″ (2.2 cm)
Marks: WW, hallmark, A
W.I. 1116/1912 (acquired from the Wiener
Werkstätte)
WWMB 68, p. 1526
Cf. no. 216

309 Brooch, after 1910
Made by Wiener Werkstätte
Made by J. Souval or J. Lauterkranz for the
Wiener Werkstätte
Enamel on copper; diameter 1³⁄₄″ (4.3 cm)
Marks: WIENER/WERK/STÄTTE
Bi 1571/1986
WWMB 29, p. 177

310 Brooch, 1910
Made by Wiener Werkstätte
Enamel on copper; 1 × 1″ (2.5 × 2.5 cm)
Marks: WIENER/WERK/STÄTTE
Bi 1564 (inventoried in 1986)
WWMB 29, p. 75

311 Pendant, 1907
Made by Wiener Werkstätte
Silver and semi-precious stones; diameter
2″ (5 cm)
Marks: WW, hallmark
Bi 1471/1933
WWMB 65, p. 687
K.I. 12144/43 (design)

312 Pendant, 1912
Made by Wiener Werkstätte
Gold and opals; height 2¹⁄₂″ (6.5 cm), width
1¹⁄₂″ (4 cm)
Marks: WW, hallmark, A
W.I. 1113/1912 (acquired from the Wiener
Werkstätte)
WWMB 68, p. 1430
WWF 92, p. 66

313 Belt buckle, 1905
Made by Wiener Werkstätte (Karl Ponocny)
Silver, opal, malachite, and coral; 2¹⁄₄ × 1″
(5.8 × 2.5 cm)
Marks: WW, rose mark, JH, KP
Bi 1302/1908 (acquired at the *Kunstschau*,
Vienna, 1908)
WWMB 3, p. 1044
WWF 91, p. 27

Textiles, Leather Objects, and Fashion Accessories

314 Block print of "Serpentin" fabric
design, 1910/15
Black and violet on coarse-grained white
paper; 5¹³⁄₁₆ × 4¹⁄₂″ (14.8 × 11.5 cm)
Inscribed (verso): Prof. Hoffmann
K.I. 11895/1

315 "Serpentin" fabric design, 1910/15
Pencil on imitation parchment; 5 × 11¹⁄₈″
(12.7 × 28.3 cm)
Wiener Werkstätte copyright stamp (lower
center): Entwurf: Prof. Hoffmann
K.I. 11895/2

316 Fabric design, 1905/10
Pencil and yellow, brown, and black water-
color on graph paper; 7¹⁵⁄₁₆ × 13¹⁄₄″
(20.2 × 33.6 cm)
Monogrammed (center left): JH
Wiener Werkstätte copyright stamp
(lower left)
WWE 34/6

317 Six fabric designs, 1901/5
Pencil, watercolor, and green crayon on
graph paper; 13³⁄₈ × 8¹⁄₄″ (33.9 × 20.9 cm)
Monogrammed (upper left and center): JH,
dated (upper left, upper right, left center,
right center, lower left, lower right): 1905
1902/1905 1901/1902/1903
K.I. 8820

318 "Carus" fabric design, 1929
Pencil and red crayon on white paper;
9¹⁄₁₆ × 11³⁄₄″ (23 × 29.9 cm)
K.I. 11870/1

319 Fabric design, 1931
Pencil on graph paper, 13³⁄₁₆ × 8¹⁄₈″
(33.5 × 20.6 cm)
Monogrammed (lower right): JH
Dated (inventory stamp): 12.X.31
K.I. 11903/8

320 Fabric design, 1931
Pencil and gray-green watercolor on graph
paper; 13¹⁄₁₆ × 8¹⁄₈″ (33.2 × 20.6 cm)
Monogrammed (lower right): JH
Dated (inventory stamp): 12.X.31
WWE 34/21

321 "Carus" fabric design, 1929
Pencil and yellow and blue body color on
cardboard; 11⁷⁄₈ × 7¹⁵⁄₁₆″ (30.2 × 20.2 cm)
Wiener Werkstätte copyright stamp
(verso): Hoffmann
K.I. 11870/2

322 "Csikos" fabric design, 1930
Pencil and green, red, and black watercolor
on graph paper; 8¹⁄₈ × 13¹⁄₄″
(20.7 × 33.6 cm)
Monogrammed and dated (lower right):
JH 30
Wiener Werkstätte copyright stamp
(lower right)
K.I. 11872/1

323 "Csikos" fabric design, 1930
Pencil and green and red crayon on
parchment, 7¹⁵⁄₁₆ × 9³⁄₁₆″ (20.1 × 23.4 cm)
Wiener Werkstätte copyright stamp
(verso): ENTW: PROF. HOFFMANN
K.I. 11872/3

324 Block print and "Kiebitz" fabric
sample, 1910/15
Block print on paper/silk; a) print
16¹⁵⁄₁₆ × 11³⁄₁₆″ (43 × 28.5 cm), b) fabric
4³⁄₁₆ × 5¹¹⁄₁₆″ (10.5 × 14.5 cm)
K.I. 11883/1,3

325 "Jordan" fabric design, ca. 1928
Pencil and yellow, red, green, and violet
watercolor on graph paper; 16³⁄₈ × 13⁵⁄₁₆″
(41.6 × 33.8 cm)
Monogrammed (lower right): JH
Dated (inventory stamp): 3.VII.28

K.I. 11881/1
Damaged

326 "Reifen" fabric design, 1928
Pencil, watercolor on graph paper;
$11^{1}/_{4} \times 16^{5}/_{16}''$ (28.6 × 41.4 cm)
Monogrammed (verso): JH
Inscribed (verso): Dessin "Reifen" Arch.
15370, Entwurf: Prof. Hoffmann
K.I. 11892/1

327 "Athos" fabric design, 1928
Pencil, watercolor on graph paper,
$13^{3}/_{8} \times 8^{1}/_{4}''$ (34 × 21 cm)
Signed and dated (lower right): Josef Hoff-
mann 3. 7. 1928
K.I. 11866/1

328 Fabric design, ca. 1928
Pencil, India ink, and yellow, red, black,
and gray body color on white cardboard;
$14^{1}/_{2} \times 10^{3}/_{8}''$ (36.8 × 26.4 cm)
K.I. 11909/3

329 "Pallas" fabric design, 1928
Pencil on graph paper; $8^{1}/_{16} \times 12^{5}/_{8}''$
(20.5 × 32.1 cm)
Monogrammed (lower left): JH
K.I. 11889/1-4

330 Fabric design, ca. 1930
Pencil and water color on graph paper
mounted on white paper; $13^{5}/_{16} \times 16^{7}/_{16}''$
(33.8 × 41.7 cm)
Signed (lower right): Josef Hoffmann
K.I. 11902/4

331 Fabric design, 1925/30
Pencil and India ink on graph paper;
$15^{11}/_{16} \times 8^{5}/_{8}''$ (39.9 × 21.9 cm)
Signed (lower right): Josef Hoffmann
K.I. 8822/1

332 Fabric design, date unknown
Pencil and India ink on imitation
parchment; $9^{3}/_{16} \times 7^{5}/_{8}''$ (23.4 × 19.3 cm)
K.I. 12166/13

333 Fabric design, date unknown
Pencil and black ink on imitation
parchment; $9^{5}/_{8} \times 8^{1}/_{16}''$ (24.5 × 20.5 cm)
K.I. 12166/18

334 "Elis" fabric design, 1925/30
Pencil and black ink on cardboard;

$9^{5}/_{8} \times 8^{1}/_{4}''$ (24.5 × 20.9 cm)
Wiener Werkstätte copyright stamp
(lower right): Entwurf: Prof. Hoffmann
K.I. 11874/1

335 "Elis" fabric design, 1925/30
Pencil and black ink on cardboard;
$6^{3}/_{8} \times 5^{5}/_{8}''$ (16.2 × 14.2 cm)
K.I. 11874/2

336 Linien basket, 1927
Pencil on graph paper; $7^{3}/_{4} \times 13^{1}/_{8}''$
(19.7 × 33.4 cm)
Monogrammed (lower right): JH
K.I. 12030/4
WWMB 51, L 4251 (model no. L 4251)

337 Fabric design, 1925/30
Pencil and brown body color on cardboard;
$15^{1}/_{2} \times 11^{5}/_{16}''$ (39.4 × 28.7 cm)
K.I. 11905/3

338 Leather handbag, 1925/29
Pencil and yellow crayon on graph paper;
$7^{3}/_{4} \times 13^{3}/_{16}''$ (19.7 × 33.5 cm)
Monogrammed (lower right): JH
Dated (inventory stamp): 7. 1. 29
K.I. 12098/21 (model no. L 4259)

339 Embroidered handbag, 1931
Pencil on graph paper; $10^{15}/_{16} \times 8^{1}/_{4}''$
(27.8 × 21.1 cm)
Monogrammed (lower right): JH
Dated (inventory stamp): 12.X.31
K.I. 12098/40

340 Embroidered handbag, 1931
Pencil on graph paper; $13^{3}/_{16} \times 8^{3}/_{16}''$
(33.4 × 20.7 cm)
Monogrammed (lower right): JH
Dated (inventory stamp): 12.X.31
K.I. 12098/41

341 Handbag clasp, 1920/23
Pencil on graph paper; $8^{1}/_{4} \times 11''$
(21 × 28.1 cm)
Monogrammed and dated (lower left):
JH 15/III/20
Executed (date unknown)
K.I. 12098/31
WWMB 51, p. 4020 (model no. L 4020)

342 Knobs for walking sticks and
umbrellas, ca. 1920
Pencil on graph paper; $8^{3}/_{8} \times 13^{3}/_{8}''$
(21.2 × 34 cm)

Monogrammed and dated (lower right):
JH12/12 21
WWE 39 (model no. S 5362, not confirmed
by Wiener Werkstätte records)

343 Leather handbag, ca. 1925 (?)
Pencil on graph paper, $8 \times 12^{7}/_{8}''$
(20.4 × 32.6 cm)
Monogrammed (lower right): JH
K.I. 12098/10

344 Umbrella knobs, ca. 1925
Pencil and red crayon on graph paper;
$8^{1}/_{8} \times 13^{3}/_{16}''$ (20.7 × 33.5 cm)
Monogrammed (lower right): JH
Executed (date unknown)
Model no. L 4120/21, not confirmed by
Wiener Werkstätte records
K.I. 12097/19

345 Walking stick handle, ca. 1910
Pencil and yellow body color on graph
paper; $8^{1}/_{4} \times 6^{5}/_{8}''$ (20.9 × 16.8 cm)
Monogrammed (lower right): JH (?)
Wiener Werkstätte stamp (lower right)
Model no. M 147, not confirmed by Wie-
ner Werkstätte records
K.I. 12097/25

346 Umbrella knobs, ca. 1925
Pencil and carmine and vermilion crayon
on graph paper; $8^{9}/_{16} \times 14''$ (21 × 34.2 cm)
Monogrammed (lower right): JH
K.I. no. 12097/22

347 Walking stick handle, ca. 1910 (?)
Pencil on graph paper; $8^{3}/_{16} \times 6^{5}/_{8}''$
(20.8 × 16.8 cm)
Monogrammed (center): JH
Wiener Werkstätte stamp (lower center)
K.I. no. 12097/26
Model no. M 146, not confirmed by
Wiener Werkstätte records

348 Leather casket, 1904
Pencil, India ink, and green and brown
crayon on graph paper; $8^{9}/_{16} \times 13^{13}/_{16}''$
(12 × 33.8 cm)
Monogrammed and dated (lower right):
JH 1904
Pencil sketches on verso
K.I. no. 12046/24
Model no. BL 34

349 Leather casket, 1905/10
Pencil on graph paper; $8^{1}/_{2} \times 13^{3}/_{16}''$

(21.5 × 33.5 cm)
Monogrammed (lower right): JH
K.I. no. 12046/17

350 Leather casket, 1905
Pencil on graph paper; 8 × 12¾″
(20.4 × 32.4 cm)
Monogrammed (lower right): JH, stamped
(upper left): JH, dated (upper center):
4/XII 05
Executed 1905
K.I. no. 12046/20
WWMB 42, p. 318 (model no. BL 318)

351 Book cover for Gerhart Hauptmann's *Hanneles Himmelfahrt,*
date unknown
Pencil and black and red oil pastel on
graph paper; 17³⁄₁₆ × 13⁷⁄₁₆″
(41.9 × 34.1 cm)
Monogrammed (lower right): JH
K.I. no. 12163/49

Fabric samples from the Wiener Werkstätte archives.
None of the printed fabrics listed below
were made by the Wiener Werkstätte.

352 "Adler," 1910/12
Block print; 2 × 1″ (5 × 2.5 cm)
Ten cotton samples
Silk pattern book: T 10621, pp. 53, 54
Linen pattern book I: T 11379 a
WWBW 1

353 "Herzblatt," 1910/15
Block print; 3³⁄₁₆ × 1⁷⁄₈″ (8 × 4.7 cm)
Four silk samples, one cotton
Silk pattern book: T 10621, pp. 69, 70
Linen pattern book I: T 11379 a
WWS 319; WWBW 80

354 Fabric sample, 1909
Made by Johann Backhausen & Söhne,
Vienna, design no. 7208
Printed linen, black and white;
29½ × 118¹⁄₈″ (75 × 300 cm)
W.I. 827/1910

355 "Ozon," 1923
Block print; 3⁹⁄₁₆ × 2¾″ (9 × 7 cm)
32 silk samples
WWS 557 A

356 "Cypern," 1910/15
Block print; 4½ × 4¾″ (11.3 × 12.1 cm)

42 silk, 4 cotton and 6 voile samples
WWS 143 a; WWBW 37; WWV 31

357 "Luchs," 1910/12
Block print; 3³⁄₈ × 6⁵⁄₁₆″ (8.5 × 16 cm)
One silk sample
Silk pattern book: T 10621, p. 80
Linen pattern book II: T 11379 b
WWS 453

358 "Wasserfall," 1910/12
Block print; 4 × 2³⁄₈″ (10 × 6 cm)
Two silk samples
Silk pattern book: T 10621, p. 84
WWS 846

359 "Miramar," 1910/15
Block print; 2½ × 1³⁄₁₆″ (6.4 × 4.5 cm)
25 silk, 4 cotton samples
WW 420

360 "Martha," 1910/15
Block print; 1⁹⁄₁₆ × ⁷⁄₈″ (4 × 2 cm)
Four silk samples
WWS 463

361 "Jordan," 1928
Block print; 13³⁄₁₆ × 8¹¹⁄₁₆″ (33.5 × 22 cm)
18 cotton samples, one voile
Bolt: T 8598/1932
WWBW 101; WWV 87

362 "Erlenzeisig," 1910/11
Block print; 2³⁄₈ × 1¾″ (flower repeat)
(6 × 4.5 cm)
One silk sample
Silk pattern book: T 10621, pp. 25, 26
WWS 199

363 "Kiebitz," 1910/15
Block print; 5 × 2¼″ (12.7 × 5.7 cm)
Three cotton samples
Silk pattern book: T 10621, p. 46
Linen pattern book II: T 11379 b
Pattern portfolio: T 11502
WWBW 109

364 "Lerche," 1910/11
Block print; ¹³⁄₁₆ × ¾″ (2.1 × 1.5 cm)
Ten silk samples
Silk pattern book: T 10621, p. 102
W.I. 1117
WWS 422 a

365 "Oder," 1928
Block print; 12 × 4″ (30.5 × 10.2 cm)

13 silk samples
Pattern portfolio: T 11502
WWS 537

366 "Ibera," 1928
Block print; 4 × 4″ (10.2 × 10.2 cm)
26 silk samples
WWS 323

367 Fabric sample, 1909/10
Made by Johann Backhausen & Söhne
(pattern no. 5113), Vienna, for the Wiener
Werkstätte
Wool and cotton in black, beige, and green;
48 × 126″ (122 × 320 cm)
T 10511/1966

368 "Montezuma," 1910/12
Block print; 9 × 4¹⁄₁₆″ (23 × 10.3 cm)
Ten silk, five cotton samples
Silk pattern book: T 10621, p. 39
Linen pattern book II: T 11379 b
WWS 488; WWBW 145

369 "Refrain," 1929
Block print; 4¹⁄₈ × 4³⁄₈″ (10.5 × 11 cm)
20 silk samples
WWS 620

370 "Tulpe," 1910/15
Block print; 1³⁄₁₆ × ¾″ (3 × 2 cm)
Three silk samples
WWS 791

371 "Mira," 1929
Block print; 6⁷⁄₈ × 6⁵⁄₁₆″ (17.5 × 16 cm)
Two cotton samples
WWBW 131

372 "Gotemba," 1925
Block print; 6⁵⁄₁₆ × 2³⁄₈″ (16.5 × 6 cm)
17 silk samples
Pattern portfolio: T 11502
WWS 280

373 "Triangel," 1910/13
Block print; 3¹⁄₈ × 3¾″ (8 × 9.5 cm)
Seven silk samples
Silk pattern book: T 10621, pp. 28, 29
Linen pattern book II: T 11379 b
WWS 772

374 Fabric sample, 1909/10
Made by Johann Backhausen & Söhne,
Vienna
Silk and cotton in gold and black;
50³⁄₈ × 59″ (128 × 150 cm)
W.I. 830/1910

375 "Schwarzblatt," 1910/12
Block print; 4¹⁄₈ × 4¹⁄₂″ (10.5 × 11.5 cm)
Four silk samples
Silk pattern book: T 10621, p. 83
WWS 722

376 "Kohleule," 1910/15
Block print; 6⁵⁄₁₆ × 3¹⁵⁄₁₆″ (16 × 10 cm)
One silk sample in red, salmon, and yellow
Silk pattern book: T 10621, p. 19
Linen pattern book II: T 11379 b
Design: K.I. 11884

377 "Biene," 1910/11
Block print; 4¹⁄₂ × 2″ (11.5 × 5 cm)
One cotton sample with black background
Silk pattern book: T 10621, p. 24
Linen pattern book I: 11379 a

378 "Nil," 1910/17
Block print; 9¹⁄₄ × 3¹⁵⁄₁₆″ (23.5 × 10 cm)
Seven silk samples
Design: K.I. 11887

379 "Hirschenzunge," 1910/12
Block print; 4³⁄₄ × 3¹⁄₈″ (12 × 8 cm)
Two silk samples
Silk pattern book: T 10621, pp. 91, 92

380 "Guido," 1929
Block print; 12 × 12″ (30.5 × 30.5 cm)
Dated (verso): 25.4.1929
Twelve silk samples
Design: K.I. 11878/1–3

381 Book cover, 1907
Made by the Wiener Werkstätte (Carl Beitel and Ludwig Willner)
Yellow kid leather with hand-gilt ornamentation; 7¹⁄₈ × 4³⁄₄″ (18.1 × 12.2 cm)
Monogrammed (rear endpaper): JH, Wiener Werkstätte, CB, LW
For *La Figlia di lorio* by Gabriele d'Annunzio, Milan, 1904
B.I. 20311

382 Book cover, 1910/14
Made by the Wiener Werkstätte (Carl Beitel and Ludwig Willner)
Dark blue kid leather with hand-gilt ornamentation; 7¹⁄₈ × 6³⁄₈″ (24.2 × 16.2 cm)
Monogrammed (back cover): JH, Wiener Werkstätte, CB, LW
For *The Gold Bug* by Edgar Allan Poe, Munich and Leipzig, 1910
B.I. 21176

383 Book cover, 1911
Printed by Brüder Rosenbaum, Vienna
Cloth with gold ornamentation; 6¹⁄₂ × 5³⁄₈″

(16.4 × 13.7 cm)
For the Wiener Werkstätte almanac, Vienna and Leipzig, 1911
B.I. 21895/1938

384 Book cover, ca. 1915
Made by the Wiener Werkstätte (Ludwig Willner)
Colored Morocco leather applied with still life and line ornament;
5¹⁄₂ × 3³⁄₈″ (13.9 × 8.5 cm)
Mark (on spine): MB
Monogrammed (on verso of front endpaper): JH, Wiener Werkstätte, LW
For *Der Bräutigam* by Max Brod, Berlin, no date
B.I. 21192

385 "Ragusa," 1910/12
Block print; 1³⁄₄ × 1⁹⁄₁₆″ (4.5 × 4 cm)
One cotton sample
Silk pattern book: T 10621, p. 34, 161
WWBW195

386 "Bremen," 1928
Block print; 6⁵⁄₁₆ × 12″ (16 × 30.5 cm)
Eleven silk samples
Pattern portfolio: T 11502
WWS 99a

387 "Tenor," 1928
Roller print; 6¹⁄₈ × 5³⁄₁₆″ (15.5 × 13.2 cm)
100 silk samples
WWS 762

388 Calling card etui, 1925/29
Kid leather with gold embossment;
3¹⁄₈ × 5¹⁄₈″ (7.9 × 13.1 cm)
Mark: WIENER/WERK/STÄTTE*
Le 545c/1932 (acquired at the Wiener Werkstätte liquidation auction)
WWMB 47, p. 1760

389 Calling card etui, 1925/29
Kid leather with gold embossment;
3¹⁄₈ × 5¹⁄₈″ (8 × 13 cm)
Mark: WIENER/WERK/STÄTTE*
Le 545b/1932 (acquired at the Wiener Werkstätte liquidation auction)

390 Wallet, ca. 1920
Kid leather with gold embossment;
5¹⁄₂ × 6³⁄₄″ (14 × 17 cm)
Mark: WIENER/WERK/STÄTTE*
Le 540b/1932 (acquired at the Wiener Werkstätte liquidation auction)

391 Handbag, 1930
Kid leather with gold embossment;
4¹⁄₂ × 7¹⁄₄″ (11.5 × 18.3 cm)

Mark: WIENER/WERK/STÄTTE*
Le 598/1972

392 Handbag, ca. 1909/10
Kid leather with gold embossment;
4³⁄₈ × 7⁷⁄₈″ (11 × 20 cm)
Mark: WIENER/WERK/STÄTTE
WWF100, p. 66 (acquired from the Wiener Werkstätte)
W.I. 975/1911

393 Calling card etui, 1929/31
Kid leather with gold embossment;
3¹⁄₈ × 5¹⁄₈″ (8 × 13 cm)
Mark: WIENER/WERK/STÄTTE*
Le 544a/1932 (acquired at the Wiener Werkstätte liquidation auction)

394 Writing case, 1927/29
Kid leather with gold embossment;
11⁷⁄₈ × 9¹⁄₄″ (30 × 23.5 cm)
Mark: WIENER/WERK/STÄTTE
Le 541a/1932 (aquired at the Wiener Werkstätte liquidation auction)

Glass and Ceramics

395 Vase, 1928
Pencil on red paper mounted on graph paper; 13¹³⁄₁₆ × 8³⁄₈″ (35.1 × 21.2 cm)
Signed (lower right): Josef Hoffmann, dated: 11.4.28
K.I. 11971/9

396 Vase, ca. 1928
Pencil on pink paper mounted on graph paper; 13¹⁄₈ × 7¹³⁄₁₆″ (33.4 × 19.8 cm)
Monogrammed (lower right): JH
Dated (inventory stamp): 9.V.1928
K.. 8848/3

397 Glass goblet, ca. 1928
Pencil on green paper mounted on graph paper; 13¹³⁄₁₆ × 8¹⁄₄″ (35.1 × 21 cm)
Monogrammed (upper right, lower right): JH
K.I. 11971/8

398 Lidded glass goblet, ca. 1928
Pencil on yellow paper mounted on graph paper; 13¹⁄₈ × 7³⁄₄″ (33.4 × 19.7 cm)
Monogrammed (center right): JH
Dated (inventory stamp): 9.V.1928
K.I.12039/5

399 Lidded glass goblet, ca. 1928
Pencil and green, yellow, and black crayon
on green paper mounted on graph paper;
$13\frac{1}{8} \times 7\frac{11}{16}$" (33.4 × 19.6 cm)
Monogrammed (lower right): JH
Dated (inventory stamp): 9.V.1928
K.I. 12039/4

400 Three glasses, 1920/24 (?)
Pencil on graph paper; $11\frac{15}{16} \times 17\frac{15}{16}$"
(30.3 × 45.4 cm)
Monogrammed (lower right): JH
K.I. 11958/1
Cf. no. 401

401 Three glasses, 1920/24 (?)
Production drawing
Pencil and green and blue body color on
imitation parchment; $9\frac{5}{8} \times 13\frac{3}{4}$"
(24.5 × 35 cm)
Wiener Werkstätte stamp (lower right)
Monogrammed and dated by Philipp
Häusler (lower left): PH 26.IV.24
K.I. 11958/2
Cf. no. 400

402 Three glasses, 1915
Pencil and blue ink on graph paper;
$8\frac{3}{16} \times 13\frac{3}{16}$" (20.8 × 33.5 cm)
Monogrammed (center): JH
Executed (date unknown)
Model nos. I/617-19
K.I. 11962/8

403 Two glasses, date unknown
Pencil on graph paper; $11\frac{1}{4} \times 8\frac{7}{8}$"
(28.5 × 22.6 cm)
Two further designs on verso
K.I. 11957/7

404 Glass, date unkown
Pencil on graph paper; $12\frac{1}{8} \times 9\frac{3}{16}$"
(30.8 × 23.3 cm)
Monogrammed (lower right): JH
K.I. 11957/11

405 Teacup, date unknown
Pencil and black and red body color on
graph paper; $8\frac{1}{16} \times 13\frac{1}{16}$" (20.5 × 33.2 cm)
Monogrammed (right center): JH
K.I. 11993/7

406 Glass, date unknown
Pencil on graph paper; $13\frac{1}{4} \times 8\frac{3}{8}$"
(33.6 × 21.3 cm)
Monogrammed (left center): JH
K.I. 11957/9

407 Two glasses, date unknown
Pencil on graph paper; $13\frac{3}{8} \times 8\frac{3}{8}$"

(33.9 × 21.2 cm)
Monogrammed (lower left): JH
Inscribed (lower right): GLÄSER DIV.
Pencil sketch on verso
K.I. 11957/8

408 Jardinière, ca. 1927
Pencil on graph paper; $9\frac{1}{8} \times 5\frac{11}{16}$"
(23.2 × 14.5 cm)
Monogrammed (lower right): JH
Inscribed (lower center): Keramik
Executed (date unknown)
Model no. KE tp 90
K.I. 12135/11

409, 410 Jar, ca. 1914
Pencil on graph paper; $7\frac{15}{16} \times 13\frac{3}{16}$"
(20.1 × 33.5 cm)
and $8 \times 5\frac{7}{8}$" (20.5 × 14.9 cm)
Monogrammed (409, right center): JH
Executed (date unknown), cf. Gl. 3112
K.I. 12039/25
Cf. no. 436

411 Jam jar, ca. 1915
Pencil on graph paper; $8\frac{1}{8} \times 7\frac{3}{8}$"
(20.7 × 18.8 cm)
Monogrammed (lower right): JH
Executed (date unknown)
K.I. 11941/2
Cf. no. 436

412 Four glasses, 1928
Pencil and crayon on graph paper;
$7\frac{13}{16} \times 13\frac{3}{16}$" (19.8 × 33.5 cm)
Signed (lower left): Josef Hoffmann,
dated: 9.5.1928
K.I. 11954/8

413 Bottle, pitcher, and glass, 1928
Pencil and crayon on graph paper;
$7\frac{13}{16} \times 13\frac{3}{16}$" (19.8 × 33.5 cm)
Signed (lower right): Josef Hoffmann,
dated: 9.5.1928
K.I. 11954/4

414 Water jug, ca. 1928
Pencil on graph paper; $13\frac{1}{16} \times 7\frac{13}{16}$"
(33.2 × 19.9 cm)
Monogrammed (lower right): JH
K.I. 12021/6

415 Punch bowl, ca. 1920
Pencil on graph paper; $8\frac{1}{16} \times 13\frac{1}{4}$"
(20.5 × 33.7 cm)
Monogrammed (lower right): JH
Wiener Werkstätte copyright stamp (verso)
K.I. 12022/2

416 Coffeepot, ca. 1925/28
Pencil and black crayon on graph paper

mounted on graph paper; $11\frac{7}{16} \times 7\frac{3}{8}$"
(29 × 18.7 cm) (design sheet), $13\frac{3}{8} \times 8\frac{1}{4}$"
(33.9 × 21 cm) (whole)
Monogrammed (lower right): JH
K.I. 8836

417 Coffeepot and cup, 1928
Pencil and red, yellow, blue, black, and
green watercolor on graph paper;
$16\frac{1}{2} \times 13\frac{3}{8}$" (42 × 34 cm)
Folded sheet, pencil design on 2nd sheet
Monogrammed and dated: JH 1928
K.I. 8844/1, 2

418 Coffeepot, 1928
Pencil and red and black watercolor on
graph paper mounted on graph paper;
$11\frac{1}{8} \times 7\frac{9}{16}$" (28.2 × 19.2 cm) (design
sheet), $13\frac{5}{16} \times 8\frac{5}{16}$" (33.8 × 21.1 cm)
(whole)
Monogrammed (lower right): JH
K.I. 8835

419 Glass, before 1914 (designed 1910)
Made by a Bohemian glass factory for
J. & L. Lobmeyr, Vienna
Cut glass; height $8\frac{5}{16}$" (21.1 cm)
W.I. 1630/2/1915 (acquired from
J. & L. Lobmeyr)
WWMB 61, p. 455

420 Glass, before 1914 (designed 1910)
Made by a Bohemian glass factory for
J. & L. Lobmeyr, Vienna
Cut glass; height $8\frac{1}{8}$" (20.7 cm)
W.I. 1267/1914 (acquired from
J. & L. Lobmeyr)
WWMB 61, p. 456

421 Glass, before 1914 (designed 1910)
Made by a Bohemian glass factory for
J. & L. Lobmeyr, Vienna
Cut glass; height $8\frac{1}{4}$" (20.9 cm)
W.I. 1630/5/1915 (acquired from
J. & L. Lobmeyr)
WWMB 61, p. 454

422 Glass, before 1914 (designed 1910)
Made by a Bohemian glass factory for
J. & L. Lobmeyr, Vienna
Cut glass; height $7\frac{1}{2}$" (19.3 cm)
W.I. 1630/1/1915 (acquired from
J. & L. Lobmeyr)
WWMB 61, p. 457

423 Vase (designed before 1923)
Made by a Bohemian glass factory for the
Wiener Werkstätte, 1923-28
Height $9\frac{5}{16}$" (23.6 cm)
Gl. 3570/1986 (bequest in memory of

Dr. Richard Ernst)
Design: K.I. 11966/17

424 Vase (designed before 1923)
Decoration designed by Julius Zimpel
Made by a Bohemian glass factory for the
Wiener Werkstätte, 1923-25
Engraved glass; height 9³/₁₆″ (23.4 cm)
Gl. 2649/1932 (acquired at the Wiener
Werkstätte liquidation auction)
Design: K.I. 11966/17 (identical form,
no decoration)

425 Tumbler, ca. 1910
Made by a Bohemian glass factory for
J. & L. Lobmeyr, Vienna
Frosted glass with broncit decoration;
height 3¹⁵/₁₆″ (10 cm)
W.I. 1162/1912 (acquired from
J. & L. Lobmeyr)

426 Tumbler, ca. 1910
Made by a Bohemian glass factory for
J. & L. Lobmeyr, Vienna
Frosted glass with broncit decoration;
heights a) 4″ (10.2 cm) b) 4¹/₈″ (10.4 cm)
Labels: a) Decor D, b) No 48 M
W.I. 1031, 1161/1912 (acquired from
J. & L. Lobmeyr)

427 Wine glass (designed ca. 1911)
Made by a Bohemian glass factory for
J. & L. Lobmeyr, Vienna
Frosted glass with broncit decoration;
height 4¹⁵/₁₆″ (12.5 cm)
Label: No 46 M
W.I. 1163/1912 (acquired from
J. & L. Lobmeyr)
WWMB 61, p. 472

428 Wine glass
(designed ca. 1911)
Made by a Bohemian glass factory for
J. & L. Lobmeyr, Vienna
Frosted glass with broncit decoration;
height 4⁵/₈″ (11.8 cm)
Labels: No 43 No 43 (round firm label)
W.I. 1675/1916 (acquired from
J. & L. Lobmeyr)

429 Liqueur glass, ca. 1911
Made by a Bohemian glass factory for
J. & L. Lobmeyr, Vienna
Frosted glass with broncit decoration;
height 2¹/₁₆″ (5.3 cm)
Gl. 3415/1983
WWMB 61, p. 473

430 Two liqueur glasses, ca. 1911
Made by a Bohemian glass factory for
J. & L. Lobmeyr, Vienna

Frosted glass with broncit decoration;
height 2¹⁵/₁₆″ (7.4 cm) (each)
Gl. 3409/1982, 3416/1982
WWMB 61, pp. 469, 465

431 Champagne glass, ca. 1911
Made by a Bohemian glass factory for
J. & L. Lobmeyr, Vienna
Frosted glass with broncit decoration;
height 4⁵/₈″ (11.8 cm)
W.I. 1633/5/1915 (acquired from
J. & L. Lobmeyr)
WWMB 61, pp. 474, 475 (identical
decoration, different forms)

432 Two liqueur glasses, 1917/25
Made by various Bohemian glass factories
for the Wiener Werkstätte
a) Glass with enameled decoration,
b) glass; height 5″ (12.7 cm) (each)
From a set of 11 liqueur glasses,
5 decorated, 6 undecorated
Gl. 3280/1967
Design: K.I. 11963/6

433 Jardinière, before 1914
Made by a Bohemian glass factory for
J. & L. Lobmeyr, Vienna
Cut glass; height of jardinière 4¹/₈″
(10.5 cm), base 4⁷/₈ × 7¹/₈″ (12.4 × 18.1 cm)
W.I. 1626/3-4/1915 (acquired from
J. & L. Lobmeyr)

434 Jardinière, before 1914
Made by a Boemian glass factory for
J. & L. Lobmeyr, Vienna
Cut glass; height of jardinière 4¹/₈″
(10.5 cm),
base 7¹/₂ × 11⁷/₈″ (19.1 × 30.2 cm)
W.I. 1626/1-2/1915 (acquired from
J. & L. Lobmeyr)

435 Bowl, from 1915
Made by various Bohemian glass factories
for the Wiener Werkstätte
Cut violet glass; height 4¹³/₁₆″ (12.2 cm)
Gl. 3111 (inventoried 1952)
WWMB 61, p. 516
Design: K.I. 12035/13

436 Jar, after 1918 (designed 1915)
Made by Moser glass factory, Karlovy Vary
(Karlsbad), Bohemia
Cut violet glass; height 5¹/₈″ (13 cm)
Marks: WW, MOSER KARLSBAD
CZECHOSLOVAKIA
Gl. 3439/1984
Cf. no. 411

437 Bottle, after 1915
Made by various Bohemian glass factories

for the Wiener Werkstätte
Cut dark green glass; height 7³/₈″ (18.7 cm)
Mark: WW (stained)
Design: K.I. 12063/7
WWMB 61, p. 528

438 Bonbonnière, before 1914
Made by a Bohemian glass factory for
J. & L. Lobmeyr, Vienna
Cut glass; height 4¹³/₁₆″ (12.2 cm)
W.I. 1631/2/1915 (acquired from
J. & L. Lobmeyr)

439 Punch glass, before 1914
Made by a Bohemian glass factory for
J. & L. Lobmeyr, Vienna
Cut glass; height 5¹/₈″ (13 cm)
W.I. 1631/1/1915 (acquired from
J. & L. Lobmeyr)

440 Punch bowl, before 1914
Made by a Bohemian glass factory for
J. & L. Lobmeyr, Vienna
Cut glass; height 13⁷/₁₆″ (34.1 cm)
W.I. 1631/3/1915 (acquired from
J. & L. Lobmeyr)

441 Vase, before 1914 (designed 1910)
Made by a Bohemian glass factory for
J.& L. Lobmeyr, Vienna
Cut glass; height 7¹/₈″ (18.1 cm)
W.I. 1630/4/1915 (acquired from
J. & L. Lobmeyr)
WWMB 61, p. 452

442 Two glasses and a decanter from a
set (designed ca. 1920)
Made by a Bohemian glass factory for
J. & L. Lobmeyr, Vienna
Muslin glass; heights a) glass 5⁵/₁₆″
(13.5 cm), b) glass 7¹/₈″ (18.3 cm),
c) decanter 13³/₈″ (34 cm)
Gl. 2989-91/1949 (acquired from
J. & L. Lobmeyr)

443 Toiletry set, ca. 1913
Made by a Bohemian glass factory for
J. & L. Lobmeyr, Vienna
Frosted glass with broncit decoration
Firm labels: 27. (c), 25 (d)
W.I. 1632/1-4/1915 (acquired from
J. & L. Lobmeyr)
WWMB 61, pp. 476 (a), 477 (b)

444 Requisites for Holy Mass,
before 1915
Made by Carl Schappel, Haida, Austria
Engraved glass; a) basin, 8⁷/₈ × 5¹/₈″
(22.5 × 13 cm), b) and c) cruets,

height 4³/₄″ (12.1 cm) (each)
W. I. 1719/1915 (acquired from Schappel)

445 Vase, ca. 1913
Made by Bohemian glass factory for
J. & L. Lobmeyr, Vienna
Frosted glass with broncit decoration;
height 5⁹/₁₆″ (14.1 cm)
Gl. 3404/1982 (bequest)
WWMB 61, pp. 476, 477 (identical
decoration, different forms)

446 Centerpiece, before 1914
Made by Joh. Lötz Witwe, Klostermühle,
near Unterreichenstein, Austria
Stained cased glass; height 6¹/₄″ (15.8 cm)
Marks: Loetz (stained),
PROF. HOFFMANN (engraved)
Label: 32/1 30.– W. I. 1594/1914 (acquired
from Joh. Lötz Witwe)

447 Tumbler (designed before 1915)
Decoration designed by Josef Hoffmann or
Dagobert Peche
Made by Joh. Oertel & Co., Haida, Austria
(in production to 1917)
Glass with enameled decoration
("Kriegsglas"); height 3¹⁵/₁₆″ (10 cm)
W. I. 1421/1915 (acquired from Oertel)
WWMB 61, p. 502

448 Lidded vase, before 1914
Made by Joh. Lötz Witwe, Klostermühle,
near Unterreichenstein, Austria
Gilded cased glass with dot decoration;
height 7¹⁵/₁₆″ (20.2 cm)
Mark: PROF. HOFFMANN (stained)
Label: firm label with arrow trademark
W. F. 1268/1914 (acquired from Joh. Lötz
Witwe)

449 Jug from a porcelain service,
1910/11
Decoration designed by Emanuel J.
Margold
Made by Pfeiffer & Löwenstein,
Schlackenwerth, Austria, for the Wiener
Werkstätte on commission from Wiener
Porzellan-Manufaktur Josef Böck
Glazed porcelain with colored decoration,
height 6⁷/₈″ (17.4 cm)
Marks: IMPERIAL PSL (stamped in gray),
WIENER WERKSTÄTTE, JOSEF BÖCK
WIEN, GESETZLICH GESCHÜTZT W. P. M.
(stamped in red), PSL (stamped)
Label: W. P. M. BÖCK WIEN (red)
W. I. 927/1911 (acquired from Josef Böck)
See also no. 452

450 Mocca service (made before 1935)
Made by Wiener Porzellan-Manufaktur
Augarten

Glazed porcelain, painted blue; a) pot,
height 6⁷/₈″ (17.5 cm), b) sugar bowl,
height 4¹/₄″ (10.8 cm), c) cups, height 1³/₄″
(4.4 cm), d) saucers, diameter 3³/₄″
(9.6 cm), e) creamer, height 3⁷/₁₆″ (8.8 cm)
Marks: mark of the Wiener Porzellan-
Manufaktur Augarten (underglaze blue)
decoration and painter number 5491/7
(underglaze blue, damaged on (c))
Ke 7347/1935 (acquired from Wiener
Porzellan-Manufaktur Augarten)

451 Mocca service (made before 1938)
Made by Wiener Porzellan-Manufaktur
Augarten
Glazed porcelain, painted yellow;
a) creamer, height 3³/₈″ (8.6 cm), b) sugar
bowl, height 4¹/₄″ (10.8 cm), c) cups, height
1³/₄″ (4.5 cm), d) saucers, diameter 3⁷/₈″
(9.8 cm), e) pot, height 6⁷/₈″ (17.4 cm)
Marks: mark of the Wiener Porzellan-
Manufaktur Augarten (underglaze blue),
Augarten Austria (red, (d)), 15/55389 (gray,
(d)), 15/55389 (green, (a), (b), (e))
Ke 10516/1985

452 Sugar bowl from a porcelain
service, 1910/11
Decoration designed by Emanuel
J. Margold
Made by Pfeiffer & Löwenstein,
Schlackenwerth, Austria, for the Wiener
Werkstätte on commission from Wiener
Porzellan-Manufaktur Josef Böck
Glazed porcelain with colored decoration;
height 3⁵/₈″ (9.2 cm)
Marks: IMPERIAL PSL (stamped in gray),
WIENER WERKSTÄTTE, JOSEF BÖCK
WIEN, GESETZLICH GESCHÜTZT W. P. M.
(stamped in red)
Label: W. P. M. BÖCK WIEN (red)
W. I. 927/1911 (acquired from Josef Böck)
See also no. 449

453 Cup, ca. 1919 (designed ca. 1910)
Decoration designed in the Wiener
Werkstätte, ca. 1911.
Made by Pfeiffer & Löwenstein,
Schlackenwerth, Austria, for the Wiener
Werkstätte
Glazed porcelain with colored painted
decoration; height 2³/₁₆″ (5.6 cm)
Marks; factory mark PL (blue), WW
(stamped in gray), II 1145/3 (blue)
Ke 10142 (inventoried in 1981)
WWMB 25, no. 1145

454 Cup, ca. 1919 (designed ca. 1910)
Decoration designed in the Wiener
Werkstätte, ca. 1919

Made by Pfeiffer & Löwenstein,
Schlackenwerth, Austria, for the Wiener
Werkstätte
Glazed porcelain with colored painted
decoration; height 2³/₁₆″ (5.6 cm)
Marks: factory mark PL (blue), WW
(stamped in gray), II 1145/10 (black)
Label: II 1145/10 (damaged)
Ke 10141 (inventoried in 1981)
WWMB 25, no. 1145

455 Wooden models for parts of a
porcelain mocca service, ca. 1910
Wood; a) sugar bowl, height 2″ (5.1 cm),
b) pot, height 6³/₄″ (17.2 cm)
Inscribed: Zuckerschale (a), Mokka (b)
Ke 10135–39 (inventoried in 1981)
Set also includes cup and saucer

Architecture and Monuments

456 Design for a high-rise building,
1927
Pencil on graph paper mounted on graph
paper; 8¹/₁₆ × 8¹/₄″ (20.5 × 20.9 cm) (design
sheet), 13³/₈ × 8⁵/₁₆″ (33.9 × 21.1 cm)
(whole)
Monogrammed (lower left): JH,
monogrammed and dated (lower right):
27 JH
K. I. 8810

457 Plan and elevation of a pavilion for
a Russian exhibition in Vienna, 1923/25 (?)
Pencil, India ink, and green, yellow, red,
and black watercolor on graph paper
mounted on graph paper; 12¹¹/₁₆″
(32.3 × 19.6 cm) (design sheet), 13³/₈ × 8¹/₄″
(34 × 21 cm) (whole)
Monogrammed (lower right): JH
Stamp of the Baubüro des österreichischen
Verbandes für Siedlungs- und
Kleingartenwesen, Vienna (lower right)
K. I. 8805/1

458 Plan and elevation of a pavilion for
a Russian exhibition in Vienna, 1923/24 (?)
Pencil, India ink, and green, yellow, red,
and black watercolor on graph paper
mounted on graph paper; 13¹/₈ × 7¹³/₁₆″
(33.4 × 19.8 cm) (design sheet),
13³/₈ × 8⁵/₁₆″ (34 × 21.1 cm) (whole)
Monogrammed (lower left): JH
Stamp of the Baubüro des österreichischen
Verbandes für Siedlungs- und
Kleingartenwesen, Vienna (lower right)
K. I. 8805/2

459 Plan of the Ast country house,
1923/24
Pencil and red, yellow, blue, and green
crayon on graph paper; $7\frac{7}{8} \times 11\frac{1}{4}''$
(20×28.5 cm)
Monogrammed (lower left): JH
K.I. 8802/2

460 Design for the facade of the
country house, 1923/24
Pencil and blue, yellow, green and orange
crayon on graph paper;
$7\frac{15}{16} \times 12\frac{13}{16}''$ (20.1×32.5 cm)
Monogrammed (lower right): JH
K.I. 8802/1

461 Design for the facade of a row
house in the Werkbund housing estate,
1930/32
Pencil and green, orange, yellow, and pink
crayon on graph paper; $8\frac{3}{16} \times 13\frac{7}{16}''$
(20.8×34.1 cm)
Monogrammed (lower right): JH
K.I. 8807/1

462 Plan of a row house in the
Werkbund housing estate, 1930/32
Pencil on graph paper; $8\frac{3}{16} \times 13\frac{7}{16}''$
(20.8×34.1 cm)
Monogrammed (lower right): JH
K.I. 8807/2

463 Plan and elevations of a row house
in the Werkbund housing estate, 1930
Pencil and red, green, and ocher crayon on
graph paper;
Signed (right center): Josef Hoffmann
Inscribed (lower left): Aufriss- und
Grundrissstudien
$16\frac{7}{16} \times 13\frac{3}{8}''$ (41.7×34 cm)
Monogrammed (right center): JH
K.I. 8812/3, 4

464 Design for the facade of an
apartment building, 1930
Pencil and blue, green, and violet crayon
on graph paper; $8\frac{5}{16} \times 13\frac{3}{8}''$
(21.1×34 cm)
K.I. 8803/1

465 Design for the facade of a three-
story apartment building, 1929
Pencil and green and red crayon on graph
paper; $8\frac{5}{16} \times 13\frac{3}{8}''$ (21.1×34 cm)
Monogrammed (lower right): JH
K.I. 8803/2

466 Design for the facade of a public
housing project in Vienna, 1929
Pencil and blue, and red crayon on graph

paper; $8\frac{5}{16} \times 13\frac{5}{16}''$ (21.1×33.9 cm)
Monogrammed and dated (lower right):
1929/JH
K.I. 8808/1

467 Plan of the Werkbund housing
estate, 1930
Pencil on graph paper; $8\frac{5}{16} \times 13\frac{3}{8}''$
(21.2×34 cm)
Monogrammed (lower right): JH,
dated: 1930
K.I. 8812/2

468 Design for the facade of a public
housing project on Billrothstrasse in
Vienna, 1923
Pencil and India ink on graph paper;
$8\frac{3}{16} \times 13\frac{1}{16}''$ (20.8×33.2 cm)
K.I. 8804/2

469 Third design for the remodeling of
the facade of the Österreichische Central
Boden Credit Bank, 1912
Pencil on imitation parchment;
$11\frac{1}{16} \times 16\frac{11}{16}''$ (28.1×42.4 cm)
Monogrammed and dated (lower right):
1912/JH
K.I. 8800

470 Elevation of a monument
to Otto Wagner, 1929/30
Pencil on graph paper; $16\frac{1}{2} \times 13\frac{3}{8}''$
(42×33.9 cm)
Monogrammed (verso): JH
K.I. 8815/3

471 Elevation of a monument
to Otto Wagner, 1929/30
Pencil on graph paper; $16\frac{1}{2} \times 13\frac{3}{8}''$
(42×33.9 cm)
K.I. 8815/6

472 Plan and elevation of a monument
to Otto Wagner, 1929/30
Pencil and blue and brown crayon;
$16\frac{5}{8} \times 13\frac{3}{8}''$ (42×33.9 cm)
Monogrammed (lower left): JH
K.I. 8815/2

473 Elevation of a monument
to Otto Wagner, 1929/30
Pencil on graph paper; $13\frac{3}{8} \times 8\frac{1}{4}''$
(33.9×21 cm)
Monogrammed (lower right): JH
K.I. 8815/8

474 Elevation of a monument
to Otto Wagner, 1929/30
Pencil on graph paper; $16\frac{1}{2} \times 13\frac{3}{8}''$
(42×33.9 cm)

Monogrammed (lower left): JH
K.I. 8815/4

475 Elevation of a monument
to Otto Wagner, 1929/30
Pencil on graph paper; $16\frac{7}{16} \times 13\frac{3}{8}''$
(42.2×33.9 cm)
Monogrammed (lower right): JH
K.I. 8815/7

476 Elevation of a monument
to Otto Wagner, 1929/30
Pencil on graph paper; $16\frac{5}{8} \times 13\frac{3}{8}''$
(42.2×33.9 cm)
Monogrammed (lower left): JH
K.I. 8815/5

477 Model of the Purkersdorf
Sanatorium, 1904/5
Reconstructed by Elfriede Huber and
Franz Hnizdo, Institute of Model
Construction (Prof. Arch. Wilhelm
Cermak), Hochschule für angewandte
Kunst, Vienna
Limewood, pear, and Finnish birch veneer;
$74\frac{3}{4} \times 43\frac{1}{4}''$ (190×110 cm)
Scale 1:50

478 Model of the Beer-Hofmann villa,
1905/6
Reconstructed by Elfriede Huber and
Franz Hnizdo, Institute of Model
Construction (Prof. Arch. Wilhelm
Cermak), Hochschule für angewandte
Kunst, Vienna
Limewood, pear, and Finnish birch veneer;
$43\frac{1}{4} \times 37\frac{3}{8}''$ (110×95 cm)
Scale 1:50

479, 480 Model of the Skywa/
Primavesi orangery and villa, 1913/15
Reconstructed by Elfriede Huber and
Franz Hnizdo, Institute of Model
Construction (Prof. Arch. Wilhelm
Cermak), Hochschule für angewandte
Kunst, Vienna
Limewood, pear, and Finnish birch veneer;
a) villa $59 \times 37\frac{3}{8}''$ (150×95 cm),
b) orangery $31\frac{1}{2} \times 27\frac{1}{2}''$ (80×70 cm)
Scale 1:50

481 Model of the Palais Stoclet,
1905/11
Reconstructed by Elfriede Huber and
Franz Hnizdo, Institute of Model
Construction (Prof. Arch. Wilhelm
Cermak), Hochschule für angewandte
Kunst, Vienna
Limewood, pear, and Finnish birch veneer;
$65 \times 51\frac{1}{8}''$ (165×130 cm)
Scale 1:50

Selected Bibliography

Barten, Siegrid. *Josef Hoffmann Wien: Jugendstil und Zwanziger Jahre.* Exh. cat. Zurich: Museum Bellerive, 1983.

Behal, Vera J. *Möbel des Jugendstils.* Collection cat. Vienna and Munich: MAK-Austrian Museum of Applied Arts, 1981.

Bortolotti, Nadine, ed. *Le Arti a Vienna: Della Secessione alla caduta dell'Impero asburgico.* Exh. cat. Venice: Palazzo Grassi, 1984.

Campbell, Sarah. *Vienna Moderne 1898-1918.* Exh. cat. Houston: Sarah Campbell Blaffer Gallery, University of Houston, 1979.

Clair, Jean. *Vienne 1880-1938: L'Apocalypse Joyeuse.* Exh. cat. Paris: Centre Georges Pompidou, 1986.

Fagiolo, Maurizio. *I mobili semplici etc.* Exh. cat. Rome: Emporio Floreale, 1977.

Fanelli, Giovanni and Ezio Godoli. *La Vienna di Hoffmann architetto di qualità.* Rome, 1981.

Fanelli, Giovanni and Rosalia Fanelli. *Il tessuto moderno.* Florence, 1976.

Frühes Industriedesign 1900-1908. Exh. cat. Vienna: Galerie nächst St. Stephan, 1977.

Gebhard, David. *Josef Hoffmann: Design Classics.* Exh. cat. Fort Worth, Texas: The Fort Worth Art Museum, 1983.

Gorsen, Peter. "Josef Hoffmann: Zur Modernität eines konservativen Baumeisters." In *Ornament und Askese*, A. Pfabigan (ed.), 69-92. Vienna, 1985.

Hoffmann, Josef. "Selbstbiographie." In *Ver Sacrum, Neue Hefte für Kunst und Literatur.* Vienna and Munich, not dated (after 1970).

Josef Hoffmann zum 60. Geburtstag. A selection of his works on the occasion of the exhibition at MAK-Austrian Museum of Applied Arts. Vienna, 1930/31.

Josef Hoffmann. Exh. cat. Vienna: Galerie Ambiente, 1978.

Josef Hoffmann: Sanatorium Purkersdorf. Exh. cat. Vienna: Galerie Metropol, 1985.

Josef Hoffmann (1870-1956): Ornament zwischen Hoffnung und Verbrechen. Exh. cat. Vienna: MAK-Austrian Museum of Applied Arts, 1987.

Josef Hoffmann: 1870-1956. Exh. cat. St. Petersburg: The Hermitage, 1991.

Kallir, Jane. *Viennese Design and the Wiener Werkstätte.* Exh. cat. New York: Galerie St. Etienne, 1986.

Kamm-Kyburz, Christine. "Tendenzen im Ornament Josef Hoffmanns." In *Grenzbereiche der Architektur: Festschrift Adolf Reichle*, 115-23. Basel, 1985.

Kleiner, Leopold. *Josef Hoffmann.* Berlin, Leipzig, and Vienna, 1927.

Lane, Terence. *Vienna 1913: Josef Hoffmann's Gallia Apartment.* Exh. cat. Melbourne: National Gallery of Victoria, 1984.

Mendelssohn, Georg. "Industrie und Ornament." In *Die Form* (Heft 2), 21-23, 1925.

Moderne Vergangenheit: Möbel-Metall-Keramik-Glas-Textil-Entwürfe aus Wien. Exh. cat. Vienna: Künstlerhaus, 1981.

Müller, Michael. *Die Verdrängung des Ornaments.* Frankfurt/Main, 1977.

Neuwirth, Waltraud. *Österreichisches Kunsthandwerk des Jugendstils: Glas, Keramik, Metall, Email.* Vienna, 1980.

———. *Josef Hoffmann: Bestecke für die Wiener Werkstätte.* Vienna, 1982.

———. *Wiener Werkstätte: Avantgarde, Art Déco, Industrial Design.* Vienna, 1984.

———. *Glas 1905-1925: Vom Jugendstil zum Art Déco.* Vol. 1: *Glas mit Schliff.* Collection cat. Vienna, 1985.

———. *Die Schutzmarken der Wiener Werkstätte.* Vol. 1: *Rosenmarke und Wortmarke.* Vienna, 1985.

———. *Die Wiener Werkstätte.* Vienna, 1985.

Österreichischer Werkbund (ed.). *Josef Hoffmann zum 60. Geburtstag.* (Almanach der Dame). Vienna, 1930.

Rochowanski, Leopold W. *Josef Hoffmann: Eine Studie geschrieben zu seinem 80. Geburtstag.* Vienna, 1950.

Schmuttermeier, Elisabeth. *Schmuck von 1900-1925.* Exh. cat. Vienna: MAK-Austrian Museum of Applied Arts, 1986.

———. *Wiener Werkstätte: Atelier Viennois 1903-1932.* Exh. cat. Brussels, 1987.

Sekler, Eduard F. and Robert Judson Clark. *Josef Hoffmann 1870-1956: Architect and Designer.* Exh. cat. London: Fischer Fine Art Ltd., 1977.

Sekler, Eduard. *Josef Hoffmann: The Architectural Work. Monograph and Catalog of Works*. Translated by John Maas. Princeton, 1985 [1982].

———. *Josef Hoffmann*. Turin, 1992.

Traum und Wirklichkeit: Wien 1870-1930. Exh. cat. Vienna: Künstlerhaus, 1985.

Varnedoe, Kirk. *Vienna 1900: Art, Architecture, and Design*. Exh. cat. New York: Museum of Modern Art, 1986.

Vergo, Peter. *Vienna 1900: Vienna, Scotland, and the European Avant-Garde*. Exh. cat. Edinburgh: National Museum of Antiquities of Scotland, 1983.

Veronesi, Giulia. *Josef Hoffmann*. Milan, 1956.

Vienna: A Birthplace of 20th Century Design. (Part 1: "1900-1905: Purism and Functionalism 'Konstruktiver Jugendstil'.") Exh. cat. London: Fischer Fine Art Ltd., 1981.

Völker, Angela and Ruperta Pichler. *Die Stoffe der Wiener Werkstätte 1910-1932*. Vienna, 1990.

Weiser, Armand. *Josef Hoffmann*. Geneva, 1930.

Die Wiener Werkstätte: Modernes Kunsthandwerk von 1903-1932. Exh. cat. Vienna: MAK-Austrian Museum of Applied Arts, 1967.

Wien um 1900. Exh. cat. Vienna: Historical Museum of the City of Vienna, Künstlerhaus, Secession, 1964.

Wien um 1900: Klimt, Schiele und ihre Zeit. Exh. cat. Tokyo: Sezon Museum of Art, 1989.

Index of Names

Numerals in *italics* refer to pages with illustrations

MAK – Austrian Museum of Applied Arts

"Art provokes conflicts, questions the existing, and facilitates new ways of seeing."

In 1986 Peter Noever, current director of the MAK-Austrian Museum of Applied Arts, Vienna, initiated a radical reorientation in the work of this, the oldest arts and crafts museum in Continental Europe. Encapsulated in the motto "Back to the Past," the new program of activities has been based on a critical evaluation of historical developments in its exploration of the interaction between "applied" and "fine" arts, between the traditional and the experimental. In this dialogue with the past emphasis is placed on the involvement of contemporary artists, creating a lively, active and receptive institution, where experimentation and spontaneity prevail.

From the outset, the MAK has challenged prevailing attitudes toward art. At its foundation in 1864 as a "Museum of Art and Industry," it promoted a daringly innovative notion of the relationship between art and craft in opposition to the academic preoccupation with antiquated, historicist values. Art was to combine basic technical ability with mental creativity while no longer standing aloof from the production of simple, everyday objects. By attempting to appeal to all sections of the population, the museum hoped to improve the taste of the public at large. This revolutionary concept, linking the utilitarian to the aesthetic, involved presenting works of art in a context relevant to the society of the day, stimulating new points of view.

After several decades of strict fulfillment of its so-called "memory function" – a reliance on its existing holdings to the detriment of the new – the MAK is now once again searching for a new dimension to art. By combining the supposedly mutually exclusive concepts of "applied" and "fine" art, the exhibition program of the MAK stimulates and promotes new approaches to historically preconceived notions. Looking back on the achievements of recent years, Peter Noever states: "This project has entailed walking on a tightrope between the traditional and the present-day. It has demanded great willingness to take risks and has required both the ability to act and react and careful planning. These demands have been met through the whole-hearted commitment and constructive cooperation of all those involved."

When it reopens its doors in 1993, after three years of extensive renovation and construction work, the MAK will possess exhibition spaces adequate to the implementation of its bold new program.